The

HIDDEN

of
YORKSHIRE AND HUMBERSIDE

Front Cover: Whitby
By
Graham Lewis

Acknowledgments

This book would not have been compiled without the dedicated help of the following: Elaine and Deborah - Administration; Joanne Les & Graham - Artists; Bob - Research; and Jennie - Writing and Production.

Map origination by Paul and Simon at Legend DTP, Stockport.

All have contributed to what we hope is an interesting, useful and enjoyable publication.

Other titles in this series:

Printed and bound by Guernsey Press, Channel Islands.
© M&M Publishing Ltd.
Tryfan House, Warwick Drive, Hale, Altrincham, Cheshire WA15 9EA.
First printed 1990.

THE HIDDEN PLACES
OF
YORKSHIRE AND HUMBERSIDE

Contents

The North York Moors

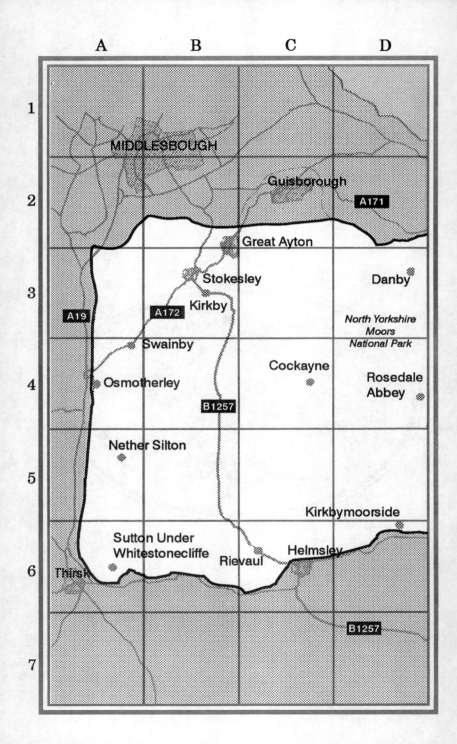

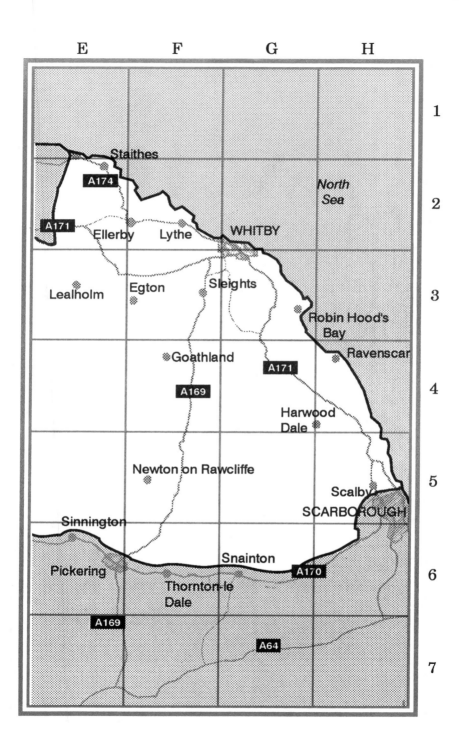

Whitby Harbour

The North York Moors

The North York Moors is an area of approximately 650 square miles, and holds expectations of a rather inhospitable, bleak terrain, which could not, as it happens, be further from the truth. As you drive around this area you will find yourselves travelling through pretty cottaged hamlets, kept in a style reminiscent of the typical English rural scenes one might associate with more southerly counties, surrounded by the more characteristic heather-clad hills. In season the flowers and greenery are profuse, and set a quite magnificent backdrop to any journey.

Danby to Osmotherley

An ideal place to start any visit to this part of Yorkshire is the village of DANBY and the nearby Danby Lodge National Moors Centre. This is an excellent facility for those who might wish to take full advantage of the recreational value of the moors. Set in 13 acres of riverside meadow, woodland and gardens there are a number of woodland walks and nature trails that can be sampled. The main centre is the major visitor centre of the Moors and there are many informative displays on natural and local history and an excellent selection of maps and guide books.

Downstream from the Visitor Centre is a narrow medieval packhorse bridge known as Duck Bridge, one of three to be found in the area of Eskdale. The name appears to have nothing to do with aquatic birds, originally being known as Castle Bridge, re-named after an 18th-century benefactor, George Duck, who had the bridge repaired.

In the nearby village you will find a great hostelry in the form of the **Duke of Wellington Inn**. This historic establishment was built in 1732 and reputedly gained its name from the Duke of Wellington himself who used the pub as a staging post and recruiting centre. A unique plaque dating from the period was recently uncovered and now hangs in the public bar. Restoration and refurbishment has improved the facilities while maintaining the character and charm of this old country inn. Owned by Tony, Pat and Steve Howat, you will be warmly welcomed into this friendly establishment. Visitors can enjoy a game of darts or dominoes in the bar while sampling the real ales, or enjoy a tasty bar meal. The food is all home-cooked and features traditional and imaginative dishes including vegetarian and children's meals. For those who require accommodation, there are 9 en-suite letting rooms available. The location of the Duke of Wellington makes it ideal for a family holiday or an activity holiday.

Duke of Wellington, Danby, Nr. Whitby Tel: 01287 660351

To the south of Duck Bridge are the remains of Danby Castle. Built in the 14th century and originally of large proportions, now serving as a farmhouse, it was formerly the home of Catherine Parr - the sixth wife of Henry VIII. Elizabethan justices met here and the Danby Court Leet and

Baron, which still administers common land and rights of way, is still held here every year in the throne room. One strange anachronism of the court is the issuing of licenses for gathering sphagnum moss - once used for stuffing mattresses but now more commonly used in flower arranging.

Danby Castle stands at the entrance to LITTLE FRYUP DALE and from here there is a pleasant journey along Crossley Sides, where bilberries ripen in late August. High in GREAT FRYUP DALE is a tiny lane with a few small dwellings, quaintly named Fryup Street. Fryup's odd name causes amusement and speculation. It was possibly derived from Friga, an old English personal name, while the 'up' or 'hop' means a small valley.

In the tiny hamlet of AINTHORPE, to the south of Danby Village, stands the former coaching inn, The Fox and Hounds. Dating back to 1555 the inn is only a short distance from Danby Castle, where Mary Queen of Scots was once held on her journey to London. One of the features of the inn today is a magnificent stone fireplace and surround which came from the castle. The inn is traditional in style and full of character, and its idyllic position offers views across the surrounding countryside. Open all week, the pub serves food every lunchtime and evening. The menu offers a good range of snacks and meals with plenty of vegetarian options. To complement your meal, there is a variety of well-kept real ales too. Gill Dickinson, the owner, can also offer bed and breakfast accommodation in one of eight cosy letting rooms.

The Fox and Hounds, Ainthorpe, Danby Tel: 01287 660218

Also in Ainthorpe is the delightful Rowan Tree Farm. Situated on a 120 acre working farm, once part of Lord Downe's estate, is the impressive farmhouse where Brenda Tindall provides bed and breakfast accommodation. A very warm welcome awaits visitors to this 200 year old farmhouse which has some most impressive views across the moors. All the rooms are snug and cosy, and the location means it is a very peaceful place to stay. Home-cooked evening meals are available by prior arrangement and packed lunches can be provided. The breakfasts are a real treat too!

Rowan Tree Farm, Ainthorpe, Nr. Danby, Whitby
Tel: 01287 660396

CASTLETON is a typical small Moors village and at one time was the largest in Eskdale with a market and busy railway station. Nearby Freeborough Hill has a curious conical shape and is believed to be named after Freya, the goddess of fertility.

The Moorlands Hotel, Castleton Tel: 01287 660206

Occupying a superb position in this picturesque village is **The Moorlands Hotel**. From it are uninterrupted views of the Esk valley and the heather moors. The 19th-century hotel has a stone exterior strong enough to withstand the severe winter winds, yet behind it there hides a comfortable hostelry with a warm and welcoming atmosphere. There are nine bedrooms, most with en-suite bathroom and all with stunning views. There is also a bar with a log fire and a romantic à la carte, candle-lit restaurant. The extensive menu changes regularly and most items are home-made. Scones and sandwiches are served at afternoon tea and there

Staithes

is a traditional Sunday lunch. The Moorlands Hotel can also offer Guided Walking Breaks and Golfing Holidays. Ring for details.

Heading west along the B173 brings you to the village of **GREAT AYTON**, the most northerly village in North Yorkshire and famous as the place where Captain James Cook spent his youth. In the centre of the village is the former site of the Cooks' family home, which was transported in 1934, brick by brick, creepers and all, to Point Hicks in Australia. A cairn of stones is all that remains to mark the site today. The skyline at Great Ayton is made distinctive by the peculiarly shaped hill known as **ROSEBERRY TOPPING**, sometimes called the Matterhorn of Yorkshire, which rises to 1000 feet above the village. Beyond that, one can also see the Captain Cook Monument on Easby Moor, a 60 foot obelisk erected by Robert Campion, a Whitby banker, in 1827.

The village has many attractions for the day visitor or holidaymaker. A popular attraction is the Captain Cook Museum which will provide an interesting afternoon's entertainment.

The Royal Oak Hotel is a former 18th-century coaching inn, situated in the centre of the village. The Royal Oak offers the best tradition of a rural hostelry and has a well-established reputation for good food and drink with comfortable accommodation. In it you will find the rustic charm of oak-beamed ceilings and log fires. There are a total of five letting rooms, all with en-suite facilities and the rooms are well-equipped with tea tray, television and telephone. The candlelit restaurant is open each evening and also for Sunday lunch. Choices can be made from either the à la carte or table d'hôte menus and you can be assured of an excellent, freshly-prepared meal. The restaurant is very popular so bookings are advisable. In the bar area food can be obtained whenever the pub is open and prices will suit every pocket. Behind the bar the selection of ales, wines and spirits include Theakstons bitter, Theakstons O.P. and Youngers No.3

traditional ales. The service is always helpful and efficient, and your hosts, Derek and Linda Monaghan, are delightful. This one is well worth a special visit.

The Royal Oak Hotel, High Green, Great Ayton
Tel: 01642 722361 Fax: 01642 724047

STOKESLEY itself is an attractive market town below the northern edge of the moors, the peace only broken on market day which is Friday. The town consists of the market square, rows of elegant Georgian houses reached by little bridges over River Leven that flows through the town and an old water wheel which marks the entrance to the town. Seven hundred years ago, the town was owned by the Balliol family, one of the descendants of which is remembered as the founder of the Oxford college of that name.

A wonderful restaurant and hotel, called Chapters, can be found opposite the Market Square. Dating back to the 18th century this former coaching inn used to have its own brewery. Alan and Catherine Thompson came here four years ago and with lots of hard work and imagination have turned this into an establishment of great character and class. There are three facets to Chapters - a bistro, restaurant and a hotel. The bedrooms are cosy and individually furnished. They all include en-suite bathrooms and are available in a variety of sizes. The bistro and the restaurant are very stylish in decor,

11

Mount Grace Priory

with the restaurant being suited to more intimate dining. Meals are served at lunch time and the evening in the Bistro, and in the evening only in the restaurant. The menus are varied and highly imaginative and there is sure to be something to suit your taste. Bookings are advisable. At the rear of Chapters flows the River Leven, and a patio area has been created which is lit up at night. Great for summer al fresco dining and the regular jazz nights and barbecues.

Chapters, 27 High Street, Stokesley Tel: 01642 711888

Easily found on the main road is the welcoming establishment of **The White Swan**. The building itself dates back to the early 18th century and has traded under many different names. Initially it was called the Racecourse, and at the time there was one here in Stokesley. Later it was called the Cleveland, but for the last 100 years has been known as The White Swan. Brian Skipp and June Harrison came here only five years ago, and despite being new to the trade have successfully created a quality establishment that is very different to the many pubs you come across today. The main reason that many people return to the pub is the quality of Brian's real ales - there are always six on tap, and all are kept in tip-top condition. Food is served, and although the menu consists solely of Ploughman's Lunches there is a range of over 30 different cheeses and patés to choose from. For entertainment there are no juke boxes or pinball machines, just the traditional pub games of bagatelle and bar billiards. This is a first class, old English Pub that is a must.

The White Swan, 1 West End, Stokesley Tel: 01642 710263

Situated in the tiny hamlet of **KIRKBY-IN-CLEVELAND**, just two miles south of Stokesley, is the very impressive **Black Swan**.

The Black Swan, Busby Lane, Kirkby-in-Cleveland Tel:
01642 712512

Renowned throughout the area for its food, the Black Swan is worth seeking out. Alan and Carole, the present
14

owners, came to the pub two years ago and this is their first venture in the business. Without doubt it has been a great success. The pub dates back to the 18th century, and although still very 'olde worlde' in parts, it is run in a modern and efficient manner. To the rear, visitors will find the delightful addition of a conservatory, a great place to sit on sunny afternoons and enjoy the views. Food is served on weekday lunch times, there is an extensive choice, and all dishes are reasonably priced. Most importantly the meals are delicious and come in hearty portions. This place is a real hidden gem.

Also in the village, adjacent to Dromonby Hall, is **Dromonby Hall Farm**. This is the delightful home of the Weighell family, who used to occupy the Hall next door. The house is modern, having been built in 1975 and is beautifully situated, offering fantastic views across the Cleveland countryside and to nearby Roseberry Topping. The garden is equally impressive and guests are of course welcome to explore it. Pat and Trevor Weighell will pamper you from the moment you arrive to ensure you enjoy your stay to the full. The three bedrooms are comfortable and Pat's breakfasts are a real treat. Evening meals are not available, but packed lunches can be supplied on request.

Dromonby Hall Farm, Kirkby-in-Cleveland, Stokesley,
Middlesborough Tel: 01642 712312

Return to the A172 and travel southwest to the village of **SWAINBY**. Although it has all the characteristics of a modern village, Swainby actually dates back to the 14th century. When the nearby settlement of **WHORLTON** was attacked by a plague, the population moved away and settled here, although it is probable that there was a settlement here already. Any signs of the ancient history that would have once been here were obliterated when the village become overrun with jet and ironstone miners in the 19th century.

The wonderfully inviting **Black Horse Inn** stands proudly by the stream in this sleepy village. Dating back to the mid-19th century, the building was almost derelict when Clive Farrand Bland and Stephen Wiper took over two years ago. Both had been in the trade for many years and have used their expertise to convert the Black Horse into an establishment that is renowned throughout the area for its excellent food and well-kept ales. The menus are very impressive, and of a very high standard. Stephen is the chef, and provides good portions of freshly prepared, home-cooked food. The interior of the pub is warm and inviting and has been traditionally furnished to great effect. Behind the bar is served a good range of real ales, wines and spirits. The pub is beautifully situated and has a large car park and beer garden.

Black Horse, Swainby, Northallerton Tel: 01642 700436

Continuing south you will come to the hamlet of **INGILBY CROSS** where you will find the very pleasant **Blue Bell Inn**. The building dates back to 1912, when it replaced the previous inn which had to be pulled down because steam engines could not negotiate the curve in the road! Now part of the Arncliffe estate, the inn is one of those old-fashioned English pubs that one doesn't come across often. Built of traditional Yorkshire stone, the atmosphere is very inviting and homely. Open every day, the inn serves good home-made, delicious pub food and keeps a good selection of well-kept real ales. In an old converted stable block there are five letting rooms for bed and breakfast accommodation. Guests can even bring their horse on holiday as there is stabling available.

Blue Bell Inn, Ingleby Cross, Northallerton
Tel: 01609 882272

Just where the A172 joins the A19 are the beautiful ruins of Mount Grace Priory, one of the best preserved examples of a Carthusian priory. Now a National Trust property the priory can be reached by a pleasant walk, along the lanes, from Osmotherley. Founded in the 14th century by Thomas Holland, Duke of Surrey, Earl of Kent and Nephew of Richard III, the full title of building is 'The House of the Assumption of the Blessed Virgin Mary and Saint Nicholas of Mount

17

Grace in Ingleby'. The foundations of most of the twenty cells in which the monks would have lived in isolation can be seen with the walls and tower of the priory church which were added in 1420.

OSMOTHERLEY itself is an attractive mixture of old stone cottages and stylish modern houses. In the centre is a heavily carved market cross and next to it is a low stone table which was probably once a market stall.

Around this particular area, the countryside is very intimate and cosy, an impression created by the closeness of the surrounding hills and trees. Of all the places you have travelled through, the areas around NETHER and OVER SILTON and Osmotherley will give perhaps the closest impression of a "hidden place". Places of note worth a visit in this area are the country park area above Osmotherley that offers splendid views over Stockton and Darlington, the lovely village of Osmotherley itself, famous as the starting point of the famous Lyke Wake Walk and the pretty church of St Mary, Over Silton, accessible only by walking across two fields.

Danby to Whitby

Returning to the North York Moors Visitor Centre at Danby, there are a number of attractive villages that can be investigated en route to Whitby.

Following the River Esk seawards will bring you to LEALHOLM, a picturesque village set on the side of the moors, and of which one foreign visitor said, "Elsewhere, you have to go in search of beautiful views; here, they come and offer themselves to be looked at.".

The village has become very popular with naturalists who are attracted by Cruckley Gill, a deep dramatic ravine which extends upstream from the village. It is rich with trees, ferns, flowers and rare plants. Sadly the ravine is privately owned and not open to the public.

Whitby Jet

Jet is a glossy black fossilised wood which has been carved and polished to make jewellery since the Bronze Age. The wood is obtained from the beaches or by digging mines into the cliff faces and it is at Whitby that the greatest quantity in England occurs.

Jet rose in popularity when Queen Victoria introduced it as a mark of mourning for Prince Albert. The trade flourished from the 1850s, and at one time there were 1500 men, women and children employed with Whitby Jet being sent to all parts of the world. The industry declined however, following the import of Jet from the continent. It is also believed that its association with mourning contributed to its decline as people began to see it as representative of death and found it distasteful to wear.

There has been some interest shown in Jet in recent years and yet today there is only one shop in Whitby which produces Jet jewellery. Each piece is handled ten times in a method that has not changed for 150 years. There are only one or two Jet workers left although craftsmen can sometimes be seen at work in the streets, engraving and carving.

A couple of miles to the north, midway between Lealholm and the coast, is the village of UGTHORPE. Ugthorpe is noted for having adhered to the Roman Catholic faith throughout the reformation. The reason for this is thought to have been a result of the number of priests who were trained overseas and brought ashore near Whitby. They would then have been smuggled to 'safe' houses en route to the north, a fact borne out by the large numbers of priest holes found in the older buildings of the village.

In the centre of the village is The Black Bull. Dating back in parts to the 1600s, there used to be a slaughter house and a smithy on either side of it. Following a fire about 100 years ago there was much rebuilding work done. Today, it is an establishment of great character much enjoyed by locals and visitors alike. It is a free house and you will find a choice of three real ales on tap, with guest beers in the summer months. There is a small restaurant to the rear, and the food available throughout is of the highest quality. There is a good choice of fare, and the restaurant can also offer a set menu. In addition, owners Bob and June Briddon offer bed and breakfast accommodation in two comfortable guest rooms.

The Black Bull, Ugthorpe, Whitby Tel: 01947 840286

Just to the north of Ugthorpe is the delightful hamlet of ELLERBY. Located here is The Ellerby Hotel, which is owned and run by David and Janet Alderson. Thanks to their vision and a great deal of hard work, a ramshackle collection of buildings has been transformed into a truly outstanding inn, hotel and restaurant. There are now nine well-appointed letting rooms, each with en-suite facilities, and to the rear, an impressive residents' conservatory looks out over a beautiful flower-filled garden to breathtaking countryside beyond. The hotel restaurant serves an excellent range of meals, including lunch on Sundays, and has become particularly renowned for its sumptuous twice-monthly Chinese banquets. The Ellerby Hotel is only a mile inland from the picturesque fishing village of Runswick Bay and is open all year round.

The Ellerby Hotel, Ellerby, Saltburn-by-the-Sea
Tel: 01947 840342

The rustic fishing port of **STAITHES** is situated on the coast, 9 miles north of Whitby. The modern village lies at the top of the cliff, alongside the main road, and visitors must leave their cars in the car park here as they are not allowed down the exceedingly steep road into the old village. As you descend towards the wharf and its enclosing cliff-face, the stone chapels and rather austere architecture bear witness to strong links with its Methodist past. Look out for the walkway called Slippery Hill; you don't need too much imagination to know why it was given this name.

21

Street Scene, Whitby

Staithes is notable as the place where the 17 year old James Cook worked in William Sanderson's haberdashery shop, before he set off to start his naval apprenticeship for Thomas Scottowe, a friend of Sanderson. The village is quiet and peaceful - there are no amusement arcades or bingo halls here. There is a small sandy beach, frequented by families and painters, and the rocky shoreline to the north and south is worthy of some exploration. In one direction you will be rewarded with small rock pools with starfish and anemones, and to other there are fossils and fools gold ingots to find.

The pretty boats that are moored in the harbour at high tide and along the river are cobles, of a design first introduced by the Vikings, and used to catch crabs and lobsters - this is one of the few fleets in England still to do so.

Further down the coast is another delightful fishing village, RUNSWICK BAY where pretty cottages cling to the steep sides of the cliff and are often painted and photographed. The attractiveness of the village has made steadily more popular with tourists.

Lythe Bank is a very steep hill which takes the A174 from Lythe down to Sandsend where the road literally runs alongside the edge of sea. The village of LYTHE, on the top of the hill, is a small collection of houses with a sturdy, clifftop church, worthy of a visit. There is an old custom practised here which takes place on special occasions, usually celebrating notable events of the family of the Marquis of Normanby of nearby Mulgrave Castle. The custom is known as 'Firing the Stiddy'. The anvil is pulled out of the blacksmith's shop, upturned, and a charge of gunpowder placed upon it. The gunpowder is then detonated with a long metal bar that has been heated to red hot at one end.

Situated on the coast road north of Whitby, at Lythe, is the charming Red Lion Inn. Run by a lovely couple, Tony and Deryn Brown, this is a typical village pub, friendly with atmosphere and character with well kept ales and wonderful food available, all home cooked by Deryn and served at reasonable prices. There are several bedrooms at the inn and it is well worth getting up early to sample the large Yorkshire breakfasts. Like all 'locals' this is a great meeting place, with conversations covering soccer and pigeon breeding and games of darts and unintelligible card games. This is a wonderful place to stay, with a friendly atmosphere and well worth going out of your way to find.

The Red Lion, High Street, Lythe, Near Whitby
Tel: 01947 893300

Adjoining the village is Mulgrave Castle, the grounds of which are open to the public and contain the ruins of Foss Castle which date back to the Conquest. Charles Dickens once enjoyed a holiday at Mulgrave Castle and it has accommodated many notable people, including members of the Royal Family.

At the bottom of Lythe Bank is the village of **SANDSEND**. A pretty village and popular holiday centre, aptly named, standing as it does at the end of a long sandy beach. Once the site of a Roman cement works, the area has also been mined for Jet and alum. A railway once served the village and although this closed in the late 1950s some of the tunnels, cuttings and embankments form part of the Sandsend Trail which is a two mile walk through the surrounding area.

The Sunflower Garden Centre can be found at RAITHWAITE, just outside Sandsend, on the A174 coast road. It provides an ideal day out for all those interested in flowers and gardens. The centre has only been open for a few years, but the gardens are mature and well-established. The centre specialises in Pelargoniums and also houses a magnificent cacti collection. In the main house, there are tea rooms which are open all day, serving refreshments and light snacks. The tea shop is open daily between Mother's Day and the end of October. Adjacent to the tea shop is a fine craft shop selling a variety of hand-made crafts and gifts. Also on sale are many local history books on the Merchant Marine enhanced by displays of model ships and memorabilia. The centre, although being near to the coast, is surrounded by attractive countryside. An unusual and enjoyable day out.

The Sunflower Garden Centre and Tea Rooms, Raithwaite, Whitby Tel: 01947 893284

The superb cliff-top Whitby Golf Course and miles of open fields separates Sandsend and Whitby. The White House Hotel commands an outstanding position overlooking the golf club, with views over the coastline and sea beyond. A former farmhouse, it has been used as a hotel since the mid-19th century. In days gone by, the Whitby-Middlesbrough railway ran alongside the property, where the golf course is now, and the stone outbuildings that are now used as storerooms and garages were once railway linemen's buildings. Today the hotel is family-run, with the emphasis on personal attention and service. The hotel doubles as an inn with a public bar that, like the rest of the establishment, is beautifully decorated and furnished. Behind the bar they keep a selection of six ales which are permanently available. The inn keeps normal licensing hours and the bar food is delicious and very well priced. The hotel can offer 12 en-suite letting rooms which include colour TV, drinks tray and telephones. The cosy and intimate restaurant seats around 30 people and is popular with hotel guests and locals. The evening menu is varied and imaginative but the restaurant can get busy, so booking is advisable. The carefully selected wine list will complement any meal.

The White House Hotel, Upgang Lane, Whitby
Tel: 01947 600469

One mile north-west of Whitby town centre and on A174 coast road, you will find the **Sandfield House Farm Caravan Park**. This quiet and friendly twelve-acre caravan park is set within lovely undulating farmland and has magnificent views over the surrounding countryside and coastline. Martin and Christine Warner have been running the site since 1985 and have created a excellent reputation.

They provide first-rate facilities for touring caravans, including electrical hook-ups, water points, coin-operated laundry facilities and a recently opened shower and toilet block. The site is only half a mile from shops and the beach, and is open to families and couples only. Open March to end of October.

Sandfield House Farm Caravan Park, Sandsend Road, Whitby Tel: 01947 602660

This region is full of landmarks of the life of its greatest son, Captain James Cook, who learnt his skills in seamanship in the town of WHITBY. This historic fishing port serves as an excellent base for jaunts around the coast, and is, in itself, worthy of several days exploration on its own.

Visitors stopping here might be forgiven for imagining that the town would be shrouded in mist and have a distinctly gothic air to it. We can, of course, blame novelist Bram Stoker for this as he based part of his Gothic horror "Dracula" in this little town. For fans there is a Dracula Walk, which takes place on a weekly basis (further information from the Tourist Information Centre).

Fiction aside there is a rich historical background to Whitby. Its traditions as a Christian settlement and whaling port are ancient and inspiring indeed. In AD664, the synod of Whitby determined the date of Easter. A few years later St

Hilda, a Northumbrian princess, founded a community for monks and nuns here. The imposing ruins of Whitby Abbey on the cliff top date mainly from the 13th century and dominate the town and harbour.

From the old town, you can climb the famous 199 steps to the Church of St Mary, next to the abbey remains, the place of worship for fishermen and seafarers for centuries. The interior has a distinctly nautical feel to it, due to alterations carried out by local shipwrights in the 17th century. Today, Whitby still retains its air of a seafarers' town, with the fishing boats and cobles anchored alongside more modern keel boats, and the yachts that one can see heading towards the marina situated up river.

The town is divided by the River Esk into two distinct areas. The old town is made up of narrow, cobbled streets and contains some small interesting shops. The newer part contains amusement arcades and souvenir shops but is worth investigating nevertheless.

The Duke of York, Bottom of 199 Steps, Church Street,
Whitby Tel: 01947 600324

The magnificent **Duke of York** stands in the old part of the town of Whitby. The 300 year old building lies at the bottom of the famous 199 steps and overlooks the busy harbour and a cobbled stone road leads you to the entrance of

Whitby Abbey

this wonderful, historic establishment. Originally built as cottages, the inn is in a real picture postcard setting. The interior is traditional and features wooden floors, beamed ceiling and exposed brick walls. The inn is renowned for its excellent food, ales and accommodation. The menu is extensive and there are plenty of extra, daily specials. There are three well-kept real ales on tap - John Smiths, Magnet and Directors. The three beautiful letting rooms are let on a room only basis and have wonderful views across the harbour. This one must not be missed.

Whitby Glass Ltd., 9 Sandgate, Whitby Tel: 01947 603553

In one of the ancient parts of Whitby called Sandgate, you will find the renowned studio of Whitby Glass Ltd., home of the world famous 'Whitby Lucky Duck'. The studio was founded in the early 1960s by Peter Rantell and today it is personally run by Dorothy Clegg, twice former Mayor of Whitby, and also a former Deputy Mayor of Scarborough. Visitors are invited to call in at the 400-year old building to observe the skilled crafts people as they draw, bend and fashion coloured glass into the intricately shaped good luck talismans. These have been exported to places as far away as Mexico and Japan, with their alleged successes including financial windfalls and the ending of a drought in southern France.

30

For those with tastes of a more nautical flavour, one can visit the cottage in Grape Lane where James Cook served his apprenticeship. In fact, reminders of the great man are never far away in one's ramblings through Whitby. A handsome monument to him stands on the West Cliff, looking down towards the Abbey, not far from the whalebone arch which is another famous landmark.

Chiltern Guest House, 13 Normanby Terrace, West Cliff, Whitby Tel: 01947 604981

Also on West Cliff, one of the older parts of Whitby, you will find a delightful bed and breakfast at **Chiltern Guest House**, an attractive Victorian property with plenty of style and class. The establishment is run by Pauline and Brian Upright who came here five years ago and have successfully created one of the foremost guest houses in the whole of Whitby. There are eight letting rooms which are available all year round, most have en-suite facilities and all are spacious and attractively furnished. There is also a cosy guests' lounge and a dining room where evening meals are served by prior arrangement. Packed lunches can also be provided. There is plenty of on-road parking available and Chiltern Guest House is only a few minutes walk from the shops and the sea front.

Situated on Whitby's Royal Crescent are the Warwick Holiday Apartments. Modelled on Bath's elegant regency houses the crescent was built by one of the great railway pioneers, Hudson, and overlooks Crescent gardens and the sea front - probably the best position in the whole of Whitby. There are a total of eight self-catering apartments available here, sleeping between four and eight people. All the flats are spacious and fully equipped with a comprehensive range of crockery, cutlery and cooking utensils and comfortably furnished to a very high standard. A passenger lift serves all floors which is ideal after a long day sightseeing. Run by Anne and Dave Atkinson, here you will find all the ingredients you need for a happy holiday. Send a stamped addressed envelope for your free brochure.

Warwick Holiday Apartments, 10 Royal Crescent, Whitby
Tel: 01947 604224

The Corner Guest House in Crescent Place in the heart of Whitby is ideally situated, being only two minutes walk from the sea front and the shops. The property has been converted from two mid-19th century houses by the resident hosts Colin and Susan Price to create this warm and friendly guest house. A former joiner by trade, most of the refurbishments have actually been carried out by Colin. Today, Corner Guest House can offer visitors the quality of establishment that one expects, but rarely finds, on holiday. On the ground floor you will find a smart yet cosy sitting room while downstairs there is a bar and the dining room. On the upper floors there are a total of 13 letting rooms of various sizes, many with en-suite facilities. All the bedrooms are spacious and have been beautifully decorated and furnished. Evening meals can be provided by prior arrangement and packed lunches can also be supplied.

The Corner Guest House, 3 & 4 Crescent Place, Whitby
Tel: 01947 602444

Another thing that one will notice in exploring Whitby, are the lovely sepia-tone photographs by Frank Meadow Sutcliffe, a nostalgic record of the sailing ship traditions and lives of the local fisherfolk of days gone by. A trip to the Whitby Museum in Pannet Park will provide more information as to the lives and industry of these people, as well as more detailed documentation on Cook's endeavours.

For those who find Sutcliffe's original photographs fascinating a visit to the Sutcliffe Gallery on Flowergate is a must. The gallery documents this remarkable man's life and works. The great love and respect he held for the hard-working locals is evident for all to see, and his portraits of such local characters are a tender and haunting reminder of a populace and way of life that would have passed unnoticed into obscurity, were it not for his efforts with his cumbersome and primitive photographic equipment. As well as a large collection of his work to view there are many prints to choose from.

Between 1753 and 1833, Whitby was the capital of the whaling industry, bringing home 2761 whales in 80 years. Much of that success was due to the skills of the great whaling captains William Scoresby and his son. William Scoresby Senior was renowned for his great daring and navigational skills, as well as for the invention of the crow's nest or mast-head lookout. His son, William, possessed leanings of a more scientific nature, and occupied himself with various experiments during his long days at sea in the icy Arctic waters. He is most noted for his discoveries of the forms of snow crystals, and the invention of the "Greenland" magnet, which made ships' compasses more reliable.

The whaling industry is now, thankfully, long dead, but fortunately the fishing industry is not, as many of Whitby's restaurants will prove, being famous for their seafood menus.

Spinks, 40-42 Flowergate, Whitby Tel: 01947 601402

Centrally situated, **Spinks Restaurant and Takeaway**, has a very special atmosphere - cosy, friendly and inviting. Owner Wilf Booth was born and has lived in Whitby all his life. After 30 years in the Fire Service he bought and opened the restaurant six years ago. It is housed within a listed building which is 200 years old and in the days of the whaling trade, used as the shipping offices. The restaurant is located on the first floor and is spacious enough to seat forty-four people comfortably. The service is efficient and well-managed and is food is excellent too. Spinks is open for morning coffee and lunch and again in the evening. The regular menus offer a good choice with seafood and fish featuring prominently. The takeaway side, available at lunchtime and in the evening, offers pizzas, pasta and curries. Bookings are preferred for the evening in the summer season and are essential for every Saturday throughout the year. So if you are in town, and need a bite to eat, give Spinks a go.

Magpie Café, 14 Pier Road, Whitby Tel: 01947 602058

In a splendid position on Whitby's bustling quayside, there is a first-rate eating house called The Magpie Café. The building dates from the 18th century and was once the home of the Scoresbys. It was then used as a shipping office for many years before being re-opened as a café in the 1950s. The Magpie is more like a top class restaurant than a café, being Egon Ronay recommended and featuring in the Good Food Guide, Wholefood Guide and British Relais Routier Guide. It has also recently been featured as the Just a Bite Guide

Restaurant of the Year. Owners Alison and Ian Robson have built their reputation on the quality of the food served and of the service provided. The house speciality is fresh, locally caught fish and seafood and it is said they serve the best fish and chips in the area. The menus offer a very wide choice, and there is much more than just fish. A variety of salads and vegetarian meals are on offer, and the dessert selection is impressive to say the least! The chefs will also cater for those on special diets without a fuss. The seating areas have an atmosphere which is relaxed and welcoming with flowers on the tables and prints of old Whitby on the walls. The upper level also has magnificent views of the harbour. Open daily March to November, 11.30am to 6.30pm.

Larpool Hall Country House Hotel, Larpool Lane, Whitby
Tel: 01947 602737

On the outskirts of Whitby, just off the Scarborough road is an elegant Georgian Mansion, steeped in local history, called **Larpool Hall**. The present mansion was built by Lady Jonathan Lacey in 1796, but records show that there has been a building on the site since the twelfth century. In recent years the Hall has been an orphanage, service quarters during the second World War and an outdoor pursuits centre until the present owners, Keith and Electra Robinson bought it in 1986.

Today Larpool Hall Hotel offers luxurious accommodation, with attentive personal service and peaceful surroundings. The hotel stands in ten acres of delightful gardens and woodland which are perfect for a relaxing or leisurely stroll. From the beautiful entrance hall visitors are led to the large and elegant bedrooms. All have en-suite bathrooms and all the facilities you would expect from a top class hotel. There are, in addition, ground floor bedrooms for those unable to climb the stairs. For very special occasions, the hotel boasts a romantic bridal suite on the top floor. The public rooms include the Cholmley Lounge which overlooks the forecourt of the hotel and the Esk Valley beyond. The Dales Restaurant is also a very beautiful room and is a lovely setting for your meal. The menu reflects Electra's wide interest and knowledge of cooking and ranges from traditional English and regional Yorkshire fare, to more exotic dishes for the adventurous. There is always a selection of vegetarian dishes and special diets are catered for with advance notice.

Eskdale

Esk Dale is the largest of the dales within the North York Moors National Park, and is unusual in that it runs east-west, rather than the more common north-south. The River Esk rises at Esklets, high up on Westerdale Moor, reaching the sea at Whitby. The landscape of this particular valley is dramatic and there are some stunning viewpoints from the surrounding moorland. The scenic Eskdale Railway follows the length of the valley running from Whitby through to Middlesbrough and the ride can provide an interesting outing for an afternoon - perhaps taking lunch or tea in one of the pretty villages along the way.

Esk Dale is renowned for its salmon fishing, however, it is worthwhile noting that should anyone wish to travel to the area with the intention of taking advantage of the abundant salmon, the inland waters are not public property, and permission must be obtained from the land-owner first. A rod licence and permit will also be required (Details of these are obtainable from the local branch of the National Rivers Authority).

Another feature of the valley that can be enjoyed is the Esk Valley Walk, a group of ten linking walks that explore the length of the valley.

One of the first villages one comes to, having left Whitby and following the route of the River Esk, is **AISLABY**. Dating back to the early 18th century, **The Huntsman Inn** is a quality establishment where you are sure to enjoy your visit. The atmosphere is full of character, added to by the wooden floors and open log fires. The landlord, Gary Moutrey, is an experienced chef so you can also be guaranteed of a good meal. Behind the bar he can also offer well-kept real ales to complement your food. During summer months, the pub can get busy so bookings for meals are advisable. At the time of writing a couple of letting rooms are planned. The decor of this establishment is traditional and the atmosphere friendly - this is one place well worth a try.

The Huntsman Inn, Aislaby, Whitby Tel: 01947 810637

On the opposite side of the river is the village of **SLEIGHTS**. In Whitby's prosperous days, the wealthy of the town built their houses here. The village is not on the main tourist trail but is worth visiting and ideally placed for a touring base.

In the village you will find The Plough. It is situated on Coach Road which was the old route taken by coaches travelling through the moors to the coast at Whitby. The Plough is, perhaps not surprisingly, a former coaching inn and dates back in parts, some 350 years. Inside, the welcome that you will receive from owners Colin, Pat, Tony and Carole will be difficult to beat. The decor is very traditional and you find plenty of good company from locals and other visitors. Behind the bar, they serve well-kept real ales some of which are hand-pulled. There is also an excellent dining area and the menus available throughout the pub are excellent. The range is good, catering for children and vegetarians, and is very reasonably priced. Upstairs there are three letting rooms available for bed and breakfast accommodation. The rooms are clean and comfortable and very good value. All in all, a great place that everyone will enjoy.

The Plough, 180 Coach Road, Sleights, Whitby
Tel: 01947 810412

The twin villages of EGTON and EGTON BRIDGE are the next stops along the valley. Egton is set higher up on the windswept moors while Egton Bridge, which is slightly smaller and somewhat more interesting, can be found at the

Beggar's Bridge, Eskdale

valley bottom. The village is dominated by the massive Church of St Hedda. Built in 1866, its roof is painted blue with gold stars and there is some fine Belgian terracotta-work on the altar. Egton Bridge is also well known for its Gooseberry Show. Established in 1800 the show is held on the first Tuesday in August. Competitors come from all over world and some of the prize specimens reach 2 oz in weight!

In this delightful village you will find the impressive traditional inn and guest house, The Wheatsheaf Inn. The inn has been owned since 1978 by Albert and Susan Latus and is now managed by their son Michael.

The Wheatsheaf Inn, Egton, Whitby Tel: 01947 895271

Parts of this fine inn date back 450 years, and inside much of its original character and charm have been retained, with beamed ceilings, open fires and a wood-panelled bar area. A good selection of bar meals is served here, and a splendid collection of bank notes from all over the world decorates the room.

A first-class restaurant has been created in the adjacent building which at one time was a cow-shed. This has magnificent stone walls, a relaxed and stylish atmosphere, and a menu which offers a extensive range of dishes. The daily specials often include such delights as pheasant braised with spring Vegetables, lemon marinated chicken or a home-made vegetarian chilli.

The resident's lounge is spacious and elegant, and the guest rooms all have en-suite facilities and are appointed to the highest modern standards. Look out for the superb room at the top of the house which has a truly unique atmosphere. The Wheatsheaf caters for fishing and shooting parties, and being situated only a mile and a half from the North Yorkshire Moors Railway terminus at Grosmont, provides the ideal base for exploring the nearby moors and coastline.

Whitby to Scarborough

Just a few miles to the south of Whitby is another of the region's great beauty spots, ROBIN HOOD'S BAY, or Bay Town, as the locals refer to it. Although fishing is no longer the main occupation, in the 18th and 19th centuries the village thrived on it. By 1920, however, there were only two fishing families left in the Bay, mainly due to lack of harbour facilities, and the industry died out. Today the interest is being revived, due to this being renowned as one of the best crab grounds on the north coast. The reputation of the young seamen in this area was held very highly indeed, and press gangs from the Royal Navy were sent here to procure men for their vessels. Apparently the local women had different ideas, and were reported to have discouraged the gangs by means of pans and rolling pins!

Because of the natural isolation of the bay, smuggling once played a great part in the prosperity of the town. The houses and inns in the Bay were said to have connecting cellars and cupboards, and it is reported that "a bale of silk could pass from the bottom of the village to the top without seeing daylight".

Shipwrecks play another major role in the history of the Bay, as the many reefs that surround the coast would indicate. A notable episode occurred in 1881, when a large

42

brig called "Visitor" was run aground. The seas were so rough that the lifeboat from Whitby had to be dragged eight miles in the snow to Robin Hood's Bay to be launched. In the end, it was the brave people of the village who rescued the crew, a much lauded event in the history of the community. The town itself has not escaped totally from the ravages of the sea, and on several occasions parts of it have been swept away.

The Victoria Hotel, Robin Hood's Bay, Nr. Whitby
Tel: 01947 880205

The magnificent Victoria Hotel stands proudly overlooking Robin Hood's Bay and beyond and offers marvellous scenic views. Built in 1897 this is a hotel that really does have everything the visitor could wish for. The eleven letting rooms are of a high quality, beautifully decorated and furnished throughout. Add to this the food and drink of the highest standard and you will need to look no further. The beautiful beer gardens overlook the sea and are an ideal spot for a drink on a summer's evening. Behind the bar there are always four real ales on tap - two are permanent and the others change regularly. The bars are open all day Friday and Saturday and all day every day in the summer season. A great establishment with a friendly service.

If you are looking for an excellent morning coffee, light lunch, afternoon tea or evening meal in this lovely village, then look out for **The Bramblewick** on the quayside. Formerly an old fisherman's cottage and bakery (at one time the baker used to charge the locals one penny for heating their roasts), parts of the building date back over 400 years. Owners, Linda and Andrew Carter, concentrate on preparing fine home-cooked dishes, especially those using fresh locally-caught fish and seafood. All the cakes and puddings are home-made and include such tempting offerings Syrup and Nut tarts, crumbles, sponges and Sticky Date and Walnut cake. Evening booking is advisable. Closed mid-November to Christmas and only open weekends to the end of February.

The Bramblewick, New Road, Robin Hoods Bay
Tel: 01947 880418

Until the summer of 1994 if you took an excursion up on to **FYLINGDALES MOOR** near to Robin Hood's Bay you wouldn't have been able to miss the famous 'golf balls' of Fylingdales Early Warning Station. Erected at the height of the Cold War they became redundant and after a long debate to decide whether they were of sufficient architectural merit to be preserved the decision was taken to dismantle one of Yorkshire's most obtrusive and dramatic attractions. The surrounding moors leave you with an impression of the grand isolation. It would be advisable, however, not to run out of petrol at this point! The most environmentally-friendly way to view it, though, must be on foot, and should one's resolve run out, a ride for the remainder of the journey can be taken on the steam train route.

There is no village of Fylingdales, but the village of **FYLINGTHORPE**, set back slightly from the coast is on the moor. A warm welcome awaits all visitors to **Croft Farm**, just outside of the village. John and Pauline Featherstone offer comfortable bed and breakfast accommodation in their 17th-century farmhouse or alternatively there is an adjacent cottage available for self-catering. In the farmhouse there are 3 letting rooms which are all cosy and inviting and Pauline's outstanding Yorkshire breakfasts are a real feast - just the thing before a long day sightseeing! Bed and breakfast is available from Easter to October. Sleeping four people, the cottage is warm and comfortable and ideal to use as a touring base. The cottage is available all year round. The location of the farm is superb and you can enjoy wonderful views of the surrounding countryside and Robin Hood's Bay.

Croft Farm, Fylingthorpe, Whitby Tel: 01947 880231

Continuing south along the coast you will shortly arrive at the cliff-top village of **RAVENSCAR**, noted for its views and wildlife walks. A plan in the 1890s to build a holiday resort here failed in the 1920s and overgrown roads are the only evidence that remains. Much of this dramatic stretch of coastline is National Trust owned and they have an information centre and shop that provide an ideal start to any visit.

Walks along the rocky beach can be dangerous, as is bathing, due to the fast-rising tide, and advice should always be taken from locals before setting out to explore.

Raven Hall, Ravenscar, Nr. Scarborough Tel: 01723 870353

Ravenscar has a long and turbulent history dating back to the fifth century, but its main claim to fame is the magnificent Raven Hall which King George III made his royal retreat. Situated 600 feet above sea level, with dramatic cliff top scenery, Raven Hall is on the edge of the North Yorkshire Moors and within easy reach of Whitby and Scarborough.

Since 1961 the Hall has been owned by the Gridley family who have carried out extensive refurbishments to the 54 bedrooms, and developed the award-winning gardens and battlement walks. There is plenty of room for guests to relax, the grounds extend to 100 acres and include a swimming pool, paddling pool, tennis courts, bowling green, clock golf, putting, a challenging 9 hole golf course, giant chess, croquet lawn, sauna and beauty salon. Indoor facilities are just as

46

comprehensive with a renowned restaurant and two bars, and plenty of entertainment. This is a fabulous hotel just waiting to be discovered.

Wrea Head House, Wrea Head Farm, Barmoor Lane, Scalby, Scarborough Tel: 01723 375844

Surrounded by beautiful countryside, on the edge of the North York Moors National Park at SCALBY, are Wrea Head House Country Cottages. The collection of self-catering cottages have been converted from red brick and pantiled farm buildings. The majority are clustered around an attractively landscaped courtyard, and they enjoy magnificent views across rolling meadows towards the sea and Scarborough Castle. There are nine cottages in all, and they vary in capacity from two to eight guests. They are comfortably furnished, very well-equipped, have full central heating and linen is included. Other facilities on the site include a superb heated indoor swimming pool, jacuzzi and sauna which are available every day all year round. The extremely high quality of the cottages has been recognised in their English Tourist Board 4 Key Highly Commended rating and they have also been awarded the Yorkshire and Humberside Tourist Board White Rose Award for Best Self-catering Cottages in the region.

SMUGGLING

The tales of smugglers associated with much of this coastline enthrall all who hear them. Houses with secret rooms still exist today, as do the moorland tracks that the smugglers and donkey trains used nearly 250 years ago.

At Robin Hood's Bay, The Smuggling Experience is a themed museum with the sound, sight and smells of the 18th century, providing a wonderful chance to discover the taste of York's smuggling history. Such scenes as the ship to France, the monastery, the old town prison, the swamp, a plot in the tavern and even the execution of the smugglers make this show totally unique and awe-inspiring.

However, often these wild men were far from romantic being mercilessly cruel as they loaded up with Dutch gin, tea, and French brandy.

The bay was particularly attractive to smugglers because of its isolation. The men were financed by local squires and although the risk was hanging, it was thought the perks were worth it.

Robin Hood's Bay is now a quiet fishing village and the maze of steps and alleys and secret passages, which were intended to outwit the excise men, can be explored by visitors today.

In addition to the cottages, Chris and Andrea Wood, the owners, can also offer bed and breakfast accommodation in their farmhouse. There are three letting rooms available, one twin and two doubles. Each bedroom has an en-suite bathroom, colour television, drinks tray, hair-dryer and individually controlled heating. The lawns, gardens and summer house are available to all guests, as is the leisure complex.

Once a village in its own right, Scalby has become a suburb of Scarborough with a large entertainment complex at Scalby Mills. Formerly the site of an old mill, visitors can now enjoy a fun park, shops, cafés, bars and pools here. The Scarborough Sea Life Centre is also located here offering a fascinating outing that all the family are sure to enjoy.

The older part of Scalby is set back from the sea and the fine Church of St Lawrence is worthy of a visit. Another reminder of the past is the Derwent Sea Cut which passes through the town. This artificial river was cut by hand between 1800 and 1810 to relieve the problems of flooding by the River Derwent.

The Plough, 21 High Street, Scalby, Scarborough
Tel: 01723 362622

Situated in the village of Scalby, just a few hundred yards off the main A170 Whitby to Scarborough road, is the very welcoming public house, The Plough. Your hosts Brian and Heather Simpson are a charming couple and have been here just a year, but have over 30 years experience in the trade. The Plough has a charming interior, beautifully decorated, with its beehive style windows being a real feature. Built in 1899 the inn retains much of its original Victorian character with the original high ceilings and feature fireplace. Added to the warm Yorkshire hospitality is the excellent food and well-kept ales which will keep all visitors well satisfied. Food is served every lunchtime and Saturday early evening. The menu is varied and complemented by daily specials. The chef's specialities are steak pie and the traditional Sunday roast dinners. The real ales include Worthington's, Stones and Bass Mild in addition to the range of lagers and spirits. To the rear of the establishment is a terraced area with tables and chairs, ideal for sunny days, and Brian's aviary is a real talking point.

Before we visit the popular seaside town of Scarborough (the first stop in Chapter Two) let us take a look at some of the villages of the central Moors.

Central Moors

GOATHLAND is located high up on the moors and has earned recent notoriety for being the setting of the TV series 'Heartbeat'. Sheltered from cold winds by the surrounding moorlands, it has a surprisingly mild climate for a village so high above sea level, and the beautiful situation certainly makes the village very special.

In a splendid location overlooking the wide expanses of Goathland Moor, you will find the Mallyan Spout Hotel, named after the waterfall of the same name, which flows into a wooded valley a short distance away. This handsome ivy-clad, stone-built hotel provides a perfect base for those interested in outdoor pursuits or the peaceful pleasures of fine food, good wine and charming hospitality.

Inside, the atmosphere is friendly and the surroundings luxurious. There is a cocktail bar and three spacious guest lounges with views over attractive gardens to the moors and beautiful Esk valley beyond. Each of the 24 individually decorated bedrooms has a private bathroom, colour television, telephone and radio. Most are decorated in cottage style and have breathtaking views over the surrounding countryside and moorland. Four rooms have recently been completely refurbished and are of a particularly high quality. They are located at the rear of the hotel and have outstanding panoramic views over the moors, towards Egton. Their facilities include electric curtains and full hi-fi systems. In the Coach House, two double and two twin rooms are available at ground floor level for those who find stairs a problem.

The hotel has been owned and personally run by Judith and Peter Heslop since the early 1970s. They ensure that their guests receive a professional standard of service which makes them feel instantly at home. The hotel restaurant is renowned for its cuisine and is open to residents and non-residents alike. The menu is long and adventurous and features freshly caught seafood from Whitby. The chef's specialities could include such delights as fresh pear poached in rosemary and lime with fresh coriander, stilton and creme fraîche mousse for starters and sautéed medallions of monkfish with a pink and green peppercorn sauce served on a bed of wild rice for a main course. All dishes are freshly cooked to order and they may require a short while to prepare. The results, however, are mouth-watering and well worth waiting for.

The Mallyan Spout Hotel provides an ideal base for exploring the many nearby beauty spots and places of historical interest.

The privately-owned North Yorkshire Moors Railway stops at nearby Goathland station and offers a fascinating excursion through heather-clad hills, wooded valleys and charming moorland villages. The hotel also runs a programme of special weekends for the gourmet or for those interested in such activities as hill-walking and fishing.

Mallyan Spout Hotel, Goathland, Nr. Whitby
Tel: 01947 896486

Many of the houses in Goathland have wonderful views of the moors, and this is especially true of Prudom House, a renovated farmhouse owned by Ian and Viv MacCaig.

The house stands on the second oldest site in the village, the original building dating back to the 12th century. The name 'Prudom' was probably that of a sheep-stealer who, it is believed, was hanged for his activities! The sheep now wander safely across the green in front of this lovely old house which provides comfortable, homely accommodation. While preserving the farmhouse feel, with exposed beams, log fires oak panelling and stone-work, the MacCaigs have incorporated modern features. Some bedrooms have en-suite shower and toilet, and tea and coffee facilities and there is central heating in all rooms. The food is home-cooked to produce out-of-the-ordinary country dishes. In addition, the MacCaigs run a tea-room alongside the house, where they serve morning coffee, hot and cold light lunches, soup, granary rolls and afternoon teas. The tea-room has recently been extended to create a sun-lounge, with wonderful views across the moorland. Within the tea-room you will also find local products on display and for sale, such as glassware, woodwork and metalwork.

Prudom House, Goathland, Nr. Whitby Tel: 01947 896368

As one might imagine with an isolated community such as this one, the traditions go back far, and none so far as the origins of the Plough Stots Service, a ritual sword dance performed in the town every January. The Nordic settlers brought this particular ceremony to these parts over a thousand years ago, the "stot" being derived from the Scandinavian word for a bullock. In the ancient procession, young men of the village drag a plough through the street, in place of the bullocks that would normally perform the task. The dancers follow, brandishing 30 inch swords, in a pagan ritual that the Norsemen were keen to retain after their invasion of the area.

You will find a particularly peaceful and relaxing hotel in a very quiet location near Goathland, called the **Whitfield House Hotel**. The hotel is situated on the edge of the delightful hamlet of **DARNHOLM** and it may be advisable to telephone the owners, John and Pauline Lusher, on 01947 896215 for directions on how to find it. The handsome hotel building is a former farmhouse dating from the 17th century. Much of its original character and charm have been retained, and inside the atmosphere is truly relaxing and welcoming.

The cottage-style bedrooms all have bathrooms en-suite and are equipped with radio-alarms, hair dryers, TV, direct-dial telephones and drinks facilities. The standard of service is high and the full English breakfasts and table d'hôte and à la carte menus offer the very best in country cooking. The hotel lies a short distance from the stepping stones at Darnholm and within easy reach of many superb woodland and moorland walks. Open March to October inclusive.

Whitfield House Hotel, Goathland Tel: 01947 896215

One of the most outstanding attractions of this area is the privately operated, steam-hauled North Yorkshire Moors Railway which runs between Pickering and Grosmont, stopping in Goathland. This spectacular line passes through some of the most dramatic landscapes in the National Park including several Sites of Special Scientific Interest. The railway was designed before the age of steam by the great railway engineer, George Stephenson, in order to provide Whitby with a modern land link with the outside world.

When the line first opened the trains were made up of stage coaches on top of simple bogies, pulled along the rails by horses. One of the most interesting features was the 1 in 10 incline from Beck Hole to Goathland where wagons were hauled by rope. The incline caused many accidents until, in 1865, the Deviation Line was blasted through solid rock.

Although the gradient is still one of the steepest rail sections in the country at 1 in 49, it opened up the line to steam trains.

To the west of here is Rosedale, a long and pleasant valley extending from the centre of the moors to the southeast. In May the road from LASTINGHAM is brightened by rhododendron bushes and deer can often be seen.

ROSEDALE ABBEY is the largest settlement of the dale. A small priory was founded here in 1158 but which was dismantled during the Dissolution. Another vanished landmark is the chimney which gave its name to Chimney Bank, a steep and twisting road, with gradients of 1 in 3, which leads to the moor. The chimney which used to be on the summit of the moor was a relic from the days of iron-ore mining, but it was declared unsafe and demolished in 1972.

The White Horse Farm Hotel, Rosedale Abbey, Nr. Pickering
Tel: 01751 417239

High on the west side of Rosedale, accessed from Chimney Bank, The White Horse Farm Hotel boasts one of the finest views in Yorkshire. The hotel dates back to 1702 and although it has seen may changes in that time, it still retains a wealth of character, and this is particularly evident in the bar and dining room. The restaurant offers an excellent choice of local game, fish, meat, poultry and vegetarian dishes served with fresh locally grown vegetables. To complement your meal, a well-stocked cellar provides interest for all palates and pockets. For quiet relaxation you may prefer the lounge to the more lively bar, in which hand-pulled real ales and a selection of over thirty malt whiskies are available. If you have not booked a table for dinner then you will be more than satisfied by the wide variety of bar meals on offer at lunch time and in the evenings. The hotel has 15 bedrooms, some in an annexe at the rear, all with private bath or shower room. Perhaps the best way to enjoy the food and character of the hotel is to try one of the 'Moorland Breaks', available all year round.

Rosedale Caravan and Camping Parks, Rosedale Abbey,
Pickering Tel: 01751 417272

Dedicated campers will find a great place to stay, at **Rosedale Caravan and Camping Parks**. Maureen and Barrie Doughty have owned and personally run this picturesque 30-acre park since 1987 and can accommodate up to 100 touring caravans and 150 tents. The site facilities include a modern shower block, laundry facilities, a popular club and restaurant and a shop selling groceries, gifts and camping accessories. A limited number of electric hook-ups are available which should be booked in advance. There is also a splendidly-equipped children's play area, and in the
56

nearby village there is a post office, newsagents and two pubs. In addition, Maureen and Barrie can now offer 2 self-catering flats sleeping four people, and a hard-standing caravan which can also accommodate four. The sites are open March to end October.

The Coach House, Rosedale Abbey, Nr. Pickering
Tel: 01751 417208

Standing opposite the Rosedale Abbey Caravan and Camping Park, is the very impressive Coach House. As the name suggests the building was for many hundreds of years where the Lord of the Manor kept his coaches, and where the coachmen would have lived. It has subsequently been refurbished, and the large front windows are where the coaches would have once entered. The house became an inn and restaurant only 3 years ago, when Ray Doyle and Jayne Alderson also took occupancy. Tastefully converted so as not to lose its character, there are three distinct areas to the building. There is a family room with lots of pub games, and where children are welcome, a bar area, and a cosy, snug restaurant area too. The food available is traditional English fare, all freshly prepared and home cooked. Jayne looks after this department, and her efforts are obviously well appreciated as the restaurant is often busy. Ray looks after the bar, and keeps a good selection of ales, many being real ales, and all in excellent condition. In addition to the restaurant menus there are bar meals and daily specials available as well.

The next valley but one, to the west, is the long, remote valley of FARNDALE. The dale is famous for its wild daffodils which every spring cover the banks of the River Dove. Yorkshire folk often refer to the daffodils as 'Lenten Lilies' because of the time of year that they bloom. The flowers, once plundered by visitors, are now protected by law and 2,000 acres of Farndale are designated as a local nature reserve.

CHAPTER TWO

Scarborough and Ryedale

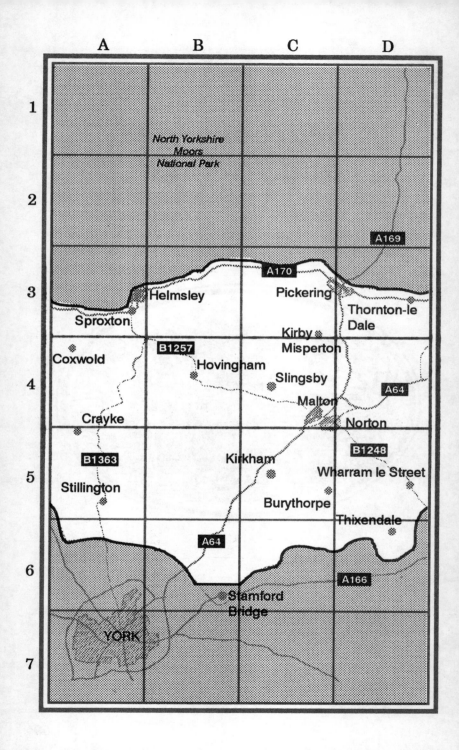

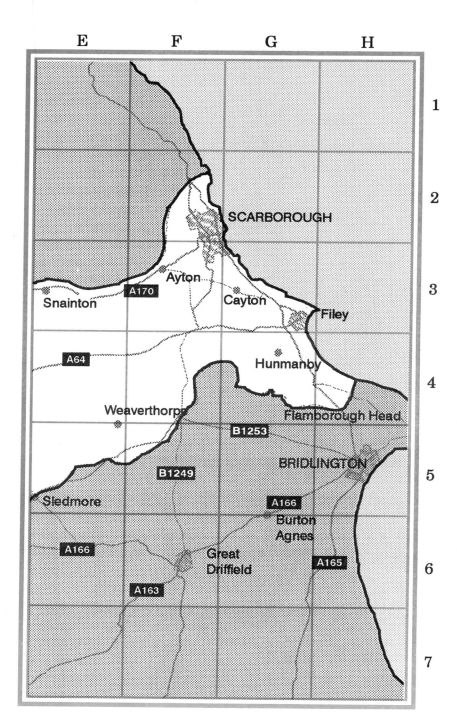

Scarborough Castle

CHAPTER TWO

Scarborough and Ryedale

Probably the best known and most popular resort in Yorkshire is SCARBOROUGH. Settlements in this area date back to the time of the Norse invaders and reminders of those less popular tourists are evident in the place names. The Vikings introduced the 'thorp's and 'by's into the vocabulary - as in Fridaythorpe, Kirkby and, of course, Scunthorpe and the Danes gave us the ' burgh' at the end of place names such as Sedburgh and 'Scarthi's Burgh' a former name of Scarborough.

Visitors to the resort today cannot fail to be impressed by the panoramic setting of the cliffs and bays and the buildings, in their latter-day splendour, seem appropriately in proportion with their setting. In fact, the popularity of Scarborough did not begin with the attractions of its seaside, but from people flocking to sample the benefits of its spring water, discovered in 1626 by Mrs Tomyzin Farrer, and later popularised in a book published by a certain Dr Wittie, who named it "Scarborough Spaw".

The connecting of the railway from York in 1846 was the factor that really transformed Scarborough into the resort we know today. People from the industrial towns of the West Riding could travel out to escape the grime and pollution caused by the Industrial Revolution, to breathe the cleaner sea air.

There is more to Scarborough though, than the candy-floss stalls and brightly painted Regency and Victorian buildings. Parts of it, notably the Castle and its environs, date back to medieval times, and were themselves built on the site of a

Roman fort and signal station. Scarborough Castle dates from the 12th century, and its gaunt remains stand high on Castle Rock Headland, dominating the two bays. Staged battles to commemorate the invasions of the Danes, Saxons and more latterly the Napoleonic incursions are often held here, along with other events, and are a popular attraction for the tourists. The cliffs around the area are also well worth exploring, forming the final part of the famous Cleveland Way.

Those visiting the resort around Shrove Tuesday might be forgiven for wondering as to the sanity of the inhabitants of Scarborough. The sight of people exercising the ancient right to skip along the highways, in competition with the more usual methods of getting from A to B, may be witnessed, although the local authorities do attempt to restrict the avid and eccentric exponents of this quaint and peculiar custom to the area along Foreshore Road. Another tradition upheld by the locals at this time is the sounding of the Pancake Bell, a custom started by the wives of the town to alert their menfolk in the fields and in the harbour that they were about to commence the cooking of the pancakes.

Scarborough, as is fitting for such a well-established holiday resort, is primed for entertainment of all kinds, from the intellectual attractions of the Rotunda Museum on Vernon Road and the art collections at the Scarborough Art Gallery, right through to the futuristic world of holograms at Corrigans Arcade on Foreshore Road. The Stephen Joseph Theatre in the Round is another lively venue, where playwright Alan Aykbourn is the director.

Another place worthy of a visit is the Wood End Museum of Natural History on the Crescent, once the home of the famous Sitwell family. There are permanent displays of their books and photographs, as well as changing exhibitions of local wildlife. Particularly worth a visit is the double-storied conservatory and aquarium.

Overlooking the North Bay in the heart of Scarborough is **The Boston Hotel**. Built during the 1880s this magnificent

Victorian property was formerly a private residence, probably owned by a wealthy businessman of the day. The magnificent view over the bay cannot be equalled and the hotel is conveniently close to all the tourist attractions in the town. This is very much a family establishment, owned and run by Mary and Malc Woodall and their family for the past seven years. The family's knowledge and experience of the hotel business is very apparent and through much hard work they have made the Boston Hotel a place to which guests return year after year. The property comprises five floors, one of which is the dining room. Like the rest of the hotel it is furnished and decorated to a very high standard. The upper floors, with a total of 28 en-suite rooms, are serviced by a lift. There are two guests' lounges - one is non-smoking, and the other features a bar and small dance area. The most important aspect of the hotel is the warm, welcoming atmosphere and it is this that will have you returning again.

The Boston Hotel, 1-2 Blenheim Terrace, Queens Parade, Scarborough Tel: 01723 360296

Another comfortable hotel is **The Red Lea Hotel** located on the fashionable South Cliff, close to the Spa and South Bay attractions. The Red Lea is one of the most popular hotels in the area having been carefully converted from six elegant Victorian terraced houses. The standard of the conversion has been maintained and improved to ensure the high level of facilities and services available to guests. All 69 bedrooms are en-suite and come with colour TV, drinks tray and telephone. A lift services all the floors, and other facilities include a licensed residential bar lounge, conference room, TV lounge and well-appointed dining room. To ensure you enjoy your stay to the full, try out the heated indoor pool, and to help you keep in trim there is also a sauna, sunbed and exercise room. Despite being such a large hotel, managers Valerie and Bruce Lee ensure that your stay is a special one.

The Red Lea Hotel, Prince of Wales Terrace, South Cliff, Scarborough Tel: 01723 362431

Should you find yourself in need of some refreshment during a day of sightseeing then head for the **Tap and Spile** pub on the edge of the town centre. Formerly known as The White Horse, the building dates back to the mid-19th century and was taken over by the Pubmaster Group and reopened as the Tap and Spile in 1993. The manager, Fred Bennett, has been here since the reopening, and has created a warm welcoming atmosphere that awaits all visitors. The furnishings are traditional and the decorative memorabilia contributes to the Tap and Spile theme. Behind the bar they keep a range of eight real ales from across the country, in addition to a good range of wines and spirits. Food is served at lunch times and a specials board complements the main menu but it is very popular, so get in early!

Tap and Spile, 94 Farsgrove, Scarborough
Tel: 01723 363837

Should you wish to escape the crowds you might try to head west across Seamer Moor towards the lovely Forge Valley. The woodlands here are among the best remaining examples of mixed woodland in northeast England. There is a rich variety of trees complemented by ground flora such as wood anemones, primroses, bluebells, orchids and many other species. Look out also for the marsh marigold and flag iris that grow in the River Derwent.

In the nearby village of **AYTON** are the ruined remains of Ayton Castle set at the side of the road near the junction of the A170 and B1261. Dating from around 1400 this was one of the many pele towers built in the region when there was great danger from invading Scottish marauders. A pele tower was a fortified building, often a farmhouse, and much more common nearer to the Scottish border. In more peaceful years, many of these towers had a more comfortable mansion added and became stately homes, but their defensive origins are easily recognisable.

In the village of **EAST AYTON** there is a fascinating place that all the family will enjoy visiting, called **The Honey Farm**. This outstanding attraction is owned and run by Steve Ryan and his wife, and has everything for a great day out. Created only three years ago, it is now a place that no-one should leave out of a trip to this part of Yorkshire. Visitors can see the bees in their natural surroundings and guided tours help you learn even more about this fascinating insect.

The Honey Farm, Betton Farm Centre, East Ayton,
Scarborough Tel: 01723 864001
Tearooms and Farmshop Tel: 01723 863143

It is the females that maintain the 'home' with meticulous care, and the exhibition allows you to see a working colony sited within a tree trunk. Children will love to see the colony established in a doll's house and even more remarkable is the colonisation of a letter box. It is an incredible fact that in central London about 28 post boxes a day become sites for colonies! Another interesting exhibit is the honey extractor which is used to spin the honey from the combs. Working on a similar principle to a spin dryer, the liquid honey is flung from the cells in the combs by centrifugal force.

One of the most surprising substances to come from a bee hive is propolis. Dark brown in colour, propolis is made up of resin from plants and trees, wax, essential oils and pollen. Bees use this to block up cracks in the hive and its antiseptic properties help keep the young bees in a sterile environment. Apparently, propolis has tremendous healing powers and has been used in recent years for blood disorders, ulcers, rashes, coughs and colds, dental problems as well as to treat some arthritic conditions. Some claim it can even prevent flu!

The Honey Farm can boast an outstanding restaurant offering welcome refreshment after a long day sightseeing. It is mainly home-cooking that is on offer, and there is a bakery on site, providing freshly baked bread and cakes. The Farm Shop sells cheeses, meat and vegetables while the craft shops offer the wares of local craftsmen. The Honey Farm Shop sells a variety of honeys, fresh from the hives and lots of other souvenirs. The shop even stocks an extensive range of cosmetics that incorporate honey and bees' wax. A recent addition is a pottery where visitors can watch the talented potter at work and of course purchase the results of his labours. This is an unusual and remarkable place - well worth going out of your way to visit.

East Ayton Lodge, Moor Lane, East Ayton, Nr. Scarborough
Tel: 01723 864227

Not far from the village of East Ayton, on the edge of the North York Moors National Park, is East Ayton Lodge. This beautifully appointed hotel is set in three acres of its own grounds close to the River Derwent. The tranquil surroundings make this an ideal place for a peaceful and relaxing holiday. A well stocked bar caters for all needs offering a good selection of beers, wines and spirits. Morning coffee is available as well as a large selection of bar meals at lunch time and in the evening. The excellent restaurant specialises in English, French and Vegetarian cuisine with fresh vegetables from the hotel garden when in season. You can dine in elegant surroundings and choose from the comprehensive à la carte or table d'hôte menus which are complemented by an extensive wine list. There are 31 comfortable bedrooms, all with en-suite bathrooms, all furnished and equipped to a high standard. Three are honeymoon suites, complete with four poster bed, are ideal for that romantic break. Whether on business or pleasure, for one night or several, owners Brian and Karry Gardner will make sure you enjoy your stay to the full.

Just to the north of East Ayton is the site of the old forge from which the Forge Valley takes its name. The forge dates back to medieval times and would have produced wrought or cast iron. A pleasant walk can be taken to the forge site from WEST AYTON returning on the other side of the river. The round trip is about 4 miles and you should allow about two and a half hours.

Near to SEAMER is the Star Carr Mesolithic lake dwelling, probably the oldest man-made dwelling in the Vale of Pickering. Excavations have revealed that a settlement existed here in about 7,500BC and was home to a tribe of hunters. The houses were built on stilts on the edge of what was once a large lake. Sadly the remains of the excavation lie on private land and are not open to the public.

In the ancient village of Seamer itself is North End Farm Guest House situated in six acres of farmland which in turn accommodates free range poultry and horses. This Tourist Board recommended 18th century farmhouse has been tastefully extended over the years.

70

North End Farm, Main Street, Seamer, Scarborough
Tel: 01723 862965

The bedrooms are pleasantly decorated in keeping with the farmhouse and have en-suite facilities, TV, tea/coffee. hair dryers, etc. To start your day a hearty English breakfast is served in the delightful dining room and a separate guests' lounge is available. To ensure comfort for all, guests are asked not to smoke.

The Copper Horse, Main Street, Seamer, Scarborough
Tel: 01723 862029

Also in the village and adjacent to the farmhouse, is **The Copper Horse** , an excellent example of an English country pub and restaurant, where evening dinner is served. This is primarily an eating establishment with decor featuring oak beams and a fine array of polished horse brasses and livery. The award-winning food can be chosen from either the à la carte menu or the daily specials board, served here at value for money prices. The dining area is separated into four cosy sections, seating in total over 100 people. The names of the dishes are highly original as well, adding that extra dimension to placing your order. Some dishes you might like to try are Henpecked, Deep Liaison or perhaps Pieces of Eight!

Killerby Old Hall, Killerby, Cayton Tel: 01723 583799

Just south of Scarborough is another sandy beach in **CAYTON BAY** , a location that is popular with surfers. Above the coast road is the village of the same name and here, midway between Scarborough and Filey, is **Killerby Old Hall**. This elegant late-16th century manor house is set in 60 acres of land, just a mile and a half from the sandy beach at Cayton Bay. The beautifully restored Hall contains some early wood panelling and a inglenook fireplace, and offers extremely comfortable accommodation for up to ten people.

Three further well-appointed cottages are available in the converted stables, each sleeping between two and six people. The properties have full central heating, some have log fires and all have year-round access to a heated indoor swimming pool, making them particularly suitable for off-season breaks. The location makes this an ideal spot for walkers, bird-watchers and families with dogs. Also on the site is a small secluded caravan park, with electric hook-ups and shower facilities. Campers also have access to the pool for a small charge. Booking is advisable during school holidays. Nearby attractions include a riding school and Valerie Green's stained glass studio and showroom.

Built on high ground, Scarborough's twin resort of FILEY looks down on a large, crescent-shaped bay that has consistently retained its attraction for the tourists over the years, and for those seeking a quieter resort than Scarborough, it presents the perfect alternative. The bay is sheltered by the protective promontory known as Filey Brigg, and once had a fishing fleet, despite the fact that it had no harbour, which necessitated the boats and cobles having to be hauled across the beach.

Filey was once a resort filled with ornate hotels to which wealthy visitors came with their families and nannies, it was considered the perfect holiday place for children, although, as is the trend with so many of these older resorts, the grandeur has been replaced by glitzy bingo halls and shops selling the usual seaside paraphernalia. Some of the vestiges of its past role as a fishing village remain, however, and one may still glimpse the occasional fishing boat beached on one of the slipways. There are also still quiet streets of traditional cottages, one of which houses the local Folk Museum, mainly around the Queen Street area.

The border between the East and North Ridings once crossed right through Filey, separating the town from the area where the parish church was situated. This unusual situation was regarded with the typical Yorkshire brand of dry humour - should you be taken seriously ill the wry comment was often heard that you might well be "Off t'North Riding" if you didn't recover!

Just a couple of miles south of Filey is the village of **HUNMANBY** where there is the Forge Craft Centre. This is a fascinating place to visit where the traditional craft of the blacksmith is still practised and you are sure to find a variety of unusual quality gifts to take home for friends and family.

Wrangham House Hotel, Stonegate, Hunmanby
Tel: 01723 891333

For a quality hotel with a very informal atmosphere, then look no further than Wrangham House Hotel in the village. The house stands in sheltered grounds near the church, and was formerly the vicarage. It is approached by a footpath known as the Church Walk, which tradition says is the remains of an old Roman road. The house is mainly late 18th century but a substantial wing was added in 1803 by Francis Wrangham, to house his books. The Reverend Francis Wrangham was Vicar of Hunmanby from 1795 to 1840 and carried out many good works in the village. He was well known for his work among the poor, formed a free dispensary, a savings bank and a free library.

The elegant house which has been converted into a comfortable hotel, is an ideal place to stay and enjoy the magnificent countryside. The hotel can offer thirteen tasteful

74

bedrooms all of which are en-suite. Each has a television, drinks tray and pleasant views over the garden. Four rooms are in the separate coach house and one of the ground floor rooms is adapted for disabled guests. There is an elegant drawing room and small bar lounge for the use of guests, both of which are quiet and peaceful. The dining room, which is housed in the wing which was built for Francis Wrangham's books, is where you can enjoy fresh, traditional home cooking.

This is an excellent establishment, homely and attractive and with an informal atmosphere.

The Vale of Pickering

The A170 road runs from Scarborough to Thirsk following, approximately, the line of the River Derwent, but located between 2 and 3 miles to the north of it. Traditionally the roads in this area are built as far away from the river as possible for there is always the danger of severe floods.

The first stop beyond East Ayton is the village of BROMPTON, home to inventor Sir George Cayley who devised the seacut for the River Derwent to relieve the problems of flooding. Among his other inventions was a successful aircraft, designed long before the Wright Brothers made their Kitty Hawk. Sir George Cayley's aircraft was a glider with a movable tailplane and undercarriage which carried a person several yards over nearby fields.

Originally a farmhouse, The Coachman Inn, a Grade II listed building of the 1700s, can be found on the western outskirts of the village of SNAINTON. Philip Mort, the present owner, retains the peat rights to nearby Snainton moor, a reminder of the inn's farming heritage. Over 200 years old, The Coachman Inn is a mature and comfortable building with a warm and friendly atmosphere. The Cocktail Bar has a cosy ambience, furnished with solid oak furniture or you could relax with an aperitif in the more intimate lounge. Informal meals are served in both bars at lunch time and in the evening. For a more substantial meal, the elegant Posthorn Restaurant offers an excellent and varied menu including vegetarian dishes and an extensive wine list. Philip can also offer bed and breakfast accommodation with 10 guest bedrooms each with private bathroom. Alternatively, you could choose one of the snug self-catering cottages that have been sympathetically converted from the original stables.

The Coachman Inn, Snainton, Nr. Scarborough
Tel: 01723 859231

Milebush Farm, just to the north of Snainton Village, is a working farm open to the public, offering a coffee shop, gift and farm shop. The coffee shop is open for morning coffee, light lunches and cream teas. Also on sale are a variety of home-made cakes and pastries including speciality pork pies. The attractive Gift and Farm shop sells hand-made marmalades, jams and chutneys, country fruit wines and local hand-made crafts. Home-cured hams and bacon, home baking, fresh eggs and much more can be found in the farm shop.

This is a working farm with a variety of farm animals. A collection of old-fashioned tools and implements can be viewed along with the attractive art gallery where local

76

artists exhibit their work. Stretch your legs with a short walk to Wydale and then relax in the 200-year old Cartshed Coffee Shop. Providing the shop facilities are used, the owners are delighted for visitors to explore the farm free of charge.

Milebush Farm is located 9 miles from Scarborough or Pickering; follow the A170 to Snainton village; the farm is one mile up Nettledale Lane by the Peacock Pub and follow the farm sign to the top of the hill. The farm is open seven days a week from April to the end of October, 10am to 5pm, and every Sunday the rest of the year.

The farm is Egon Ronay Recommended 1994 and winner of the White Rose Award from the local Tourist Board in 1990. There are facilities for the disabled.

Milebush Farm, Nettledale Lane, Snainton,
Nr. Scarborough Tel: 01723 859203

YEDINGHAM is a small typical Yorkshire Wolds village situated almost halfway between the A64 and A170 roads leading towards Scarborough. The village is an ancient crossing point of the River Derwent and was once the site of a nunnery founded in the 12th century. The Providence Inn was once a local coaching stop and the stables and blacksmith's shop can still be seen. The coaches would have been garaged in what is now the lounge!

Al Wheldon has run The Providence for 11 years and provides guests and visitors with good food, drink and accommodation. The lounge has a friendly ambience and features an open fire and wooden beams. There is a small dining room where tables may be reserved for visitors who prefer a more intimate atmosphere. The menu is extensive and includes such dishes as venison casserole, steaks, chilli and pizzas. The house speciality, consisting of no less than fourteen different items of food on the same dish has to be seen to be believed and is certainly not for the faint hearted! A variety of sweets and a choice of 4 special coffees round off the meal all of which is home-cooked by Al. Accommodation consists of five letting rooms as well as a small touring caravan site at the back of the inn. Children are well provided for by a very extensive play area with a wide variety of equipment. Day fishing both on the Inn's own water (free of charge) and by day-ticket locally provide outdoor sport while pool and darts are there for the indoor sportsman!

The Providence Inn, Yedingham, Nr. Malton
Tel: 01944 728231

THORNTON-LE-DALE is a 'picture postcard' village and the boundary of the North York Moors National Park actually loops southwards to include it. As long ago as 1907 it was voted most beautiful village in Yorkshire, a title which

Helmsley

according to many still applies. Just off the A170, near the Parish Church of All Saints, is one of the most photographed houses in Britain, regularly appearing on chocolate boxes, jigsaws and calendars.

If you have difficulty locating this particular village on your map, it could be that it is marked as Thornton Dale. There are many arguments about which is the correct form.

Easthill House and Gardens, Thornton-le-Dale,
Nr. Pickering Tel: 01751 474561

Ideally situated for a touring base is **Easthill House and Gardens** in this pretty village . Standing in over two acres of grounds on the eastern edge of the village, a warm welcome awaits. This beautiful family home has been carefully and sympathetically converted to provide three attractive apartments accommodating between two and eight people. An adjoining cottage has been converted from the coachhouse and stables and sleeps four and in the woodland there are three Scandinavian-style chalets. All the apartments, chalets and the cottage are self-contained and have been traditionally and comfortably furnished. The kitchens are very well-equipped and most bedrooms are en-suite. The surrounding landscaped gardens and woodland include a grass tennis court and putting green and an adventure playground for children. In the garden there is also a games room with table tennis, darts and a pool table. All the accommodation holds 3/4 keys, Highly Commended ETB rating and is available for short self-catering breaks or longer lets. Ring for details and availability.

Situated 20 yards off the main road is **Warrington Guest House and Tea Rooms**. Tim and Amanda Brennan have only recently taken over this old coaching inn and have completely refurbished it, successfully creating an establishment of great style. Whether you are after a meal or in need of accommodation you will not be disappointed. The cosy, snug tea rooms and restaurant offer freshly prepared and delicious meals and snacks all at very reasonable prices. The accommodation comprises eight bedrooms all pleasantly decorated and with television and tea tray. One room even features a four poster bed for a more romantic stay. For a taste of good old Yorkshire hospitality you can't go wrong here.

Warrington Guest House and Tea Rooms, Whitbygate, Thornton-le-Dale Tel: 01751 475028

Eatwell Café, Carvery and Restaurant is very easy to find, being the only eating establishment on the Pickering to Whitby Road, next to the Fox and Rabbit Inn. The situation, at one of the gateways to the North Yorkshire Moors means this is a busy route - but don't worry, there is plenty of room and parking. Eatwell was built in 1990 by the farmers who owned the land, using stone from a demolished outbuilding. The establishment opens each day at 10 in the morning and can offer anything from a cup of tea to a full Sunday lunch, with plenty to choose from in between. There are, in addition, a wide variety of daily specials and sweets and the ham and egg teas are very popular! Eatwell is also licensed, so those who aren't driving can enjoy a glass of wine or a pint of Riding Best Bitter with their meal. Managed by Gill, Hazel and Ruth, who are ably assisted by their friendly staff, you are sure to be welcomed, and once discovered you sure to stop here again.

Eatwell, Fox and Rabbit Farm, Lockton, Nr. Pickering
Tel: 01751 460201/265

Keld Head Farm is situated in open countryside at the edge of the North Yorkshire Moors, and less than a mile to the north of the centre of Pickering. The **Keld Head Farm Cottages** are the result of careful restoration of traditional stone-built stables and barns by local craftsmen. The former farm buildings have been transformed into seven individually designed cottages retaining many of their original features. The cottage layouts range from traditional and single storey, to an 'upside down' style which takes advantage of the countryside views. All the cottages have

82

been fitted out to the highest standards of modern comfort, they are spacious and well decorated and include a fully equipped kitchen. Furthermore the properties are double-glazed and centrally heated throughout to ensure maximum comfort all year round. Six of the cottages have two bedrooms and can accommodate from two to five people. The Stables has three bedrooms and can sleep up to seven people. Other facilities on the site include a children's play area, barbecue, mountain bike hire, parking, laundry and pay phone. A range of frozen food is available and groceries can be ordered in advance. Rather unusually, the owners also provide a catering service suitable for all occasions - so why not celebrate a birthday or anniversary in style, or simply save yourselves the trouble of cooking after a long day sight-seeing. On warmer evenings a barbecue can even be prepared for you.

Keld Head Farm Cottages, Keld Head, Pickering
Tel: 01751 473974

Personally-run and supervised, the owners, Julian and Penny Fearn, will go out of their way to ensure your holiday is one you will remember, and make Keld Head Farm Cottages a place you will return to again and again. This is much more than your usual self-catering holiday, no 'here's your keys and see you next week' either! The full service

83

Julian and Penny offers even runs to a baby sitting and listening service. A stock of indoor and outdoor games for children and grown-ups can also be made available to residents.

If its peace and quiet you're after, then there is plenty of that too. The cottages' rural location takes care of that, and a short drive will take you even further into some of the best countryside Yorkshire can offer. This self-catering establishment is both unusual and special, and the well-informed and caring hosts make Keld Head Farm Cottages somewhere you will enjoy and remember.

Pickering Castle

PICKERING is situated in the heart of the area known as Ryedale and is the largest of the four market towns. It is possibly one of the oldest towns in the area too, claiming to date from 270BC when it was founded by the ancient King of the Brigantes, Peredurus.

Due to its location at the crossroads of the Whitby-Malton and Scarborough-Thirsk roads, Pickering was an important coaching stop. There are numerous medieval inns and posting houses, some of which were used by Cromwell in the Civil War.

Pickering Castle, originally a motte and bailey type, dates back to William I's attempts to dominate the area. Originally, the town's reputation was based on its pigs and horses, the pork being transported to Whitby, salted, and used aboard the ships that sailed from there. Horse-breeding was very important also, and the famous Cleveland Bay which was extensively bred in the area, was much in demand for the pulling of handsome cabs and street-cars.

In 1106, Henry 1 visited Pickering Castle and founded the Royal Forest of Pickering, which at this time was a vast domain, covering most of the southern region of what is now the North Yorkshire Moors. Many other reminders of the town's medieval past still remain, including the famous 15th-century murals in the local parish church of St Peter and St Paul. The murals were uncovered in 1851 but were promptly concealed beneath whitewash because the vicar feared they would encourage idolatry. Thankfully, they were rediscovered in 1878. They depict scenes from the Bible, history and legend ranging from St George slaying the dragon to the martyrdom of St Thomas à Becket.

Bramwood, an 18th-century Grade II listed house is situated in the centre of Pickering. Built in 1734 the guest house is in a peaceful area just a few minutes walk from the town centre. Ann and Brian Lane give very personal service in this homely guest house. The interior is very cosy and spotlessly clean throughout with lots of personal touches. Ann is renowned for her home-cooking, so it is well worth staying in for an evening meal. Home-grown or local produce is used when available, and vegetarian dishes can be prepared on request. There are 6 letting rooms which are very comfortable and some have a private shower. For relaxation guests are welcome to explore the walled garden or just sit in the lounge with the TV and open log fire. Non-smoking.

Bramwood Guest House, 19 Hallgarth, Pickering
Tel: 01751 474066

Situated opposite Pickering Railway Station, from which the North Yorkshire Moors Steam Railway runs to Grosmont, is the appropriately named Station Hotel. Originally there was an inn, a cottage and garage on the site, but these were all knocked into one to create a large inn. It was first called the Victoria Inn later becoming the Railway Inn when the railway was opened in 1836. During renovations in 1961 a gravestone was discovered in a concealed ceiling and this was believed to bring good fortune to those who lived there. During the building work two boxed railway lines were used to underpin the upper floor and these are still in position.

The Station Hotel is a real treat and will be enjoyed by people from all walks of life. The bar area is the original pub, and is still a place for locals and visitors to chat. The adjacent lounge area was once the cottage, and the extension that contains the restaurant was the site of the garage. Jim Hunter, the owner, keeps an excellent range of ales with Tetley's and Theakston's featuring regularly. Meals are served at lunch time and during the evening in summer. The menu offers traditional pub fare, and the Sunday carvery is very popular. In addition, Jim and his wife Chris have six comfortable letting rooms available. Who could wish for more - this is a real gem.

The Station Hotel, 11 Park Street, Pickering
Tel: 01751 472171

Opposite the Tourist Information Centre, in the heart of Pickering, keep an eye out for the **Eastgate Coffee Lounge and Tea Rooms**. The site which the building occupies was once the cattle market and freight railhead, but these have now long gone.

Eastgate Coffee Lounge and Tea Rooms, Eastgate Square,
Pickering Tel: 01751 475431

Owned and personally run by Ian and Christine Pearson with the help of their friendly staff the restaurant, coffee lounge and tea rooms that you see today were created from a disused building. Spotlessly clean and elegantly furnished and decorated, the fare comprises top quality food and drinks at a price to suit all pockets. The main menu is wide ranging and is supplemented by daily blackboard specials. An ideal place to stop for a meal or snack.

A popular visitor attraction in Pickering is the Beck Isle Museum of Rural Life. Housed in a Regency mansion are exhibits that will interest all the family. The 24 rooms are packed with collections from the Victorian era and are laid out to create typical rooms, shops and workshops of that period. Outside there is a display of old farming equipment.

The White Swan, The Market Place, Pickering
Tel: 01751 472288

Opposite the old post office in the market place, you will come across the historic inn and hotel, **The White Swan**. Here the accommodation comprises twelve delightful guest rooms each with a private bathroom, colour television and direct-dial telephone. The St. Emilion restaurant is renowned for the quality of its cuisine and takes pride in using locally-sourced produce, including pink-fleshed trout, duckling, game and Farndale goat's cheese. The owner, Mrs

Deirdre Buchanan, is a knowledgeable wine buff and has put together an extensive list which includes over seventy bins from St Emilion, probably more extensive than any other establishment in the country. The bar is welcoming and cosy and serves real ales. There is an excellent range of bar meals available and the puddings are legendary.

Continuing the watery theme, an unusual day out can be enjoyed at the Pickering Trout Lake and Fun Fishing. The fishing lake offers fun fishing for all the family with rods available for hire. There is also a café and tackle shop on the site. A good catch of trout is almost guaranteed! Further along the same road is Moorland Trout Farm where you can see the fish and feed them.

The Blacksmith's Arms, Aislaby, Pickering
Tel: 01751 472182

On the outskirts of the village of AISLABY, one and a half miles west of Pickering, is The Blacksmith's Arms. This is a not a pub, as you might expect from the name, but a small restaurant which has established a reputation for its excellent food. As a licensed public house the Blacksmith's Arms dates back to the reign of Elizabeth I, and parts of it were used as a smithy until the second World War. Much of the blacksmith's equipment can still be seen decorating the bar area, including the bellows, the forge and even the blacksmith's apron!

The food served in the present restaurant, for which The Blacksmith's Arms is renowned, is of a very high standard. The menu is changed frequently to make full use of the fresh local produce available and always contains a vegetarian option. The Forge Bar is a great place to relax with a drink, and owners Janet and Ken Bullock also provide bed and breakfast accommodation. There are five bedrooms, all simply but comfortably furnished, and three have an en-suite bathroom.

Helmsley Area

If you are looking for an outstanding hotel and restaurant then you should make a point of finding Cottage Leas, near MIDDLETON, which has superb views over the Vale of Pickering.

Cottage Leas, Middleton, Pickering Tel: 01751 472129

This delightful 18th century converted farmhouse stands in a delightfully peaceful location one mile north of Middleton village along a quiet country lane and is surrounded by attractive gardens. The hotel offers twelve luxurious guest rooms (one with a four-poster bed), all equipped with private shower or bathroom, colour television, telephone and tea/coffee making facilities. There is also a relaxing guests' lounge with an impressive inglenook fireplace and open log fire, a cosy bar area and the pleasant 'Jug and Platter' dining room. The separate restaurant enjoys splendid views over the gardens and surrounding countryside and offers a first class menu and wine list. Recommended.

Dating back to 1666, and situated just off the main A170 in the village of **WRELTON**, is the wonderful **Buck Inn**. If it is an old-fashioned traditional English pub you're after - then you need look no further. The inn does not serve food and only opens in the evenings except for Sunday. It is often busy though, because of two things. The first is the high quality of the ale, which is very well kept, and the second is the personalities of the owners, Chas and Kate Atkinson, who have been here for 19 years. Tastefully decorated throughout, very warm, comfy and inviting.

The Buck Inn, Wrelton, Pickering Tel: 01751 477144

Midway between Kirbymoorside and Pickering, the hamlet of **SINNINGTON** has now been bypassed by the A170 and it is here that the River Leven leaves the moors and the valley of Rosedale for the more open country to the south. The main part of the village features houses

91

Yorkshire - home of English cricket

Cricket has long been seen as England's national Summer sport being a game of skill played with bat and ball between two teams of 11 players on a large field. Yorkshire claims itself as the home of English Cricket, although as any schoolboy would tell you, the headquarters are now at the Marylebone Cricket Club in London. Yorkshire has always set itself slightly apart, not only in its regular successes, but until recently they would only accept true 'Yorkshiremen' onto the county team.

The following explanation is an amusing, though mostly accurate, description of the game and is subtitled 'as explained to a foreign visitor'!

You have two sides - one out in the field and one in.

Each man that's in goes out and when he's out he comes in and the next man goes in until he's out.

When they are all out the side that's out comes in and the side that's been in goes out and tries to get those coming in out.

Sometimes you get men still in and not out.

When both sides have been in and out including the not outs - that's the end of the game.

overlooking a broad green with the river running alongside and the tiny packhorse bridge in the middle of the green presumably served a purpose at one time but it now spans a dry watercourse.

Green Lea is a beautiful country house in Sinnington. Standing within a five acre smallholding where Ian Turnbull grows mainly corn, the house was purpose-built for Ian and his wife, Joan, 31 years ago. It stands in what was the pasture land opposite the village green, hence the name, Green Lea.

Green Lea, Sinnington Tel: 01751 432008

Ian and Joan are a lovely Yorkshire couple, in fact Ian has lived in Sinnington all his life, and they started providing first rate bed and breakfast accommodation 5 years ago. Their front garden is a picture all year round but really excels during the spring and summer. Open from 1st March through to the end of October, they can offer three lettings rooms - a family room, a double and a twin. All the rooms are spacious yet cosy and have lots of personal touches. One asset is that all the rooms available to guests are on one level. The guests' lounge/dining room boasts a roaring log fire when required and a magnificent acorn dining suite. If the smell of cooking is enough to tempt you, then you will need travel no further for your evening meal either.

KIRKBYMOORSIDE is pleasant, quiet market town on the edge of the National Park, with narrow twisting streets, fine Georgian houses and cobbled market square. The town has a long heritage, but probably earns its place in the history books by providing the notorious George Villiers, the Duke of Buckingham and one time royal favourite of Charles II, with his death bed. There are stories about his demise. One says that he fell from his horse while hunting and another that he caught a severe chill.

Known locally as 'Kirkby', one of the town's problems is how to spell its name. It means 'church-by-the-moorside' but there are disputes over the second 'k'!

George and Dragon, Market Place, Kirkbymoorside
Tel: 01751 433334

In the heart of picturesque village of Kirkbymoorside, and just a quarter of a mile from the main road is the George and Dragon. Since the 1600s, this has been a coaching inn, a natural stopping place on the Great North Road providing a haven of warmth, refreshment, good cheer and rest. Today, the hospitality is just as good, especially from owners Stephen and Francis Colling. The food has an excellent reputation, with a wide range of meals always on offer. There are three fully qualified chefs employed, and their handiwork can be sampled in the bar and the candlelit restaurant.

Behind the bar, there is always a good range of real ales available, and the pub has recently been awarded the 'Best Newcomer of the Year' award by the Good Beer Guide. In addition there is an excellent wine list, due in the main to Stephen's background as a wine merchant. The decor has a sporting theme throughout, and the George and Dragon frequently holds dinners hosted by sporting personalities. To the rear are a converted corn mill and rectory which now house 19 bedrooms. All the rooms have en-suite facilities and many also feature four poster beds. Most enjoy the benefit of views over the pretty walled garden.

King's Head Hotel, Market Place, Kirkbymoorside
Tel: 01751 431340

Back on the main street you will find **The King's Head Hotel**, a former 17th-century coaching inn. In the past coaches would have rumbled through what is now the entrance hall, and a bell, which now hangs in the bar, would have been rung to summon passengers to the coach. The second Duke of Buckingham, the notorious George Villiers, is said to have died at adjoining Buckingham House, once part of the King's Head Hotel. An entry in the parish register verifies the date with an entry in 1687 reading, "April 17th George Viluas: Lord Dooke of Bookingham".

Today, the hotel is run by the Riby family - Sheila, Tony and their daughter Louise. There are two bar areas to choose from. Duke's bar features the original flagstone floors and a log fires while the Hiker's bar in the brewhouse offers pool and darts for the young at heart. The distinctive and eye-catching restaurant area can seat up to 40 and offers freshly prepared and home-cooked food. The varied menu is accompanied by daily blackboard specials. There is accommodation available with nine letting rooms and half the rooms have en-suite facilities. The breakfasts are highly recommended, but make sure you allow plenty of time to enjoy them to the full!

Nunnington Hall

HELMSLEY, situated on the bank of the River Rye, straddling the boundary of the National Park, is one of the most popular and attractive of Yorkshire's market towns. Buildings of mixed architectural styles surround a substantial market square with a simple market cross and a gothic memorial to the second Earl of Feversham by Sir Giles Gilbert Scott.

Helmsley Castle, located not far from the market square, was founded in the early 12th century and was extensively added to in around 1200. Held by the Dukes of Buckingham in the 17th century, the estate was bought by a London banker, Sir Thomas Duncombe, from whom the Fevershams are descended. The tower still stands to its full height, despite the fact that half the castle was blasted away during the Civil War. The castle is now in the care of English Heritage and is open to the public.

The Royal Oak, Market Place, Helmsley, York
Tel: 01439 770450

Sitting on the market square of Helmsley, the **Royal Oak** is as attractive inside as it is on the outside. Formerly a coaching inn and posting house, the inn was rebuilt in 1896 and taken over four years ago by Alan and Di Brearley. Together they have a wealth of experience of the licensing and catering trade and through much hard work have turned this into an establishment that visitors return to again and again. The welcome you receive, the excellent ale, delicious and food and outstanding accommodation make it the equal of anywhere.

The interior is Victorian and as well as being excellently decorated and furnished there are some unusual ornaments and memorabilia to be admired. Once a Grenadier Guard, Alan has an excellent collection of militaria, the main feature being a display of military drums which now hang from the ceiling of the bar.

The Royal Oak can boast 5 letting rooms which are of the highest quality. Each room has en-suite facilities, some feature four poster beds, and all are spacious and comfortable. The food available is of an equally good quality. The menu offers a good selection with extra daily specials detailed on the blackboard and all dishes are good value for money. Behind the bar, there is a fine array of well-kept real ales and of course the usual selection of beers and spirits.

The inn is open 11am-11pm, daily, except Sunday when the normal licensing hours are kept. Food is served all day, every day, except Sunday evening when live music is often provided as entertainment. Although the excellent accommodation, food and ales should be enough to entice you into the Royal Oak, the best feature is the atmosphere which is always warm and welcoming. Give this one a try - you won't regret it.

On Bridge Street, just off the market place, Monet's Restaurant must be the ultimate hidden place for dining out in this area. To dine here is an experience comparable with anywhere else in the country. John Dyson and Heather came here in 1988 and have created a very friendly, intimate little restaurant which reflects both their talents and their enthusiasm. Their aim is to create an establishment of excellence and originality. Both John and Heather have had training and experience in London and abroad and they have brought to Helmsley many of the ideas and dishes they discovered on their travels. Such is their determination to be original, they have developed a special vocabulary to describe many of their dishes.

The idea for the name, Monet's, came from the recognition that Monet painted as he saw and interpreted his subjects

98

and John and Heather believe in creating dishes in the same way. Even the plates are chosen individually for each dish so as to complement the colours in the food. Consequently customers at the same table may well be given completely different plates for the same course. The menus change with the seasons, and are dependent on the ingredients that are available. Only fresh produce is used and only top quality goods accepted from their suppliers. Meat comes from a local butcher and fish from the east coast and London. John and Heather even have a contract supplier who makes the journey from France each week with products such as truffles, caviar, fois-gras and wild mushrooms.

Monet's, 19 Bridge Street, Helmsley Tel: 01439 770618

John Dyson is never happier than when he is creating new dishes, especially fish and pastry - and the wide range of fish used in the restaurant lends itself to creativity. Even the ice cream - which is all home-made - is given very individual flavourings - Pernod and Liquorice to name but two.

The restaurant also offers a lounge area with large easy chairs in which to relax after a wonderful meal. If you over-indulge you can even stay overnight, as there are three letting rooms available on the first floor. In warmer weather there is an outside terrace which is ideal for al fresco dining. The restaurant can get busy so booking is advisable at weekends. John and Heather's philosophy is that they now have the opportunity to use their experience and training to create a restaurant that is unique, certainly in North Yorkshire, and which offers something completely different. As John says, "We are aiming to make people who come through our doors very happy". What better philosophy could they have?

Church Farm Holidays, Church Farm, High Street, Helmsley Tel: 01439 770331

Church Farm Holidays, based in Helmsley, offer a superb selection of well-equipped, smartly furnished accommodation. Each of the cottages and apartments has been newly built using traditional local stone and have been designed to form a quiet secluded courtyard. The self-catering accommodation ranges from a flat for two people to a cottage which can sleep up to six.

Church Farm has been home to the Otterburn family for generations. Although it is no longer a working farm, Christine and Richard Otterburn now run a thriving home-made ice cream parlour called **Ryeburn Ice Cream** from buildings which have been carefully converted and sympathetically constructed. All the ice cream, and other products, including fudge, are made in the factory and are on sale. The dairy is open to the public as well, so they can see

100

Rievaulx Abbey

the ice cream and sorbets being processed. There is also a café selling refreshments and snacks.

Ryeburn Ice Cream, Church Farm, Cleveland Way, Helmsley
Tel: 01439 770331

The beautiful Georgian property, Stilworth House, situated in the heart of Helmsley has just about everything a visitor could wish for. The five letting rooms are beautiful, expertly decorated and furnished to the highest standards.

Stilworth House, 1 Church Street, Helmsley
Tel: 01439 771072

A guests' lounge, dining room and conservatory are equally luxurious and make this an ideal base while touring. Your hostess, Carol Swift, is charming and will immediately make you feel right at home. No evening meals are available, but Carol and her husband run the local fish and chip shop so you could always give that a try instead. Stilworth House also has plenty of off road parking to the rear which is very necessary in the centre of Helmsley.

The mansion of Duncombe Park dates from 1713 and although designed by Vanburgh, was most probably built by amateur architect William Wakefield. Sadly, the house was largely destroyed by fire in 1879 but rebuilt to the original designs a few years later. Home of the Duncombe family, now the Fevershams, this recently renovated stately home is surrounded by landscaped gardens, parkland and National Nature Reserve. Still the property of the Fevershams, Duncombe Park is open to the public. Many visitors may find the exterior slightly familiar, and this is probably because the mansion was used just a few years ago for the Anthony Hopkins film, The Remains of the Day.

The Carlton Lodge, Bondgate, Helmsley Tel: 01439 770557

On the A170 Thirsk to Pickering road, just outside Helmsley, is the impressive Carlton Lodge. This delightful hotel dates back to 1870 when it was originally built as a private house for a local builder's merchant - it was converted to a hotel in the early 1970s. All twelve bedrooms are tastefully and individually furnished to a high standard and have en-suite facilities. There are a number of rooms on the ground floor with wide doorways and no steps, making them ideal for guests with walking difficulties. The lounge is an ideal place to relax on the comfortable sofa in front of the open fire. The cuisine in the 'Stirrings' restaurant has won critical acclaim by combining a unique culinary flair and fresh local produce. It is a recognised oasis in the locality, and booking is advisable for most evenings. With advance warning nearly all types of dietary requirements can be accommodated. Personally run by the resident owners, this is a real gem.

To the south of Helmsley lies the village of **NUNNINGTON** and the National Trust-owned Nunnington Hall. This 17th-century house contains a remarkable collection of miniature rooms, known as the Carlisle Collection, fully furnished in different periods. There is also a magnificent panelled hall, fine tapestries and collections of china. The house is open to the public.

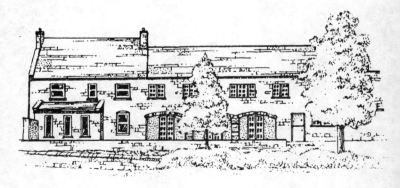

The Pheasant Hotel, Harome, Helmsley Tel: 01439 771241

On a minor road near Nunnington Hall, and two and a half miles south-east of Helmsley, you will come to the charming village of HAROME, where, in a superb position overlooking the village pond, is the extremely well-appointed Pheasant Hotel. This splendidly renovated and extended country hotel occupies the former village blacksmith's workshop, a shop, and two cottages. Today it has twelve bedrooms, all with private bathroom, colour televisions and tea/coffee making facilities, as well as two self-contained suites and two attractive cottages which are run as a fully-serviced part of the hotel. A large garden and paddock provide fresh produce for the hotel kitchen where the preparation of the finest English food is supervised by the owner, Mrs Tricia Binks. The hotel has a heated, indoor swimming pool. Unfortunately credit cards cannot be accepted.

Just to the west of Helmsley are the marvellous remains of Rievaulx Abbey, said to be one of the most beautiful monasteries in the country and now in the care of English Heritage. The original Abbey was founded in 1132 and was the first Cistercian Abbey in the north of England. The most famous Abbot of Rievaulx was Aelred, originally an Anglo-Saxon nobleman from Hexham in Northumberland, and a statue dedicated to him stands in the centre of Helmsley. The Abbey was razed to the ground during the Reformation and the stones were taken to construct a number of local buildings. Like many of the ancient ruins in the area the Abbey is occasionally used for musical and theatrical events - ask at Tourist Information Centres for details of future events. Looking down on the ruins of the Abbey is Rievaulx Terrace (National Trust), a beautiful example of landscape gardening completed in 1758 and featuring two classical temples.

Continue along the A170 and turn north at Sutton-under-Whitestonecliffe to come to the charming village of THIRLBY, home of the internationally renowned furniture workshop, Pear Tree House.

In 1979, Bob Hunter and his family acquired some farm buildings in the centre of the village which, after several months of hard work, were converted into woodworking and carving workshops. These are now known as the 'Home of the Wren' after the little birds which frequented the buildings during their restoration and which later became the trademark which is carved onto all pieces of finished oak furniture. Visitors are invited to tour the workshops and to view the completed work.

The Whitestonecliffe Inn, Sutton-under-Whitestonecliffe, Nr. Thirsk Tel: 01845 597271

The village with the longest name in England, SUTTON-UNDER-WHITESTONECLIFFE, is blessed with one of the finest inns you are likely to come across. Dating back to the 17th century, The Whitestonecliffe Inn is packed full of character, charm, class and most of all a warm, inviting atmosphere. The outside is very pretty, and the inside is just as appealing with the furnishings and decorations adding to the ambience. The recently added self-catering cottages at the rear of the inn make this an ideal spot for the visitor and tourist. The cottages are of an excellent quality and come very well equipped, available for 2 or 3 day short breaks and week-long rentals all year round. Back in the main building, there is a large restaurant area serving a good variety of freshly prepared meals. The food is reasonably priced and the portions are of a good size and booking at weekends is
106

advisable. Behind the bar, the beers are well-kept, and bar food is available. This is an inn that will suit customers of all ages and from all walks of life. Give it a try!

Sutton Bank, above, is a ridge on the western edge of the North York Moors, often soared by sleek gliders and colourful hang-gliders. There are superb views from the ridge of the Vale of Mowbray and the Pennines. In the village you will find a craftsman who, like Thompson, marks his works with an animal. Colin Almack is based at the Beaver Lodge and produces hand-made furniture marked with a beaver.

KILBURN, just a couple of miles south is the home of the most famous Yorkshire craftsman - Robert Thompson. His mark of a mouse can be found all over the world often crawling up table legs, playing on bread boards or prowling a cheese board.

Newburgh Priory

Robert Thompson was born in the village, the son of a carpenter, and was initially apprenticed to be an engineer. At the age of 20 he returned to Kilburn and begged to be trained as a carpenter by his father. Inspired by some carvings in Ripon Cathedral, the young man taught himself to carve. A turning point came when he was commissioned by a monk of Ampleforth Abbey to carve a cross. After this, there quickly followed orders for a table and chair for Ampleforth College which are still in use today.

Gradually Thompson's reputation spread and the orders began to come in requiring other men to be trained to cope with the demand. On one occasion, Robert was working in a church with one of his carvers when the man happened to use the phrase 'as poor as a church mouse'. Thompson carved a mouse there and then and remains as his trade mark to this day. (It must be said that the use of a trademark in carving was not a new one - Grinling Gibbons, a 17th-century woodcarver - used a pod of peas!).

Robert Thompson died in 1955 but his work is carried on by his two grandsons. His former home is now used as a showroom and is open to the public.

Before leaving Kilburn, look up to the Hambleton Hills to see the White Horse, on the side of Sutton Bank. It is said to have originally been the idea of one Thomas Taylor, who had seen the White Horse at Uffingham in Berkshire, although the actual work was engineered half a century later, in 1857, by local schoolmaster John Hodgson, with the help of his pupils and local villagers. It is 314 feet long and 228 feet high and can be seen from as far away as Harrogate and Otley. The Horse has one drawback, set on limestone it has to be "groomed" regularly by means of lime-washing and covering in chalk chippings to prevent it going grey, unlike the ones in Berkshire which are carved in chalk and remain white.

To the south is the tiny hamlet of CARLTON HUSTHWAITE which shelters in the lee of the gorse-covered mound which is an ancient earthwork. This is yet another place with a craftsman who signs his work! The Fox's Den produces handmade furniture using seasoned English oak with a fox's mask carved on every item.

108

In Carlton Husthwaite you will find the quaint 17th century Carlton Inn. Formerly a farmhouse, it was at one time called The Spinning Jenny, later the Black Lion before finally becoming the Carlton Inn. Owned and personally run by Maureen and Brian Lowe the inn is a welcoming sign for the tired, thirsty or hungry visitor, and without a doubt a warm welcome is assured. The inn can boast delicious food with a varied menu and fine well-kept ales. Maureen is the chef and the meals are hearty and well-priced.

The Carlton Inn, Carlton Husthwaite, Thirsk
Tel: 01845 501265

COXWOLD is the most southerly village in the North York Moors National Park boasting a variety of stone buildings which present a charming rural scene. At one end of the village lies Shandy Hall, home of Laurence Sterne, one-time vicar of Coxwold and author of "The Life and Opinions of Tristram Shandy, Gentleman" and "Sentimental Journey". Today, the hall draws literary pilgrims from all over the world who come to see Sterne's books and manuscripts. The house, Tudor in origin, contains many eccentricities which seem to have been tailor-made for Laurence Sterne. The peculiar features include the strangely-shaped balustrades on the wooden staircases, the unusual Heath Robinson-type contraption in the bedroom powder-closet, whereby Sterne could reach through a hatch and draw pails of water for his ablutions and a tiny eye-like window in the huge chimney stack, located in the study to the right of the entrance.

A beautiful old church is visible from the windows of the hall and features an octagonal perpendicular tower, three-decker pulpit and the Fauconberg family tombs. One item in the church that causes some amusement, regards the floor-brass in the nave recording the death of Sir John Manston in 1464. A space was left encouragingly for his wife Elizabeth's name to be added at a later date, but after all these years, the space is still blank.

At the other end of the village is Newburgh Priory, founded in 1145 as an Augustinian Friary and now a beautiful country house. It is believed that Oliver Cromwell's body is entombed here, having been brought here by his daughter. The house and grounds, which contain a fine water garden, are open to the public.

School House, Coxwold, York Tel: 01347 868356

School House in Coxwold, owned by Jean and John Richardson is a very well appointed 17th century cottage of considerable character and charm. It was once a coaching house and now under their personal supervision offers accommodation of the highest quality and is also noted for its home cooking. School House has three double bedrooms
110

pleasantly decorated and containing many pieces of period furniture. Each is equipped with wash basins, TV and drinks facilities. There are two guest bathrooms with showers that are close to the bedrooms. Packed lunches can be provided and evening meals are available on request. Part of the house opens as a tea room each afternoon from Easter to the end of October. The menu offers traditional afternoon teas and all the food is freshly prepared and home-made.

Just to the south of Coxwold and two miles east of Easingwold, a country road will lead you to the charming village of CRAYKE. Crayke is an interesting little village, situated on the crest of a hill with the houses clustered around the church and castle on top, visible right across the vale of York. A Saxon fortress was said to have marked this spot many years ago. There is also little left of the Norman castle once sited here, save the foundations; the battlemented house we now see amongst the trees behind the church is the tower house known as the Great Chamber built in the 15th century. It has a beautiful garden and a splendid view from its windows. By it are the remains of the New Tower, a majestic ruin cloaked in ivy.

The church is said to mark the place where St Cuthbert's body was finally laid to rest after its long wanderings and there are many fine features, including two stone figures, said to be Sir John Gibson and his wife who lived here in Elizabethan days. The fact that St Cuthbert's body was taken from here to Durham Cathedral is thought to give rise the name of the local inn.

In the centre of the village you will find this fine 18th-century inn called The Durham Ox, which is ideal for those looking for good food and traditional Yorkshire hospitality. Inside, the inn has stone-flagged floors, old-fashioned settles and an impressive inglenook fireplace. A varied range of well-prepared home-cooked dishes is available seven days a week (excluding Sunday evenings) on the bar menus. In addition, a new restaurant area serves full meals on Friday and Saturday evenings and Sunday lunches. The atmosphere is one of an old parlour, and the room is packed with memorabilia. The restaurant can, however, get busy so booking is recommended. Upstairs there are a number of clean and bright guest rooms equipped with colour television and tea/coffee making facilities. The Durham Ox also has three self-catering holiday cottages available which are grouped around a courtyard at the rear.

The Durham Ox, Crayke Tel: 01347 821506

A little further south on the B1363 is Sutton Park, well worth a visit if you are in these parts. The house was built in 1730 by Thomas Atkinson, and was almost certainly one of the regular haunts of such notable local people as Lawrence Sterne. It contains some exceptionally fine examples of Sheraton and Chippendale furniture and magnificent plasterwork by the Italian craftsman Cortese. The gardens and parkland are particularly attractive, having been designed by the grand master of landscape, Capability Brown. You will come across a Georgian ice-house, beautiful woodland walks and nature trails on your visit here, and you may also notice that the house itself is always full of flowers from the gardens. There is a gift shop and cafe, which sells wonderful home-made cakes and scones. Lunches and teas are catered for if you are travelling as a party, booking in advance.

Malton

The busy market town of MALTON sits at the most eastern edge of the Howardian Hills, with the twin village of Norton facing it across the River Derwent. Its Roman name was 'Derventio', a settlement of some note, and in the museum, just off the market square, are many Roman relics that have been excavated from this area. Malton has been the historic centre of Ryedale since Roman times. North of the Roman fort site is the original town of Old Malton, with ancient stone houses and quaint dwellings in the centre of which stands the beautiful fragment of the only remaining Gilbertine Priory in use in England - St Mary's, founded by Eustace Fitzjohn in the 12th century. On a stout oak door of the church you can see the famous mouse design of Robert Thompson of Kilburn and his work is also evident on the pulpit and lectern. Most of the wooden furniture and stalls are carved elaborately with all manner of wondrous beasts and historical/mythical scenes.

The building of a Norman castle near to the river crossing encouraged the growth of a second town, the modern day Malton.

Alongside farming, brewing is a traditional Malton industry. At one time nine breweries flourished below the main street to the Derwent, now only the Malton Brewery Company survives.

The neighbouring town of NORTON is famous as a centre for training racehorses and thoroughbreds are often seen on their way to and from the gallops on Langton Wold.

The town's present name is said to have been given 800 years ago on the occasion of its rebuilding after it had been burned to drive off the Scots. Malton today comprises of a number of yellow houses, narrow streets, a spacious market place and the old Church of St Michael. A building of note is Malton Lodge, a charming folly, with battlements and mullioned windows. Much of the stone with which it is built is said to have come from a local manor house, which was pulled down in an attempt to settle a dispute over the property by two heiresses.

Less prominent than St Michael's is the Church of St Leonard, with its mixture of Norman and Jacobean architecture. Over the high arches in the nave are many grotesque carvings and the East window displays some wonderful examples of stained-glass art. In the cemetery lies one of the unsung heroes of Malton, Dr G.C. Parkin, who devoted all his energies to fighting a typhoid epidemic in 1933 and who died as a consequence.

New Globe Inn, Yorkersgate, Malton Tel: 01653 692395

In the centre of the market town of Malton, at the crossroads, is the delightful New Globe Inn. Dating back to 1808, this was originally a coaching inn, which at that time included the shop next door. Today, the upper part of the next door property still belongs to the inn and this is where the letting rooms are located. As they are not directly over the pub, they are relatively quiet, ensuring an undisturbed sleep. The pub has a lively mix of clientele comprising regular local visitors and tourists. The decor is attractive and full of character and owners, Barry and Suzanne Hodgson offer a warm welcome to all. Food is available at lunch times only, with a good range of bar snacks on offer. There is a car park to the rear and a beer garden with a 'Wendy' house for the kids.

On the main street of Norton, you will come across an award-winning establishment called Cornucopia. It is hard to believe that only ten years ago, this was a derelict building, having been empty for nine months. Harold Quinton, the present owner, took it over fulfilling a dream to have his own pub where he could develop the catering side. Through sheer hard work, determination and imagination and of course, his all important culinary expertise, he has successfully created a far-reaching reputation for Cornucopia. Shortly after it was re-opened, the pub was awarded the 'Pub Caterer of the Year' award and has regularly featured in the Les Routiers guide ever since.

Cornucopia, Commercial Street, Norton, Nr. Malton
Tel: 01653 693456

King of the kitchen, Harold provides a fantastic-sounding menu that really lives up to the pub's name, and although this is a pub and restaurant, most of the clientele come here to enjoy the food. The cosy and atmospheric establishment can seat up to 80 people, but booking at weekends is advisable. To complement your meal, or if you really can only stay long enough for a drink, the bar can offer a good range of ales, lagers, spirits and wines to suit all palates. If you can't find your way to Norton, or aren't staying in the area, then you could try the sister establishment, The Copper Horse at Seamer near Scarborough - its just as good! Cornucopia is closed Mondays.

Just outside Malton and Norton, on the B1248 at the junction with the Settrington road, is Newstead Grange. Owned and run by Pat and Paul Williams, Newstead Grange is an elegant Georgian Country House set in two acres of grounds surrounded by mature chestnut, copper beech and sycamore trees. Situated in the heart of race-horse training country, the hotel offers delightful views across the Wolds and the North Yorkshire Moors.

Newstead Grange, Norton-on-Derwent, Malton
Tel: 01653 692502

Newstead Grange maintains the quality and style of a period country house and has original features throughout which include authentic shutters, and antique furniture and fireplaces in the two lounges. Each of the eight bedrooms has its own character and is furnished with period furniture, paintings and prints. All rooms are en-suite and include a colour TV and hospitality tray. A fine antique mahogany half-tester bed is the focal point of the spacious celebration suite.
116

Pat and Paul pride themselves on the quality of the cuisine available to guests each evening. The table d'hôte menu features fresh quality meat, local trout and organic vegetables from the hotel garden in season, and wine has been carefully selected to complement the food served. A very special place that you are certain to enjoy.

In an isolated location, yet only two miles away from Malton, is the Harvest Mouse, home of Sarah and Peter Monkman. Harvest Mouse is a working mixed farm of 150 acres and its situation offers tremendous views in every direction. Peter has lived here all his life, and his parents farmed the land before him. In this picturesque setting, Peter and Sarah offer bed and breakfast accommodation in the main farmhouse. There are two letting rooms which are delightful, and guests also have the use of a lounge and dining room. Sarah provides a full, traditional English breakfast and packed lunches can be provided but evening meals are not available. Guests are welcome to explore the farm and use the garden. There is also a livery stables so guests can bring their own horse!

Harvest Mouse, Norton Parks, Norton, Nr. Malton
Tel: 01653 692738

The road between Malton and Hovingham is a former Roman road resulting in the 'le-street' featured a couple of times along its route. A mile or so along this road, the B1257, is the village of **AMOTHERBY**, where, set in two and a half acres of wonderful gardens is Greenacres. This is a beautiful guest house offering an opportunity to relax and unwind in a delightful part of the country. The owners are Martyn and Margaret Goodwill and they will provide a warm and friendly welcome so that you feel immediately at home. All nine en-suite bedrooms are south facing and overlook the gardens. Four rooms are on the ground floor and have French windows that open onto the patio. The bedrooms are individually decorated and have all the modern comforts you expect in a quality hotel. There are double, twin and single rooms and a suite is available for families. The dining room, open to residents only, is light and airy and a delightful place in which to enjoy the traditional home-cooking that features on the menu. Both the dining room and the guest's lounge extend into the conservatory which is ideal for that before or after dinner drink. A real hidden gem.

Greenacres, Amotherby, Malton Tel: 01653 693623

Most famous of this area's attractions must surely be Castle Howard, the main location used in the filming of the popular TV series "Brideshead Revisited". The house is not so much a stately home but more like a magnificent baroque palace.

Kirkham Priory

Charles Howard, third Earl of Carlisle, commissioned Sir John Vanbrugh, who consequently made his reputation on the project, to build Castle Howard on the site of a former castle. The main part of the construction took place between 1699 and 1726, when Vanbrugh worked in close association with Nicholas Hawksmoor.

Castle Howard

Between them they designed the first private house with a dome. The interior is rich with all manner of art treasures; paintings by Holbein, Van Dyck, Kneller, Lawrence, furnishings by Adam, Sheraton and Chippendale. Also in the main hall are some beautiful frescoes; the originals were unfortunately destroyed in a fire in 1940, but repainted by Canadian-born artist Scott Nedd in 1962-63. In the chapel is the alter from the Temple at Delphi which Nelson wrested from the French at Naples. In the Stable Court are the Costume Galleries containing fashions from the 18th to the 20th centuries.

Our next stop along the B1257 is the limestone-built village of **SLINGSBY** which consists of a main street with church, village green and ruined castle. All Saints' Church, originally 13th century contains a monument to an early 14th-century knight with crossed legs, holding his heart in his praying hands. This figure is supposedly William Wycliffe

120

who allegedly killed a serpent (dragon) which preyed on travellers along this road.

Slingsby Castle which is now in ruins, is substantial and impressive. Not actually a castle, but a house, it was built in the 1620s for Sir Charles Cavendish in the Elizabethan style.

In the village is **Lowry's Restaurant and Guest House**. The restaurant offers an excellent range of meals and snacks featuring plenty of fresh local produce and home-cooked food. The restaurant is open for lunches and teas every day except Tuesday and Wednesday. Evening meals, with an à la carte menu to choose from, are available each day except Tuesday and Sunday and booking ahead is advisable. The service is friendly and efficient, and owner, Sue Hinds has recently been presented with the 'Afternoon Tea of the Year' award by Ryedale District Council. Comfortable bed and breakfast accommodation is available in four spacious bedrooms with en-suite facilities. The decor and furnishings are of an excellent quality and there are many personal touches to help guests feel right at home. An excellent place to stop for a bite to eat or to use as a touring base.

Lowry's, Malton Road, Slingsby, York Tel: 01653 628417

The Hall, in the centre of Slingsby, was built about 1830 for a Captain Ward of the Royal Navy who had been a midshipman on the ship that brought Nelson's body back from Gibraltar after the Battle of Trafalgar. This beautiful Regency house stands in 5 acres of grounds and gardens and offers country house accommodation. There are seven en-suite rooms and there is a guests' lounge and dining room. Throughout, the house is decorated with antiques and eye-catching ornaments, and is very peaceful and classy. This is an ideal place to get away from it all and enjoy a quiet break. The location also makes The Hall an ideal touring base. Guests can enjoy a traditional cooked breakfast and the evening meals, available by arrangement, feature real English cooking. Packed lunches can be provided and diets can be catered for. The owners, Peter and Cynthia Fell are a delightful couple and offer a warm welcome to all.

The Hall, Slingsby Tel: 01653 628375

Continuing west you will soon come to the peaceful village of **HOVINGHAM** and **The Worsley Arms Hotel**, an attractive stone-built Georgian coaching inn, now a fine country house hotel. The hotel overlooks the village green and is surrounded by delightful gardens. Every Saturday during the summer months, the local cricket team play on the private cricket ground of Hovingham Hall - what better way to spend a summer's afternoon than to enjoy afternoon tea watching a good match and, in the evening, the hotel feeds the team in their appropriately named Cricketer's Bar.

Having been built in 1841 by Sir William Worsley, the first Baronet, the hotel is still owned and run by the Worsley family whose home, Hovingham Hall, stands in nearby wooded park land. This was the birthplace and childhood home of the duchess of Kent and today her brother and his family reside at the hall.

The Worsley Arms Hotel, Hovingham Tel: 01653 628234

Elegant traditional furnishings and open log fires give The Worsley Arms the welcoming and restful atmosphere of a pleasant and comfortable country house. The graceful sitting rooms are a haven of peace and tranquillity and the ideal place in which to relax with a cup of coffee or an aperitif. There is also a comfortable bar where residents and locals mix freely. There are a number of delightful bedrooms, each with private bathroom and each individually and tastefully decorated, providing every comfort and modern facility. The 2 AA rosette restaurant, featuring 18th-century paintings and fresh flowers, has a reputation for imaginative food prepared from fresh local produce. Game from the estate is a particular speciality. The emphasis on delicacy of preparation and careful presentation, with intriguing combinations of flavour and texture will satisfy the most discriminating palate. The menu is complemented by an extensive wine list.

Hovingham Hall, also in the heart of the village, was built on the site of a Roman villa by Thomas Worsley, a friend of George III, who also gave him the statue depicting Samson slaying the Philistine. The 18th century house is surrounded by larch and beech woodland, and still retains its Saxon tower. The village itself is well-known for the annual cricket festival which has been held here for over a hundred years and the ancient church dates back to the days of the Saxons.

North of Malton, on the A169, is the village of KIRBY MISPERTON. Here, the 350 acres of wooded parkland of Kirby Misperton Hall contain Flamingoland Zoo and Fun Park, an ideal stop-off point and interesting day out should you have any young members of the family in tow. The park contains over 1,000 birds, animals and reptiles. However, the most spectacular sight is that of the pink flamingos, which give the park its name, standing in an attractive lake surrounded by willow trees. Other features are a fun fair, an adventure playground and a real working farm.

The Bean Sheaf, Kirby Misperton, Pickering, Malton
Tel: 01653 668614

Situated on the main A19 Pickering to Malton Road, in the centre of Kirby Misperton, you will find The Bean Sheaf Restaurant and Hotel. The hotel is spacious, comfortable and modern, complementing the original restaurant, parts of

124

which date back to the 17th century. There are 20 en-suite bedrooms available, all furnished and equipped to a luxurious standard. There are double, twin and family rooms, a special four poster suite for special occasions and two specially designed rooms for the disabled. The hotel features a sauna, and is set within 2 acres of grounds with attractive gardens and a fish pond. Attached to the hotel, so that guests have no need to go outside, is the Bean Sheaf Restaurant. Run by Liz and Michele Sardone, who also run the hotel, here Michele reigns supreme. Having trained in Switzerland, he is an outstanding chef offering English and Continental cuisine of a high standard. The menus are wide ranging and reasonably priced and all dishes feature the best of fresh local produce and vegetables from the hotel garden. You can be assured of a warm, family welcome, and you are guaranteed to enjoy your visit.

Ashfield Country Manor Hotel, Kirby Misperton, Nr. Malton
Tel: 01653 668221

Opposite the handsome 15th-century Church of St Lawrence you will find the Ashfield Country Manor Hotel. This former, spacious country farmhouse has only recently been converted into a hotel, where proprietors Noel and Molly Bulmer and their staff provide guests with a high standard of comfort and service. The seven bedrooms all have en-suite facilities and are appointed to a high modern standard, and the restaurant offers a first-rate à la carte menu which includes a choice of vegetarian dishes. The hotel incorporates The Ashfield Bar which can provide bar snacks and good real ales. Adjoining the hotel there is also a small and pleasant caravan park which is under the same ownership - there are pitches for up to 50 caravans all with electric hook-up points. Nearby there is also a log-cabin available for self-catering hire and can sleep up to six people. The land extends to 50 acres and includes a new, small, nine hole golf course which is available to all residents.

Burythorpe House, Burythorpe, Malton Tel: 01653 658200

To the south of Malton are the remains of Kirkham Priory. Kirkham, unlike other priories and abbeys already mentioned, was presided over by the Augustinian order of monks. The founder in the early 1120s was Walter Espec, who was also responsible for Rievaulx, and there are many similarities with the Cistercian house, in particular the integration of a waterway as a part of the design. Espec at one time had threatened to give Kirkham over to the Cistercian order, but this fortunately came to nothing and in the 13th century the Order were made custodians of the De Roos family sepulchres (at this time the De Roos were the lords of Helmsley Castle), a responsibility which gave them

126

this influential family's patronage and ensured their survival. The family's heraldry is prominent on many of the remaining structures we can see today.

Hidden in the country lanes, three miles east of KIRKHAM, is the small village of BURYTHORPE, home of the exceptional country house hotel and restaurant, Burythorpe House. This outstanding George II residence was built around 1750 and stands within large, delightfully wooded grounds. All the bedrooms are individually decorated, sumptuously furnished and equipped with en-suite bathroom, colour television and beverage facilities.

The oak-panelled restaurant (open to non-residents) offers an extensive à la carte menu, and after dinner guests can relax in the lounge or enjoy a game of snooker on the full size table. There is also a tennis court and a large heated indoor swimming pool with an adjoining sauna, solarium and fitness room.

The Jolly Farmers, Main Street, Leavening, Near Malton
Tel: 01653 658276

On the main street of the little village of LEAVENING, to the south, lies The Jolly Farmers public house. Dating back over many hundreds of years it is believed that the building started life as a blacksmith's shop. At some point the blacksmith began brewing his own beer and it has been

127

an inn ever since. Inside there is a cosy, old world atmosphere generated by the delightful couple, John and Janet Parkinson, your hosts. The bars feature low beams and there are also roaring fires in the colder months. The two small, snug bar areas are complimented by a 25-seater restaurant. The food, looked after by Janet, is delicious and the interesting menu contains some traditional game dishes such as jugged hare and rabbit pie. The real ales and guest beers are kept in tip top condition by John. This pub, which has won awards for its food and hospitality, is a pleasure to visit and there are also two bedrooms for overnight guests.

Not far from here is the deserted medieval village of **WHARRAM PERCY**, a fascinating place of historical and archaeological interest. If you wish actually to watch the team of diggers go about their business, then you will be able to do so for three weeks in July of each year, when professor Maurice Beresford and John Hurst, Inspector of Ancient Monuments organise their stalwart teams of volunteers. Below the remains of the medieval village have been found artefacts of both the Saxon and Roman eras.

For many years it was assumed that Wharram Percy was one of the many casualties of the Black Death, but in fact, it was merely the more expedient measure of providing land for intensive sheep-farming that led to its demise. At the site one can see peasant houses that date from between the 13th and 16th centuries, the manor house of the Percy family who gave the village its name, a 12th century church, cemetery (complete with exposed skeletons!), medieval and Tudor vicarages, a mill and older Anglo-Saxon and Roman sites.

The magnificent **Middleton Arms** stands in the small hamlet of **NORTH GRIMSTON**, just a couple of miles north of here. Dating back to the early 18th century it was originally a small-holding. The property has always been a part of the Birdsall estate and was named after the landowner. Beautifully decorated and furnished throughout, the pub is a real credit to the present owner, Kathleen Grayston, and her staff. Open every day of the week, it is advisable to book if you wish to eat on a Friday or a weekend, as it gets very busy. The menus certainly sound delicious with a good selection at very reasonable prices. The ales are just as good and well-kept. There is also bed and breakfast accommodation available with three letting rooms. One is en-suite and the other two have showers.

The Middleton Arms, North Grimston, Malton
Tel: 01944 768255

Sitting proudly alongside the A64 Malton to Scarborough Road at **RILLINGTON** is the historic **Coach and Horses Inn**. This is an established coaching inn which dates back to the 18th century replacing inns on the same site which go back to the Domesday Book. More recently the inn was used as a billet for soldiers during the Second World War. The Coach and Horses has become well known for another reason too. It has a collection of cats (of the china variety) which numbers over 500! The collection was started by previous owners 20 years ago and some are more than 100 years old. The whole of the establishment is as pretty as a picture with the interior being traditionally styled with wood panelled walls and a feature fireplace. There is even another collection - this time of ceramic and glass bells. Food is served each lunch time and evening and the meals are delicious, come in good-sized portions and are reasonably priced. A telephone call to book before you arrive will avoid disappointment. There is also a good selection of traditional ales with Tetley's and Youngers being a permanent feature. Outside, visitors will find a pets corner and aviary and an attractive beer garden. A recent addition has been the three letting rooms which are available for bed and breakfast. The quality of the establishment has been recognised by the achievement of two awards by Ken and Liz McArthur since their arrival six years ago. They have won The Grand Master Trophy for Quality Traditional Ales from Wm. Youngers and the Inaugural Yorkshire Evening Press Pub of the Year award.

Coach and Horses, Rillington, Malton Tel: 01944 758373

The Humberside Coast and the City of Hull

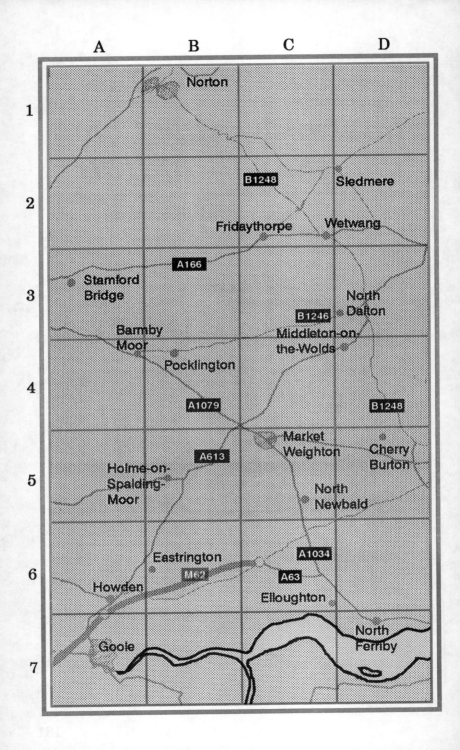

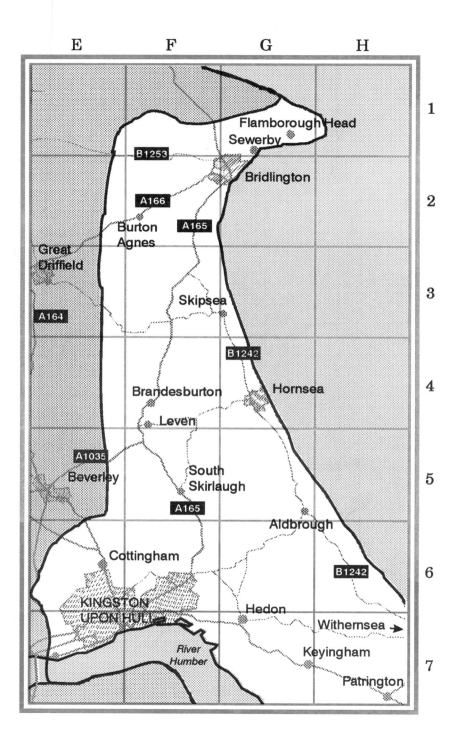

North Landing, Flamborough Head

CHAPTER THREE

The Humberside Coast and the City of Hull

In 1979 the Countryside Commission officially designated Flamborough Head and the surroundings as a Heritage Coast setting in motion a scheme to preserve this splendid section of Yorkshire's coast. There is a bird sanctuary to discover and numerous geological features of great interest too. To enjoy your visit to the full, pay a visit to the Heritage Coast Information Centre at South Landing, Flamborough.

Flamborough Head and Bridlington

Travelling to the south of Filey and just beyond its large bay, is the RSPB reserve of Bempton Cliffs, sanctuary to more than 30 species of seabirds who use the cliffs as a breeding ground. It is estimated that at any one time there are around 30,000 birds making this the largest colony in Britain. Visitors are well catered for with a good car park and information centre. If you should take a walk up here then bring a bird book with a good section on seabirds and a pair of binoculars - and get spotting.

The cliffs here reach up to 400 feet in height and mark the eastern extreme of the Yorkshire Wolds. From the cliffs a quiet road leads to BEMPTON village on the B1299 which has lots of winding lanes lined with attractive and colourful cottages. A well-known landmark in the village is the White Horse pub which features a bright blue roof.

In the 18th century the village was famous for its 'climmers', daring men who worked the cliffs of this area

135

collecting the eggs of the nesting birds. In Victorian times, however, a popular holiday sport was to shoot the seabirds from boats which affected the 'climmers' livelihood. Egg collectors came from all over the world to buy the eggs from the 'climmers' at the cliff top until the practice was made illegal in 1954.

On the Bempton side of Flamborough, set well back from the main road, is **The Grange**, a prime example of Georgian architecture approached by a wide drive. Strong and square, the clean lines of this elegant building are softened by the creeper extending around the door and the lush green of the large lawn at the front of the house. The house is also surrounded by extensive gardens which can be explored by guests at their leisure.

The Grange, Bempton Lane, Flamborough, Bridlington
Tel: 01262 850207 Fax: 01262 851359

The Grange is a working mixed farm with 475 acres of land. There is a camping site and a small caravan park which can take up to 25 tents and caravans. The site is quiet and sheltered providing an ideal position in which to stay. The site facilities include toilets, showers and electric hook-ups. The accommodation at the house, in large airy rooms, consists of a double bedroom, a family room and a twin-bedded room. Mr and Mrs Thompson, the owners, cater for bed and breakfast only but can recommend some establishments nearby for your evening meals.

Visitors to The Grange will enjoy the wonderful views of the surrounding countryside and appreciate the proximity to the Bempton bird sanctuaries where there is much to see and do and, of course, the Flamborough Heritage Coast which is within easy driving distance.

Flamborough Head must be one of the most famous sights in England, as distinctive as the cliffs at Dover. The chalk that it consists of probably covered most of Yorkshire at a time when this part of the world was a vast sea, the remains of which are evident in the fossil deposits that can be found in abundance all along this coastline.

The peninsula must have had some ancient significance for it is dotted with curious mounds. Another reminder of this region's ancient past, is the deceptively named Dane's Dyke, which is, in fact the much older site of an Iron Age entrenchment. The wooded ditch is two and a half miles long and extends from Cat Nab on the northern side to Sewerby rocks on the eastern side of Bridlington.

The village of **FLAMBOROUGH** was once rife with superstition, inhabited by fishermen and their families who scarcely ever ventured beyond the Dyke. They were clannish, resenting intrusion and regarding visitors as 'foreigners'. The 40 to 50 boats would land their catch on the beach where it was auctioned off to fish-buyers. The fishermen always wore a navy-blue jersey knitted by their wives in a cable, diamond and mesh, peculiar to the village. The pattern has passed down through the generations and is still worn by local fishermen today.

Some of the strange customs practised here make one wonder how anything was ever completed. Apparently nothing could be started on a Friday, not boat ever sailed on a Sunday, wool could not be wound in lamplight, and anyone who mentioned a hare or pig while they were baiting the lines was asking for bad luck!

The village is another place where the sword-dancing festival, introduced by the Nordic settlers, has been retained. Originally it was the fishermen who performed the rite, but now, with the decline in the fishing community, it is the boys of the local Primary School who have taken over and their navy-blue fishermen's jerseys, white trousers and red caps are a familiar sight during local events.

Thankfully, over the centuries, the superstitions and clannishness have died away - as has the fishing fleet. The villagers are still proud of their heritage, but are happy to share it with visitors.

Timoneer Country Manor Hotel, South Sea Road,
Flamborough, Bridlington Tel: 01262 850219

Built by the Duke of Norfolk for a son who died before he could live here, the Timoneer Country Manor Hotel, formerly called Cliffe House, sits in eight acres of magnificent parkland overlooking the cliffs and the sea. This grand country house is a real gem, hidden away, but well worth discovering. Recently refurbished by the present owners the hotel can offer the luxury and conveniences you would expect while successfully retaining the charm and character of the original house. The emphasis today is on the highest quality of facilities and service.

138

The restaurant can seat up to 70 and can offer both an à la carte and table d'hôte menu with a wide range of tempting dishes freshly prepared with local produce. To complement your meal there is an extensive wine list. There are two bar areas, one converted from the former study, and bar meals are served daily. In warmer weather drinks can be enjoyed in the gardens where children will find an outdoor play area. The bedrooms are as luxurious as the rest of the hotel, and all have en-suite facilities, television, tea-maker and a telephone. The honeymoon suite is one of the most impressive rooms, featuring a four poster bed and large bay window with views out to sea.

A warm welcome awaits all visitors, not just from the staff, but also from the roaring log fire in the entrance lobby, and The Timoneer is a real credit to its owners.

The North Star Hotel, North Marine Road, Flamborough
Tel: 01262 850379

Situated just a few minutes from Flamborough's famous North Landing, you will come across The North Star Hotel. If you are trying this hotel for the first time, then rest assured that you will receive a warm and friendly reception, and you will feel right at home as soon as you walk through the door. Personally-owned and run by Michael and Karen Johnston, this delightful establishment can offer unbeatable views of the North Sea. The North Star has not always been a hotel, though - it started life as a farm and stables, then became a private house, then a Methodist Temperance Hotel, then a private house, finally becoming a hotel in the 1930s. Sadly when Michael and Karen took over three years ago the hotel was in a very poor condition so it has just undergone an extensive programme of refurbishment. Upstairs, they have created seven luxury en-suite bedrooms of class and character while downstairs the popular restaurant is intimate and appealing.

The three menus - a bar menu, à la carte and table d'hôte - are outstanding and offer plenty of choice. The meals are freshly and carefully prepared, well served and offer excellent value for money. Meals are available every lunchtime and evening and although the restaurant can seat 50 people comfortably, booking for Saturday evening and Sunday lunch is advisable.

The bar lounge is just as comfortable, and to the rear of the hotel are pleasant gardens where you can enjoy a meal or a drink on sunny days. Both the bar lounge and restaurant are open to non-residents.

This is a great place where all visitors are treated as friends by the owners and staff - you are sure to return!

If you are staying in Flamborough then pay a visit to the Parish Church which contains two interesting monuments. One is to St Oswald, the patron saint of fishermen and an obvious choice for a former fishing village. The other shows a man baring his heart, recalling the death of Sir Marmaduke Constable who reputedly swallowed a toad which ate his heart!

Flamborough Head's first, and England's oldest surviving lighthouse, is the chalk tower on the landward side of the present lighthouse. Built in 1674 its beacon was a basket of burning coal. The lighthouse that is still is use was built in 1806. Originally signalling four white flashes developments over the years have included a fog horn in 1859 and in more recent years, a signal of radio bleeps.

140

At SEWERBY, between Flamborough and Bridlington, are Sewerby Hall and Gardens where there is plenty to interest visitors of all ages. The magnificent Queen Anne/Georgian mansion, built in 1714-20, is set in 50 acres of garden and parkland. There is an elegant Italian-style clock tower and the neo-Norman church was designed by Sir Gilbert Scott.

Sewerby Hall and Gardens, Bridlington Tel: 01262 673769

The house was first opened to the public by Amy Johnson in 1936 and the museum contains an extensive exhibition of some of her belongings. The Museum and Art Gallery has a varied and rich collection with displays of motor vehicles and archaeological finds. There is also a famous portrait of Queen Henrietta Maria, wife of Charles I. Legend has it that she gave the picture to the Strickland family of Boynton Hall in exchange for their gold and silver which was melted down to help the Royalist cause. The picture was later moved to Sewerby Hall.

Surrounding the hall there are acres of attractive gardens to explore and a small zoo which will delight all. There are also regular special events held in the grounds. For refreshments, pay a visit to the Clock Tower Tea Rooms which offer a good selection of snacks and drinks.

The gardens and zoo are open all year round. The Hall, Art Gallery and Museum are open Easter to September. There is an admission charge.

Also, in the village of Sewerby, is Portminion - a unique miniature village with one acre of tiny buildings set in a miniature landscape.

Travelling west, along the B1255, is the well-known seaside resort of **BRIDLINGTON**, noted particularly for its sands, which stretch along the coast for at least ten miles. Not so long ago, it was still the traditional Yorkshire fishing harbour, with rows of terraced stone-built houses and uncluttered beaches. The bustling harbour thronged with the strong dialects of local fishermen conducting their sales of the day's catch, and holiday-makers could entertain themselves aboard the large steam-boat, or hire their own small rowing skiff.

Nowadays it is the bingo hall and fruit-machine arcade that beckons, and the tourist trade these attractions bring in has lured the offspring of the old fishermen away from their original livelihood.

The miles of clean, safe beaches within Bridlington Bay are much enjoyed by the thousands of visitors that come here each year - many with just a bucket and spade for entertainment. A number of other facilities are available here too, helping you enjoy your stay to the full. On the beach there are fishing facilities and for the more energetic, jet-skis, sail boards, water-skis, rowing boats and speed boats for hire. Leisure World on the promenade incorporates a fun fair and indoor pools - ideal for when the weather turns wet!

In a seaside town like this, it is not surprising that there are a large number of high quality hotels to choose from. You will find a large variety of sizes and styles, and you are sure to find one that will suit your requirements.

One important priority in the selection of a seaside holiday is a view of the sea, and The Royal Hotel on Shaftesbury Road offers exactly that. A modern, luxury hotel situated adjacent to the beautiful South Bay sea front in a select part of Bridlington, more than half of the 15 bedrooms enjoy sea views.

The Royal Hotel, 1 Shaftesbury Road, Bridlington
Tel: 01262 672433

The beautifully maintained red brick exterior with large bay windows is adorned with flower baskets and combines with an interior furnished and decorated to the highest standard to give a sense of comfort and well-being. Mrs Jean Bath, the resident proprietor, provides a warm and friendly welcome and attentive service in spotless accommodation which includes a honeymoon suite with extra facilities such as corner-bath suite, colour television and safety deposit box.

Licensed for residents, the Royal has a cosy bar lounge with an oak fireplace and open fire and a separate television lounge which boasts a 46 inch television (this particular room is for non-smokers). The dining-room, which has separate tables and tureen service, offers traditional English fare and opens onto a large dance floor which can double as a function area. Local sequence and amateur dance clubs often use this splendid dance floor out of season. Sequence dancing weeks are held throughout the year, by group booking only (ideal for dancing clubs). Many well known personalities have stayed at the Royal including Bobby Crush, Paul Shane and Joe Loss and his Orchestra.

Apart from breakfast and an evening meal, Mrs Bath is happy to supply packed lunches, and to fill flasks with hot drinks as well as provide a light supper and a pot of tea for 'late-nighters'.

A completely self-contained ground floor holiday home is a newly opened, welcome addition to the main hotel and has all the facilities a family need to enjoy a relaxing stay in very pleasant surroundings. The Royal Hotel is convenient for the Spa Theatre and Ballroom, the golf course, bowling green and other town amenities, and the essential holiday ingredient - the sea - is merely a stone's throw away.

The Londesborough Hotel, West Street, Bridlington
Tel: 01262 672074

Built during the mid-1860s, **The Londesborough Hotel** has been accommodating visitors to Bridlington for over 130 years. Today, it continues in this tradition with a strong emphasis on providing entertainment. Within the two lounge bar areas, which can seat up to 120 people, there is a small stage where entertainment - musical, comedy, etc. - is held every evening in summer, and Wednesday, Saturday and Sunday evenings in winter. The entertainment is open to non-residents. There is also a front bar area and a games room, and all are tastefully decorated and furnished. There are 15 bedrooms, of varying sizes, and these have all the usual facilities. Pat and Gwen Smith, the resident managers, are a delightful couple and will ensure that your stay is one that you will remember.

Built during the late 19th century, the Black Swan Licensed Guest House is just two minutes walk from the shops and the beach, in the heart of Bridlington. Christine and Stuart Monks, the owners, have been here just two years. Stuart is a butcher by trade and had worked as a chef in hotels and industrial catering before settling here. A home from home, your stay here is sure to be an enjoyable one. The accommodation comprises seven rooms, three with en-suite facilities. They are all spacious and inviting and are kept warm and clean. Downstairs there is a cosy breakfast and dining room where hearty breakfasts and freshly prepared evening meals are served. The food is excellent and the portions are of a good size. There is also a cosy bar area which is fully licensed.

Black Swan, 54 Marshall Avenue, Bridlington
Tel: 01262 674423

The Caytonville Hotel on Wellington Road in the north part of Bridlington, is a small, comfortable bed and breakfast establishment. Owned and personally run by Elaine Braithwaite, who took over four years ago, this former Victorian house is warm and welcoming. Whether you are

145

just passing through or decide to stay for a while, your visit is sure to be an enjoyable. You will be well looked after and pampered with all the splendid facilities and good wholesome food. There are ten letting rooms of varying sizes which are all kept spotlessly clean. In addition there is a comfortable residents' lounge and breakfast/dining room. Evening meals are available by prior arrangement and packed lunches can also be provided. The location, just five minutes from North Bay beach and the shops, makes this ideal.

Caytonville Hotel, 11 Wellington Road, Bridlington
Tel: 01262 675034

Bridlington is still somewhat dominated by its boats and the harbour is always full of hustle and bustle. There are many fishermen who continue to work out of the port so there is plenty to see. There is even an Harbour Museum which gives a detailed history covering hundreds of years. For example, did you know that Bridlington once exported Irish gold to the continent?

The surrounding coastline itself has suffered over the years from the devastations of erosion caused by the sea. Huge sections of this coastline as far as Withernsea have disappeared in an alarmingly short period of time. Complete towns with names such as Auburn, Hartburn and Owlthorne,

146

spoken of in old records as "places of fair fame" now lie beneath the waves of the North Sea, never to be seen again.

There are many other interesting and eccentric stories in the history of Bridlington. During the reign of King Stephen the town was granted a peculiar source of revenue - the right to the goods and chattels of all fugitives and felons coming to the town, together with all the goods aboard any ship wrecked on its shores. As one may imagine, this statute was subject to a great deal of abuse by various corrupt individuals.

Carved Figures, St Mary's Church, Bridlington

In 1643 when Queen Henrietta-Maria, the wife of Charles I, was forced into Bridlington Harbour by a savage storm that threatened to overwhelm her ship, she was greeted by a bombardment of enemy cannonballs. She then retreated to nearby Boynton Hall.

The Spa, on South Beach, directly on the sea front, is one of the most prominent buildings in Bridlington. Dating from

1932, the Spa houses a theatre and the Royal Hall, renowned for its splendid ballroom and offering not only music and dancing but also celebrity concerts, children's shows, wrestling, exhibitions, displays and much more. The Spa Theatre hosts shows that will suit all tastes in quality entertainment - variety, drama, comedy, classical, pantomime and cinema. Also available at the Spa is refreshment in either The Conservatory or The Tillie Morrison Bar. Both offer a good variety, The Conservatory in a cafeteria style, with hot and cold snacks and confectionery. The bar serves a full range of beers and spirits and also offers a carvery. Outside there is a large play area at The Spa Children's Corner with all the latest kiddie rides, or alternatively the whole family can take a ride in a motor boat.

The Spa, Bridlington Tel: 01262 678255
Box Office: 01262 678258

After a long morning sight-seeing, a good restaurant is what is needed. There are of course plenty to choose from in Bridlington ranging from small fish and chip shops to Egon Ronay recommended establishments. Here are few that we can recommend.

Standing on the harbourside, with unbeatable views from the restaurant and most of the bedrooms, is the very

148

impressive Blue Lobster Hotel and Restaurant. The main room is the Lawrence Bar, named after Lawrence of Arabia, who, seeking anonymity transferred to the R.A.F. and served as Aircraftsman Shaw in this building from 1919 until shortly before his death in 1935. Some memorabilia can be seen in the foyer. Upstairs is the magnificent restaurant area decorated with old pictures of Bridlington and its fishermen. Mick and Gwyn Baron, the owners, have created a unique establishment with a far-reaching reputation. Some regulars even come from Australia! There are six bedrooms, providing overnight accommodation, located on the upper floors. The rooms are all en-suite and are spacious and beautifully furnished. This really is a wonderful place that caters to everyone's needs and where you will be looked after by charming hosts.

The Blue Lobster, South Pier, Bridlington Tel: 01262 674729

Ideally situated right on the sea front, in the centre of Bridlington, is The Captain's Table Restaurant. The location makes this establishment ideal for visitors, commanding a magnificent view of the harbour and South Bay. Seating up to 250 people, The Captain's Table can offer a sit down meal in the two restaurants, good ale and bar snacks in the Tavern Inn downstairs, or a take-away from the adjoining fish and chip shop called the 'Frying Pan'.

Whatever you choose, the food is excellent, especially the fish and chips, which have been described as the best in Bridlington. The main restaurant offers a variety of meals, all of which are available all day and the waitress service is efficient and friendly. The Tavern Inn is more traditionally styled and decorated in a nautical theme. The restaurant and fish and chip shop are open every day, between March and the end of October. The inn is open all year.

The Captains Table and Tavern Inn, 20 South Cliff Road, Bridlington Tel: 01262 678125

In the old town, one can see the Bayle or gatehouse of 1388, one of the only monastic buildings left in Bridlington. In its time, it has been used as a jail and a courtroom, and is now used as a museum for priceless antiques and memorabilia of the local East Yorkshire Regiment, the Green Howards. The Parish Church which incorporates parts of the Priory of St Mary is another building of interest, easily overlooked amidst the entertainment halls that surround it.

In the old part of Bridlington, on the High Street, you will find **Burlingtons**. Part of the building in which this restaurant is housed, dates back to the 16th century and was formerly cottages. David Hall, one of the owners, took over 5 years ago, coming from a position as a head chef at a local country house hotel. Together with his wife, Judy, this was

150

his first solo venture, which has been a great success. The reputation of the restaurant reaches far beyond Bridlington and many regulars travel quite some distance to enjoy a meal here.

The restaurant has been divided up into three separate areas. On entering you will first come to the comfortable lounge area which is ideal for a drink before or after your meal. The other two areas are for dining and both are cosy and intimate. The food is of a superlative quality, and David has won many awards. The menus offer an excellent selection but the chef's speciality is fish. A popular dish is the Triple Fish Platter which features a choice of seven fish dishes - from which you can choose three! The house specials include Guinea Fowl, cooked in two different ways - the breast in a brandy and tarragon and the leg in the red wine sauce with bacon - and "Caribbean" Chicken - filled with pineapple, coconut and ginger cooked in a sweet and sour style sauce.

The restaurant is open evenings only from Tuesday to Saturday (inclusive) and booking is recommended for Saturdays. It is also open for Sunday lunch.

Burlingtons, 91-93 High Street, Bridlington
Tel: 01262 400383

Situated in Westgate, also in the old town of Bridlington, is **Ye Olde Star Inn and Restaurant**. Dating back to the

16th century, the inn has recently been renovated and extended but the olde worlde character and traditional appearance has been retained throughout. The exposed ceiling beams still adorn the bar areas - there is a public bar and an adjoining luncheon bar where hot and cold meals and snacks are available. The cosy cocktail bar compliments the attractive dining room which can seat up to 130 guests. The size of the room makes it suitable for parties, meetings and wedding receptions. Full function menus can be found at reception or ring for full details. The luxurious accommodation comprises 11 rooms which all have en-suite facilities. Full credit must go to the brewery which owns Ye Olde Star, and to the experienced manager, Ron Wathey.

Ye Olde Star Inn, 17 Westgate, Bridlington
Tel: 01262 676039

Situated on an old Roman road at **WOLDGATE**, just half a mile off the A166 and only a few minutes drive from Bridlington, is **Woldgate Trekking Centre**. The centre has been owned and personally run by Kathy and Billy Pickering for the past nine years. Here, trekking is the name of the game, and with so many green roads, bridle paths and terrific countryside, the hacks can last anything from one hour to a whole day. You are sure to enjoy your ride, whether you are a novice or an experienced rider. There are plenty of safe,

152

friendly horses to suit all ages and sizes, and all hacks are accompanied. There is an outdoor arena which is soon to be roofed, and there are plans to provide residential holidays which should commence in 1996. A caravan and camping site adjoins the centre which can take five tourers or tents. Facilities include showers, toilets and electric hook-ups. The riding centre is expertly run and licensed by the local council and approved by the Association of British Riding Schools. Hard hats are provided, and to avoid disappointment it is best to call ahead.

Woldgate Trekking and Livery Centre, Woldgate, Bridlington Tel: 01262 673086

Continuing out of Bridlington along the A166 will shortly bring you **John Bull's World of Rock** which has become a premier tourist attraction in this part of East Yorkshire and really is a great day out. Whether you are young or old you will be fascinated as you discover the history and delights of rock making. Animation and taped conversation accompany you as you explore the establishment. Admission charge is just £1.

As you enter you will discover an imaginative picture show where the managing director's grandfather, the founder of the business, tells how the company was established and came to be called John Bull. You then walk through into where the rock is actually made and watch the process from raw ingredients to the finished product while a guide provides a commentary. From here you pass the original shop, transported here from Prince's Street, and a Victorian kitchen which shows how rock was made many years ago. The next section covers the history of sweet making and there are a number of puzzles specially designed for the children. The next stop is Charlie's Chocolate Room and no mums or dads are allowed in here. Next there is a section devoted to fudge and toffee making with videos of the stages that are involved. Finally (phew!), there is a large shop where souvenirs of your visit can be purchased. This is a unique and educational attraction that is well worth a visit.

John Bull's World of Rock, Lancaster Road, Carnaby, Bridlington Tel: 01262 678525

Park Rose Pottery Leisure Park is only two minutes from John Bull's World of Rock, two miles outside of Bridlington. Park Rose Pottery has become very popular in recent years and can often be found in high street gift shops. Here, in the Park Rose Craftsroom, you can see the items being made - from mould-making, glazing and firing through to the finished product. If something takes your eye, then take a look in the well-stocked gift shop which not only displays the wide range of ceramic goods, but also houses many other gift ideas from clothes and linens to toiletries and children's novelties. For even greater bargains, there is also a Factory Seconds Warehouse.

Some of the other attractions will delight adults and children - like the Owl Sanctuary and Woodland Conservation Area. With birds of prey, a hatchery and an owl breeding programme, the sanctuary is both fascinating and informative. Also for the children is a supervised adventure playground (small daily charge). For some less strenuous relaxation the grounds can be explored and a licensed café provides refreshments. A great day out for all to enjoy.

Park Rose Pottery Leisure Park, Carnaby Covert Lane, Bridlington Tel: 01262 602823

Burton Agnes Hall, in the village of the same name, is a delightful Wolds stately home. An outstanding Elizabethan house, built between 1598 and 1610 and little altered, Burton Agnes is particularly famous for its splendid Jacobean gatehouse, ceilings and overmantles carved in oak, plaster and alabaster. It also has a valuable collection of paintings and furniture from between the 17th and 19th centuries - including a portrait of Oliver Cromwell 'warts and all' - and a large collection of Impressionist paintings. The gardens are extensive with over 2,000 plants, a maze and giant board games in the Coloured Gardens. Other visitor facilities

155

include a new ice-cream parlour, a dried flower and herb shop, a children's animal corner and an artists' studio. A very popular recent addition is the plant sales where many uncommon varieties can be obtained. In high season, there is a café. An interesting day out for all the family.

Burton Agnes Hall, Burton Agnes, Driffield
Tel: 01262 490324

The village itself is lovely, centred on a tree-fringed pond. Although Burton Agnes Hall is the main attraction here, there is also Burton Agnes Manor House which is worth visiting. Now in the care of English Heritage, this is a rare example of a Norman house, altered and encased in brick during the 17th and 18th centuries.

Set in the tiny and peaceful hamlet of **HARPHAM** the **St Quintin Arms Inn** was taken over by the present owners, Liz and Philip Curtis, eight years ago and during this time through sheer hard work they have turned it into an inn of excellence, with quality in every area. Dating back nearly 300 years the inn was once part of a feudal estate and owned by the St Quintin family. The inn is beautifully decorated and furnished throughout, and has a warm, cosy and friendly atmosphere that is very apparent. The food is varied and in addition to the extensive menu there is a daily specials board, featuring such dishes as Cantonese Prawns and Cider Baked

Ham. All the meals are prepared by Liz and only the freshest ingredients are used. Behind the bar there are well-kept ales on tap and also two cask ales.

The four letting rooms are excellent, three are en-suite and the fourth has a private bathroom. The bedrooms are each individually designed and are comfortable and cosy with plenty of personal touches. All the rooms have fabulous views across the surrounding countryside and the front room features an antique brass half tester bed. The inn can also offer tennis to guests on an adjacent court and there is an attractive rear garden to be enjoyed in sunny weather.

The inn is situated just 1 mile off the A166 Bridlington to Great Driffield Road in Harpham.

St Quintin Arms Inn, Harpham, Nr. Driffield
Tel: 01262 490329

There are two wells in the village which both have a story behind their names. The first is known as St John's and reputedly contains healing waters. It is named after St John who was born in the village in AD640 and went on to found a Christian community on the site of the present town of Beverley. His tomb can be found within Beverley Minster and each year it is decorated with primroses gathered in Harpham woods by local schoolchildren. The second well goes under the more unusual name of the Drummerboy's Well.

157

Legend has it that the Lord of the Manor, St Quintin, was watching his soldiers at the butts when he suddenly knocked his drummerboy who promptly lost his balance and fell down the well. Tradition has it that the 'rat-a-tat-tat' of his drum can be heard when a member of the St Quintin family is about to die.

Hornsea to Spurn Head

The Wolds, to the west of Bridlington, were once described by Daniel Defoe in his travels, as "very thin of towns and people", although he recorded a great number of sheep, cattle and horses. The Sykes family were largely responsible for its civilisation and reclamation; before then, as recently as the 17th century, there were recordings of wolves roaming the region, ravaging the local sheep folds and villages.

To the south of the village of Harpham you will find FOSTON-ON-THE-WOLDS and if you confuse a Saddleback with a Gloucester Old Spot, or a Belted Galloway with a Belgian Blue, then take a trip to Cruckley Animal Farm where all will become clear. This working farm supports many different varieties of cattle, sheep, pigs, poultry and horses. Some of the animals are endangered species whose numbers are being protected by the work at the farm. Some species are very rare like the Longhorn Cattle, Greyfaced Dartmoor and Whitefaced Woodland Sheep and the farm also keeps examples of all seven breeds of rare British pigs. In 1994 Cruckley became a Rare Breed Survival Trust approved farm park - the only one in East Yorkshire. There are daily milking demonstrations and a chance to see sheep being dipped and clipped. There is a special children's paddock, where the animals can be hand-fed, and Pet's Corner, as well as a nature trail and waterfowl lake. In the hatchery, all the family will enjoy the fluffy chicks and ducklings. The farm is open daily between the end of April and the beginning of October, it is also very easy to find as it is clearly signposted. This is an enjoyable and informative day out for all the family.

Cruckley Animal Farm, Foston-on-the-Wolds, Nr. Driffield
Tel: 01262 488337

East of Foston, one can rejoin the A165 at BEEFORD. With a main street that extends for over a mile and surrounded by very flat landscape, Beeford cannot be described as picturesque. The old stone Church of St Leonard is worthy of some inspection though, having a 15th-century battlemented tower with crocketed pinnacles and containing three bells. In the chancel is a well-known effigy of Reverend Thomas Tonge dated 1472 which is of great interest to brass rubbers.

Sitting directly on the A165 at Beeford is the very impressive Yorkshire Rose Inn. Victorian in construction it has a mock Tudor façade which looks very impressive. Owned and personally run by Charlie and Jane Cleaver for the last seven years it is well established and full of character. There is food available each lunchtime and evening and the menu comprises traditional pub fayre all freshly prepared and home-cooked. The dining area can get busy so it is advisable to book at weekends and throughout the summer. Behind the bar there is the usual range of beers, wines and spirits with three hand-pulled real ales. Charlie and Jane arrange

159

entertainment at least once a week so you may find a live band playing or a quiz in progress when you visit. Often the entertainment is in aid of a charity. A welcoming establishment, which you are sure to enjoy visiting.

Yorkshire Rose, 16 Bridlington Road, Beeford
Tel: 01262 488756

BRANDESBURTON is pleasantly situated 8 miles northeast of Beverley and 6 miles west of Hornsea on the Bridlington road. The village first prospered under the church of St John of Beverley who was given the land by King Athelstan. It later passed into the hands of the St Quintin family who also owned the village of Harpham. The Church of St Mary even contains two brasses to St John Quintin, who died in 1397, and his wife Lora. The brasses, which are on a large blue stone slab in the chancel, are life size and depict beautifully decorated costume.

Near Brandesburton there is an ideal place to stay at the **Burton Lodge Hotel**. Set within two acres of landscaped grounds, this splendid country house hotel has its own 6 hole pitch and putt course and a grass tennis court. It also adjoins an attractive parkland golf course where guests can enjoy reduced green fees. All the beautifully decorated guest rooms in this recently extended and remodelled hotel have private bathroom, colour television, telephone and tea/coffee making

The Punch Hotel is a managed public house, owned by the Mansfield Brewery, situated in the centre of Hull and adjacent to the impressive Princes Quay shopping centre. Open all day, the Punch Hotel is enjoyed by locals and visitors alike. The impressive exterior is complemented by an equally attractive interior which features panelled walls and decorated ceilings. The furnishings are comfortable and the atmosphere homely and welcoming. The lighting on the bar is also very eye-catching with tall brass stems topped with coloured glass lamp-shades. A good range of food is available and a specials board is changed daily. The specials are half price for Senior Citizens.

The location of The Punch Hotel, next to a large shopping centre and opposite the Tourist Information Centre, makes it an ideal place to stop for refreshment while touring the city.

The River Humber, which drains one-fifth of all England's river water, is one of the country's largest estuaries and commercial waterways. The Humber Bridge, a well-known landmark of this city, was the longest single span suspension bridge in the world at its opening in 1981. A toll is payable on the bridge, which has a total span of 2220 metres. The towers above the supporting piers are 510 feet high. and interestingly, although both are vertical, because of the curvature of the earth they actually lean away from each other by several inches. At night the bridge is lit up with arc lights that are placed all over it.

At the north end of the bridge is the Humber Bridge Country Park which gives the visitor a true 'back to nature' tour only a short distance from one of man's greatest feats of engineering. Walks through woodlands, meadows and ponds are plentiful, with a nature trail. The Park itself has an interesting history too - it was used for chalk extraction as far back as 1317.

The Old Mill on Hessle foreshore is also worthy of a visit. Built in the early 19th century to power a whiting works, driving crushing rollers and two pumps, the windmill tower and most of the internal machinery have been preserved and

173

it is now a prominent feature of the Humber Bridge Country Park.

Historically, HESSLE was one of the great crossing points of the Humber estuary, right up until the building of the bridge. Even the Romans had a ferry here which they called 'Transitus Maximus' linking the vital route between Lincoln and York. Ferries continued until the building of the Humber Bridge and one of the paddle-steamers, Lincoln Castle, has been preserved as a floating hotel and restaurant and is now at Grimsby.

The town of Hessle is an excellent point from which to take a train or car through the picturesque Wolds villages on this side of the Humber. Like its neighbour, KIRKELLA, the town was founded by the heathen son of the Saxon King Ida, who invaded in AD547 and who established the kingdom of Northumbria, which stretched from the Humber to the Firth of Forth. Hessle is an attractive market town these days with some fine Georgian houses.

COTTINGHAM, to the north of Hull, has international acclaim as the university village, being home to around 2,000 students as well as a large number of academic staff of Hull University. This large University influence contributes to the fact that Cottingham is the largest village in England with a total population of around 17,000.

Humberside

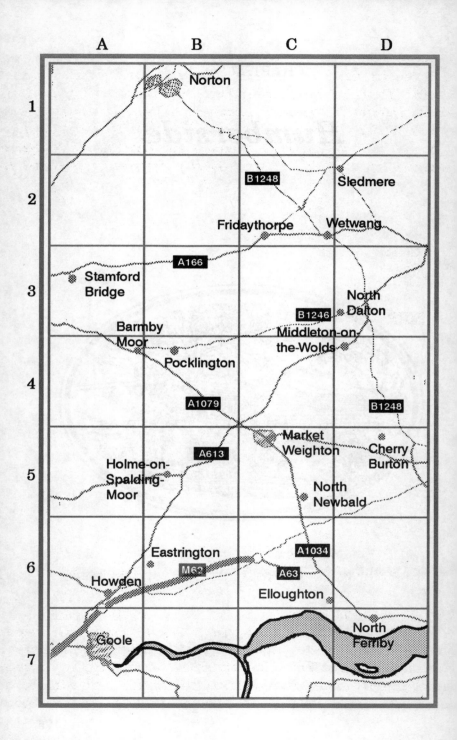

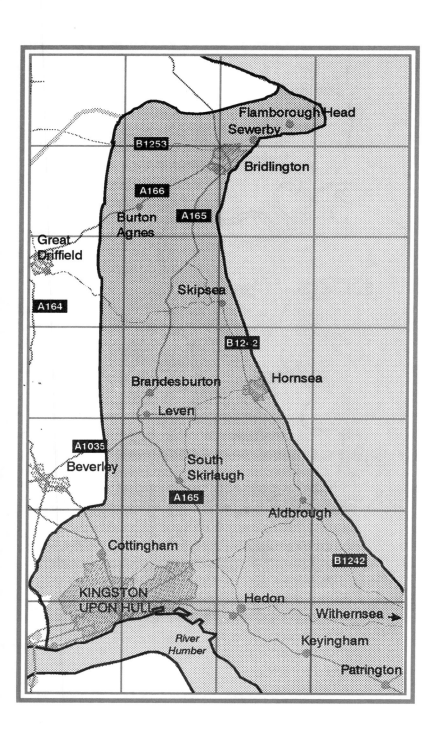

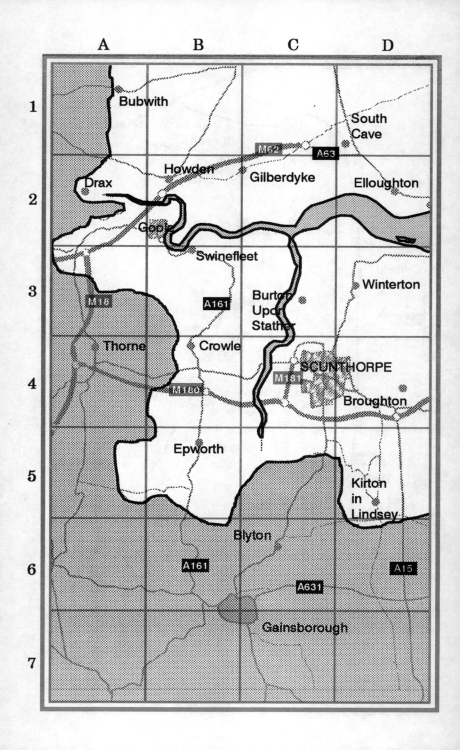

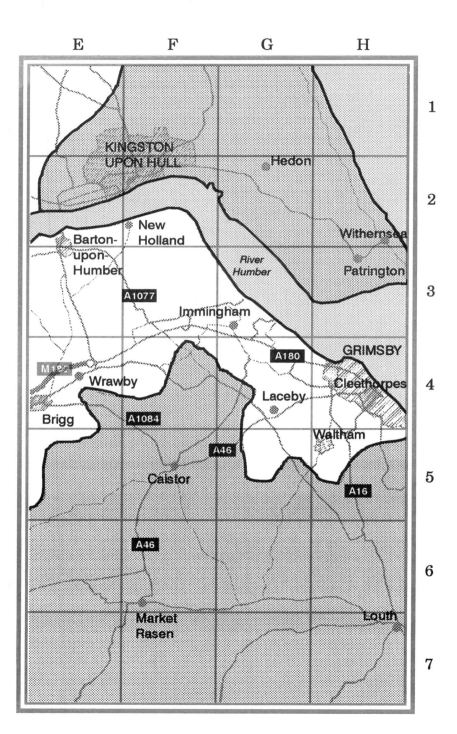

Beverley Minster

Humberside

Some of the finest countryside in Britain can be found in Humberside. Rolling hills and valleys, flat-lands criss-crossed by country lanes and ancient paths, patchwork fields and woodland provide a scenic back-cloth to many attractive villages and hamlets.

Predominantly an agricultural area, Humberside has a long history of reaping the fruits of the land. The past is preserved in many ways, not only museums.

The Wolds of East Yorkshire form a gentle rolling landscape enclosing many delightful villages in an area of great charm and natural beauty. From the north bank of the Humber to the chalk cliffs of Flamborough, the hills of the Yorkshire Wolds extend in the form of a crescent of high ground. These chalk hills were shaped by the glaciers that once linked Britain with mainland Europe and over the years have developed into rich agricultural land.

The earliest settlers in the area could have arrived as long ago as 10,000 years leaving behind tumuli, earthworks, deserted villages and farmsteads for their successors to interpret.

Beverley

Just to the west of Hessle, two nearby villages provide delightful establishments in which to enjoy some refreshment.

The delightfully named **Swan and Cygnet** can be found, rather appropriately, in **SWANLAND** overlooking the village pond, which is itself frequently visited by swans, ducks and other wild birds. This popular pub also has superb views to the Humber Bridge. A property of the Mansfield Brewery Company you can be sure of getting a good pint, and you may want to try some of the great pub food as well. The menu is varied and exceedingly well-priced. Some dishes you may want to try are the traditional Cumberland Sausage, a toasted sandwich or perhaps a Jacket Potato filled with Mexican Salsa. There is also a choice of interesting vegetarian options. To the rear is a beer garden and there is a large off-road private car park.

Swan and Cygnet, Main Street, Swanland, North Ferriby
Tel: 01482 634571

Nearby is the pretty village of **WELTON** where a stream flows past the green, under bridges and into a tree-lined duck pond. The imposing Welton Grange was built in 1741 for a Hull merchant, complete with its Venetian style windows. In fact the whole of Welton was a retreat for the wealthy shipping merchants of Hull, and the architecture reflects this.

The Church of St Helen dates from Norman times, but was almost totally rebuilt by Sir Giles Gilbert Scott in 1862-3, the Victorian architect who designed St Pancras Station. It is particularly noted for its 13th-century doorway and the intricate Pre-Raphaelite windows made by William Morris'
182

company of craftsmen. In the graveyard is the memorial of Jeremiah Found, a resilient local reputed to have out-lived eight wives!

The Green Dragon can also be found in the village of Welton. Local legend has it that this establishment gave hospitality to Dick Turpin, the notorious highwayman, prior to his committal in York Castle in 1739. The inn has since been carefully restored and today can provide superb accommodation in traditional surroundings. There are 11 rooms, all with en-suite facilities and beautifully furnished. They are well-equipped, with colour television, drinks tray, trouser press, telephone and complimentary newspaper. The bar areas are comfortable and spacious and the service is excellent. Here you can enjoy a delicious pint from the Mansfield Brewery and choose a meal from the extensive menu. All the dishes are freshly prepared and come in hearty portions. Children and vegetarians are also catered for. An ideal place to stay, conveniently situated for the city of Hull.

The Green Dragon Hotel, Cowgate, Welton, Nr. Brough
Tel: 01482 666700

Situated just on the outskirts of the village of Welton, only five minutes from the main road leading into Hull, is the Welton Heights Riding Centre. Whether you are after hacking, riding lessons or livery then you need look no further. Owned and personally-run by Dallas Tongue, herself an experienced rider, Welton Heights is a place where novices and competent riders mix in a family-like atmosphere. The centre is home to a variety of horses to suit all sizes and abilities. Hacks last from one hour upwards and a small lesson is given to gauge the standard of riders before the hack starts. There is an outdoor arena and a cross country course in addition to the many bridleways in the surrounding area. Disabled riders are very welcome with advance notice. During summer months camping/riding holidays are available. If you like riding then this is a great place to try.

Welton Heights Riding Centre, Beverley Road, Welton, Nr. Brough Tel: 01482 665248

A little way up the A63 is **BRANTINGHAM**, with a church that nestles between two hillsides. The village's war memorial is particularly unusual, and of heroic proportions, built from masonry rescued from Cuthbert Broderick's Guildhall in Hull during its reconstruction in 1914. Various stone urns located around the town were also part of the salvage.

Continuing along the A63 and turning off onto the A1034 you will come to the village of **SOUTH CAVE**. An agricultural settlement, South Cave is strictly a town, having a town hall in the market place. The name of the town is said

184

to be a corruption of South Cove, due to its southern parish being located in a back-water of the Humber.

The village is separated into two distinct parts by the grounds of the Cave Castle Golf Hotel. Built in 1586, legend has it that there are tunnels under the grounds that were used for escaping! The building is a splendid example of the Gothic style and was once the home of George Washington's great grandfather.

To be mentioned in the Domesday Book is pedigree indeed - a piece of English history which sets certain places apart. **Rudstone Walk Farm**, 400 years old, is one such place, its name coming from the medieval hamlet of 'Rudtope', which was mentioned in that great survey of England.

Set in its own 300 acres on the edge of the Wolds, this beautifully furnished family home is the centre piece of a number of accommodation options. The Greenwood family started with the original farm holiday cottages and have now added a small group of luxurious, architect-designed units to the farmhouse, all offering an attractive, relaxing country retreat.

The four cottages were built to a very high standard and incorporate every possible comfort and facility. French windows in each cosy lounge open onto a west-facing terrace where, on a clear, warm summer evening, guests can enjoy spectacular sunsets across the Vale of York. Superbly equipped and furnished, all have fitted carpets, excellent bathrooms and luxury kitchens. Linen, towels and tea towels are supplied and changed weekly. These cottages are of varying sizes - Teal sleeps two, Kingfisher and Snipe can sleep four while Mallard can sleep up to six. In 1992 a further set of farm buildings were converted into seven cottages based around a lawned courtyard. Of an equally high standard, each has a double or twin bedroom.

The self-catering units are totally self-contained but guests who prefer may take advantage of dining in the house or having their meals delivered to their cottage. The elegant, farmhouse dining-room and lounge certainly entice the visitor to join with house-guests in the relaxed warm atmosphere created by Pauline Greenwood. Rudstone Walk Farm provides holiday or business accommodation to please the most discerning visitor - peaceful, relaxing and warmly welcoming.

Rudstone Walk Farm, South Cave, Nr. Brough
Tel: 01430 422230 Fax: 01430 424552

At **NORTH NEWBALD**, just to the north, you can see working horses in their natural surroundings at Flower Hill Farm. There is an interesting collection of horse drawn implements and vehicles as well as a harness room which houses a fine display of horse brasses and other artefacts. A Bygones Museum, Victorian Kitchen and Clothing displays are other recent additions.

MARKET WEIGHTON is another quiet town where the 18th-century houses cluster around a church which was established long before the Norman conquerors moved north. William Bradley, England's tallest ever recorded man, was born in Market Weighton in 1787. He grew to 7 feet 8 inches (2.3 metres) and weighed 378 pounds (172 kilograms). Once, when in London, William was introduced to the Royal family and King George liked him so much that he gave him a huge gold watch chain to wear across his chest.

186

The **Londesborough Arms Hotel**, in the heart of Market Weighton, is an historic, listed building dating back to 1700. A former coaching and posting inn, it has been known as the Londesborough Arms since 1850, named after the Lords of the Manor of Market Weighton. Completely refurbished, the hotel has retained the charm and character of bygone days while offering today's visitor every luxury. The atmosphere is friendly and efficient and the surroundings luxurious - the hotel is furnished throughout with antiques, paintings and prints. The Cocktail Bar features an unusual carved bar as well as a superbly decorated ceiling and is an ideal place to enjoy a pre-dinner drink. The Bradley Room is a comfortable lounge for residents, named after Market Weighton's most famous son, the 'Giant' Bradley, while the Devonshire Bar is open to all guests.

Londesborough Arms Hotel, High Street, Market Weighton,
York Tel: 01430 872214

The restaurant is both magnificent and intimate and the enthusiastic staff will be on hand to ensure that you enjoy your meal. The food is of a superb quality and is offered on both a table d'hôte and à la carte menu. A particular speciality are the flambé dishes which are cooked at the table. Attached to hotel is the Grapes Bistro which is open for breakfast and lunch and again in the evening. The food is of the same high quality and ideal for a snack or more informal dining. The accommodation of the hotel comprises 17 en-suite bedrooms all beautifully decorated and equipped with every facility. All feature wood panelling and an open fireplace while the Bridal Suite includes an impressive four poster bed.

The work that has been carried out at the hotel by owners Susan and Stuart Giles has resulted in numerous awards for its sensitive planning and skilful restoration - all well deserved. This is a fabulous hotel and ideal for using as a base while touring the Wolds or for a special weekend away.

Heading east from here the A1079 will shortly bring you to the village of **BISHOP BURTON**. Lying in a dip of the Wolds the many tumuli in the area are evidence of early occupation. The name is a derivative of the Old English Burgh-tun meaning a fortified place of which there are several instances in the area.

Altisidora, Main Street, Bishop Burton, Nr. Beverley
Tel: 01964 550284

Sitting proudly opposite the village pond in this tranquil village is the impressive establishment of Altisidora. Named after a famous racehorse which came from the village, the inn provides delicious food and good ales - what more could one need?

188

Part of the Mansfield Brewery Company, the Altisidora is managed by Colin and Wendy Mountain who will ensure that you enjoy every moment of your visit. A recent addition to this establishment is a beautiful conservatory where you can enjoy your meal from a Landlord's Table menu. The menu offers a good choice of reasonably priced dishes and there are also vegetarian options. This is a traditional inn where you will find good service and a great atmosphere.

The Ferguson Fawsitt Arms, Walkington, near Beverley
Tel: 01482 882665

Situated in the village of WALKINGTON, due south, is The Ferguson Fawsitt Arms, an inn that dates back to the 17th century. Formerly a blacksmiths, the pub was named in 1868 after a wealthy landowner, Major Daniel Ferguson Fawsitt. The interior is splendid, featuring dark wooden panelling and fire surrounds. The pub has a far-reaching reputation for its food, and it is worth going out of your way to try it for lunch or for dinner. Food is available at every session and is served from a buffet, and in the evenings there is also a carvery. The separate restaurant is open Tuesday to Saturday evenings and although it seats 90, bookings are advisable. The restaurant menu is à la carte and every dish sounds delicious. To complement your meal, the wine list is excellent, with over 35 bins to choose from. The atmosphere

189

throughout is cosy and full of character. The walls in every rooms are adorned with numerous coats of arms which, set on the wooden panelling, make an interesting feature.

The village is famous for its Victorian Hayride, a parade of heavy horses, traditional hay wagons and costumed villagers every summer. This is just one of the many unique events held in Humberside every year. For a full programme, contact the nearest Tourist Information Centre.

The village of **SKIDBY** is situated to the west of the A164 about five miles from Beverley. The village has a long history, believed to have been founded by the Danish invaders around AD890. At the Dissolution of Monasteries, Henry VIII gave the manor of Skidby to Trinity College, Cambridge, in whose ownership it remained until recent years.

The Half Moon Inn, 16 Main Street, Skidby, Nr. Hull
Tel: 01482 843403

There is a fine windmill here which stands on the hill above the village and makes an outstanding local landmark. The mill was built in 1821 and is one of the few surviving working tower mills in the country. It is a listed building and is put into operation producing stone-ground flour for sale to visitors. The adjacent mill buildings house a museum of old implements and materials associated with corn production and milling.

Close to the windmill The Half Moon Inn is just as well known for its excellent bar food as for a good pint. Dating back in parts to the 17th century the property was formerly two cottages. The surroundings are pleasantly welcoming and the interior is decorated with displays of foreign beer bottles and miniatures. The Half Moon's customers are obviously amply satisfied with the pub's speciality - 'man sized' Yorkshire puddings served with a variety of fillings. For those with a less hearty appetite there are other dishes to choose from. Your host, Pete Madeley, also lays on regular entertainment, so most nights there is usually something going on - maybe some live music, a quiz or some traditional pub games.

To the rear there is 'Sproggies Bar' which is a play area for children. Here they can play safely and purchase soft drinks, crisps, sweets and ice-cream. What a good idea!

The gracious and ancient market town of BEVERLEY, a place of curious and eccentric place-names steeped in history, is also county town of Humberside. It gained its power as the centre of trade and industry that served the port of Hull during medieval times but was tightly controlled by the 38 trade guilds that implemented a complex set of ordinances. One of the more curious rules was that bakers were not allowed to employ Scotsmen - whether or not this was due to the bad feelings generated by the many invasions by their more northerly neighbours, or whether it was simply because their culinary abilities were considered rather inadequate, we will never know!

Around the town there were four (or maybe five!) gateways or bars. Unlike most other towns and cities in England at this time, Beverley was not encircled by a wall, but by a ditch, the remains of which are still being researched. The only surviving gateway is the North Bar and it was at the adjoining Bar House that King Charles I and his sons stayed in the mid-17th century.

The cloth weaving, dyeing and tanning were all represented in the ancient guilds who staged mystery plays and attracted traders from as far afield as London to their Cross fair. In fact it was these guilds that paid for the building of St Mary's Church in the 13th century. Sadly, 400 years later the tower collapsed killing 400 worshippers, but it was rebuilt and can be seen still standing below the North Bar. Full of medieval carvings, many of them brightly coloured, the interior has to be carefully savoured. The magnificent panels on the ceiling, for example, depict the Kings of England from Sigebert (623-37) to Henry VI. Four legendary kings were also shown at one time but one was removed in favour of George VI. Among the smaller details are the musical carvings, the Beverley Imp above one doorway and the Pilgrim Rabbit which supposedly inspired Lewis Carroll's White Rabbit in 'Alice in Wonderland'.

The Beverley Arms, North Bar Within, Beverley
Tel: 01482 869241 Fax: 01482 870907

The Beverley Arms, a Forte Hotel, stands proudly opposite the impressive St Mary's Church in North Bar Within. Over 300 years old, The Beverley Arms is the principal inn of this former capital of the East Riding of Yorkshire. Originally known as the Blue Bell Inn, it was here that the elusive Dick Turpin, masquerading under a false name, once stabled his horse. The horse was later identified as having been stolen, and Turpin was subsequently brought

192

before the magistrate, committed to the Beverley House of Correction and sent for trial.

The inn was rebuilt in 1794 by William Middleton, who added the Georgian façade and renamed it the Beverley Arms. Middleton was a local builder and did much to give Beverley its distinctive character as an elegant town. The hotel has also been immortalised in the paintings of the old kitchens by F.W. Elwell, the distinguished member of the Royal Academy who for 42 years lived at the Bar House. The novelist Anthony Trollope also played a part in the inn's history. He stayed at the Beverley Arms when he stood, unsuccessfully, as a parliamentary candidate in 1868. A few years later, the Beverley Arms appears as The Percy Standard, in his novel 'Ralph the Heir'.

Today, the Beverley Arms is still a centre of social life in the area, and offers a warm welcome to travellers and visitors. The hotel boasts 55 bedrooms, all comfortably furnished and with private bathroom and full facilities. There are also two suites. The downstairs lounge area is an ideal place for guests to relax with a cup of tea or light snack at any time of day. There are two bars - The Elwell Bar, where you can enjoy some local ale, and the Turpin Bar which is more intimate, and ideal for a pre-dinner drink. The Beverley Arms restaurant can offer fixed price and seasonal menus which feature traditional English fayre and local specialities.

The market place, in the centre of Beverley, is separated into three sections. There is the Saturday Market Place on one side and the Wednesday Market Place to the other. The Butterdings pavement, which as the name implies was once reserved for the sales of butter and dairy produce, lies in the centre, separating the two. Dominating this central area is the 270-year old market cross bearing the arms of Queen Anne. Local legend says that it replaces an earlier cross which was large enough for stage-coaches to pass beneath it.

One place that comes highly recommended in this particular spot is the splendid **Kings Head Hotel**. This historic inn dates from Georgian times and during its recent refurbishment, great care was taken to preserve the genuine character and atmosphere of the building. There are now twelve beautifully appointed bedrooms, all furnished in an attractive country style and equipped with en-suite bathroom, colour television with satellite and Sky link, trouser press and tea/coffee making facilities. On the ground floor there are two pleasant bars, both very cosy, offering a wide range of traditional beers, wines and delicious bar meals.

The Kings Head Hotel, 38 Saturday Market Place, Beverley
Tel: 01482 868103 Fax: 01482 871201

The hotel's charming country kitchen restaurant is open both to residents and non-residents and serves an excellent range of continental and traditional English dishes which are prepared using fresh locally-sourced ingredients wherever possible. In addition, on Sundays, excellent roast lunches are served. To accompany your meal there is an extensive wine list offering selections from most wine-producing areas of the world. The Kings Head also has an attractive conservatory room where guests can enjoy a drink or light meal in relaxed plant-filled surroundings. Within the hotel is a delightful coffee shop and bistro serving a range of tasty sandwiches,

194

snacks, pastries and cakes, along with a selection of specialist coffees and teas.

Adjacent to the Market Square, in Ladygate, is the welcoming **Dog and Duck Inn**. Built in 1936 to replace the previous pub, also called the Dog and Duck, it has recently been extended to incorporate six attractively decorated letting rooms. Each room is en-suite and offers TV and drinks-making facilities. The pub itself is characterful and a warm welcoming atmosphere is created by the manager, Mark McMullen. Real ales are served and good pub food is served every lunchtime. There is private parking to the rear, an important amenity in the centre of Beverley.

The Dog and Duck, Ladygate, Beverley Tel: 01482 886079

Most of the town's ancient timber buildings are now hidden under Georgian façades, which were used to 'gentrify' the town in the 1700s. It is the legacy of this time that we are still able to enjoy in the elegant terraces, promenades and overall planning of the town. This pleasing blend of different centuries' architecture has shaped the Beverley we know today.

The town is surrounded by 'common pastures', which are still supervised by pasture-masters and a 'regular neat-herd'. Across this green belt, the soaring twin towers of Beverley Minster can be seen for miles around. Beverley Beck, the waterway where ships were once built and along which goods were exported, today lies quiet.

A whole gallery of interesting historical, literary and artistic figures have connections with Beverley. One of the towns most famous sons was James Edward Elwell, the creator of the Gothic-style screen, as well as some of the house frontages in North Bar Without. The house once occupied by him has carvings of his, based on subject matter from Punch magazine. In conservative Beverley, these created a stir in their day, as one can see such national leaders as Disraeli and Gladstone graphically and irreverently depicted. His son Frederick W. Elwell R.A. was another famous and versatile artist and his works can be seen at Beverley Heritage Centre.

Mary Woolstonecroft, pioneer feminist and mother of Mary Shelley, lived as a child in one of the Market Places, and Anthony Trollope stood as a Parliamentary candidate in the infamous corrupt election of 1868 and later satirised the town in a novel.

The Windmill Inn can be found situated in Lairgate, just a few minutes walk from Beverley's town centre. This impressive establishment is family-run and offers the very best in food, ales and accommodation. The present owners are Alan and Joanne Wilkinson, and Alan's brother, David. The Wilkinson family have been running The Windmill for over 19 years, the previous owners being Alan's parents, David and Audrey.

The Windmill Inn, 53 Lairgate, Beverley Tel: 01482 862817

The building which houses The Windmill dates back to the early 18th century and was formerly a row of cottages, becoming an inn at the end of the 19th century. Today, the inn retains much of its character and features wood panelled walls and pew-style seating. Food is served every lunch time and the bar menu offers a good choice supplemented by the daily specials board. Evening meals are only by private

196

arrangement and for residents. On tap, Alan keeps five real ales with Theakstons, Tetleys, John Smiths and Old Peculier permanently available. The overnight accommodation comprises eleven rooms in all, of varying sizes and all individually styled. Each has en-suite facilities and comes with colour TV and drinks tray. The inn has a very homely, family atmosphere and is enjoyed by locals and visitors.

The town's Guildhall, built in 1762 replacing a Tudor predecessor and part of a panelled medieval wall has also been recently exposed. Open to the public, there is an impressive courtroom, which deals with offenders today, public gallery and a Mayor's parlour. The figure of Justice overlooking the building is unusual in that she does not wear a blindfold, contrary to the norm. In answer to a query about this a town clerk was said to have replied "In Beverley, justice is not blind".

The Minster is possibly best viewed from Westwood, one of the common pastures that encircle the town, its twin west towers rising in pale splendour from the plain that surrounds it. Its wonderful and distinctive Gothic lines provide excellent material for photographers, and good views are also to be found from the neighbouring streets that lead up to it.

The Minster was begun in the 8th century on land given by King Athelstan; in 1220 it was extended to its present magnificent Gothic proportions.

The interior is notable for its splendid carvings, all produced by the Ripon school of woodcarvers before the Reformation took place. Carvings of musicians feature throughout as an indication of an active musical life which continues to this day.

Near to the High Altar is the 1,000 year old Fridstol, or sanctuary chair used by men on the run as a haven of safety. Carved out of the solid stone, there are only two others in existence in the British Isles, one at Hexham Priory, the other at Sprotborough Church, near Doncaster. It was originally designated for the purpose it is known for today by King Athelstan in AD937. Offenders using this cold, unyielding seat, usually found they were given board and lodging for 30 days, and then given a safe escort to the county boundary or the nearest port.

The magnesian limestone that the Minster is built from, as are so many of the stone structures in this region, often seems to glow, especially in the evenings, bringing the wonderful carvings within and without to life. Try not to overlook the quirky representations of the ailments Stomach Ache, Toothache, Sciatica and Lumbago, surely more terrifying to any medieval or modern onlooker than the most grimly threatening gargoyle, more often seen in such settings.

Under the shadow of the Minster in Beverley's Highgate, there is a real find, the labyrinth of shops and small retail units collectively known as 'And Albert'. One of the first things that will attract you to this fascinating Victorian arcade will be the imaginative 3D sign which hangs on the wall to the right of the doorway. This shows a dozen of the shops in miniature and has a charming 'doll's house' quality, reminiscent of one of Richard Hamilton's pop art creations. Inside, the building has the compelling atmosphere of an Arabian bazaar. The air is filled with such evocative aromas as freshly-ground coffee, perfumed candles and newly-worked leather, adding to the feeling that one is entering a vast Aladdin's Cave.

All three storeys are overflowing with a fascinating array of crafts and artefacts, some produced locally and some originating from as far away as Africa and the Far East. Altogether, there are twenty-five shop units offering an astonishing variety of high quality products of every description.

The shop called Magpie stocks a beautiful selection of cards, clocks, candles and gifts, and within its upstairs room is a fascinating range of etchings from the antique print shop. An interesting range of plants, terracotta pots and frost-proof planters can be found throughout the whole building. Those interested in studio glass and crystal cutting should look out

198

for the Little Glass Studio, and upstairs, a unique range of handmade and imported jewellery is on view at Sirocco. The Africana Room imports batiks from Uganda, paintings from Tanzania and tapestries from Losotho and Transkei, while Turning World sells top quality hand-worked wooden bowls and giftware.

Leather Craft specialises in belts and leatherware made from the finest British hides, and at Quilling Cards, beautiful handmade stationery and cards can be personalised by their helpful staff. If you are interested in minerals and semi-precious stones, head for Merlin's Crystal Cave, and collectors of second-hand books should seek out Books on the first floor. Also on this floor are The Honey Pot and Reflections, shops which offer a varied choice of original gift ideas including framed prints, mirrors and clocks. If you are after fine linen, lace and beadwork you should make a point of finding Broderies, and those with a fascination for beautifully detailed miniature buildings should look for the premises run by M. James. The Sugar Craft Shop stocks everything for the cake decorator and sugar craft artists and wouthwatering handmade fudge and chocolates are available at Hideaway Wood. Also on view is a display of kitchens and kitchen furniture by Stirling and Jones Traditional Interiors. Should you need some refreshment after all this hard work, then head for the Butler's Parlour, Victorian Tea and Coffee Rooms to enjoy a delicious home-made cake, sandwich or light meal accompanied by a cup of speciality tea or coffee.

The proprietor of 'And Albert' is Cottingham-born David Murden. After completing a Master's degree in clinical psychology his intention was to return to the area to practise his chosen profession. His plans were changed however, when he discovered that in Beverley a number of small traders were being prevented from obtaining retail premises due to the inflated rents brought on by the property boom. He then took up an offer to purchase the premises in Highgate and set out to convert the building for use as a Victorian arcade while still practising as a psychologist. This plan was not without its problems - the building turned out to require a substantial amount of reconstruction work which led to a great deal of financial pressure being placed on David's shoulders. However, by the end of 1987, the project was successfully completed and the building opened its doors to the public for the first time.

'And Albert', 33 Highgate, Beverley Tel: 01482 871251

Such has been the success of the project since then, that David has opened a second 'And Albert' in York's Stonegate, although this new operation differs from the first in that it is run as a large retail unit rather that as a number of small ones. The York shop also acts as a showroom and test-market for David's latest project, the 'And Albert' World Crafts Trade Warehouse at Market Weighton, where a huge variety of traditional crafts and modern artefacts are imported from the Third World to sell to the trade. What is perhaps even more incredible is that David is not entirely satisfied merely to involve himself with the UK end of the operation. He also travels to such countries as Nigeria, Niger, Guana, Cambodia, Burma, Java and Bali on buying expeditions for the warehouse. Part entrepreneur and part adventurer, David's exploits will undoubtedly lead to further successful and worthwhile enterprises in the future.

Beyond Beverley in the hamlet of ARRAM, set in over three acres of grounds, is the delightful Crow Tree Farm. Some of the outbuildings of the farm date back to the late 18th century but the main house wasn't built until Queen Victoria's Jubilee. Within the friendly farmhouse, furnished with antiques, Margaret and George Hart can offer two comfortable letting rooms. The bedrooms are spacious, contain lots of personal touches and the views across the surrounding countryside are unbeatable. The breakfasts are excellent and home cooked evening meals are available on request. Within the outbuildings there is a smashing self-catering unit that is full of character; "The Fold" has all the facilities you would need and the old manger has been retained as an attractive feature. There are plans to convert another outbuilding into a room where bunk beds can be used, ideal for children and offering parents some peace and quiet. A warm welcome awaits visitors here in the heart of the English countryside and for children there is a variety of animals to handle.

Crow Tree Farm, Arram, Beverley Tel: 01964 550167

The magnificent Crown and Anchor stands proudly beside the River Hull at Hull Bridge, near TICKTON. The appearance both inside and out goes hand in hand with its setting and position which is delightful, particularly in summer months when there is lots of river traffic. Within the inn you will find a number of alcoves which make up the main bar area, a games room and, up a couple of steps, a restaurant which looks out over the river. Lee Chester is the landlord and he is particularly proud of his popular establishment. It is decorated and furnished to a high quality, the atmosphere is friendly and the staff are happy and helpful. The inn is renowned for its food as well as its well-kept ales. The menu is written on the blackboard each day and offers an excellent selection of starters, main courses and, if you have any room left, desserts. The style is that of traditional pub fare with some more exotic dishes as well. The portions are of a good size and the meals are very reasonably priced. The ales come from the Mansfield Brewery Company, one of the best in the area. The gardens and terraces are by the riverbank and are delightful in summer. Bookings for the restaurant are taken for Monday to Thursday, but not for weekends.

The Crown and Anchor, Hull Bridge, Tickton, Beverley
Tel: 01964 542816

To one side of the pub is a small camping and caravan park which can accommodate up to six tourers. Facilities include electric hook-ups, water and a children's play area.

The Crown and Anchor can be found by taking the A1035 out of Beverley towards Bridlington. About two miles out, turn right at the Tickton Village sign and immediately turn right again. Follow this road to the end and the Crown and Anchor stands in front of you.

Great Driffield

Located on the A166 York to Bridlington road, is the busy agricultural town of GREAT DRIFFIELD, known as the Capital of the Wolds. It is a town of ancient origins and was once the capital of the kingdom of Deira. However, it was the opening of the Driffield Canal in 1772 which was the major turning point in the development of the town. Grain and goods could be shipped by barge or keel directly to Hull, instead of having to be taken on the badly made roads by horse and wagon.

All Saint's Parish Church is a good example of Perpendicular architecture, parts of it dating back to the 12th century. Inside, it has beautiful stained glass windows, medieval in origin, portraying local nobility.

There is still a cattle market held on Thursdays as well as a general market on Thursdays and Saturdays. The annual Agricultural Show, first held in 1854, and the pedigree sheep sales have helped make Great Driffield into one of the most important small towns in the area.

The Blue Bell Riverside Restaurant, is located near the canal-head in a quiet corner of Driffield and yet still near the centre of the town. An attractive and unusual feature is the bar which is a scale replica of an old type of keel-boat, and the sail, complete with boom, is lowered when 'time' is called, thus completing the marine effect. In the inn a varied selection of good food is available each lunchtime and Tuesday to Saturday evenings. Real ales are served - John Smiths is the permanent brew - and there is always a guest ale as well. The inn is open all day every day. The restaurant, to the rear, is open every lunchtime and evening and live entertainment and dancing is held each Saturday and Sunday night. The menu is impressive and extensive and caters well for vegetarians. The inlaid dining tables, manufactured by hand in Italian craft workshops, are an indication of the standards of this enterprise. One only has to enter the premises to be aware that the inn and restaurant, under the guidance of Marlene and Bill Edgar, are a considerable asset to the local residential, tourist and business community.

The Blue Bell Riverside Restaurant, 5 Riverhead, Driffield
Tel: 01377 253209

Back in the centre of Driffield is The Bell Hotel, a traditional coaching inn that dates back to the early 1700s. The earliest recorded landlord was a William Porter who also promoted the canal which eventually linked Driffield with Hull and brought prosperity to the town. At that time the courtyard opened onto the main street through an arch, and the stables were located where the car park is now. In Victorian times the name was changed from 'The Blue Bell' to 'The Bell Hotel' and the archway was closed off.

The establishment has been privately owned for most of its lifetime, and for the last 19 years has been run by Mr Riggs. The Bell is renowned throughout the area, and beyond, as being one of the premier hotels in this part of Yorkshire, and it certainly lives up to its reputation. Throughout the hotel much of the decor retains original features, in particular the wood panelling in the Oak room and billiard room and the plasterwork in the hall. The fourteen bedrooms continue the standards of decor, all are en-suite and some feature four poster beds.

However, the main reason that guests return again and again to The Bell, is the outstanding cuisine. Whether you choose something from the lunchtime buffet or sit in the dining room and select from the à la carte menu, you will not be disappointed. An extra attraction is the newly opened leisure complex. Traditionally styled, the complex provides a spacious and luxurious environment exclusively for the enjoyment of hotel guests. Here guests will find a swimming pool, whirlpool sauna and steam room.

The Bell is ideally situated to use as a base for touring, and even if you just stop for a drink, you are sure to be impressed.

The Bell Hotel, Market Place, Driffield Tel: 01377 256661

In the heart of the Wolds, nestling in a valley surrounded by rolling countryside, lies the village of LANGTOFT. The settlement is perhaps notorious for its record of freak weather conditions and violent storms. Many of these are recorded by J. Dennis Hood in his book "Waterspouts on the Yorkshire Wolds" which was published in 1892.

In May 1853 a terrific thunderstorm broke over the village and destroyed the two ploughs and three of the horses of the men who were ploughing on the hills. A waterspout burst over the village in June 1888 washing soil from the surrounding hills and depositing mud and boulders in the street. Numerous other such events are detailed in the book of Dennis Hood's but a modern drainage system means that such events are no longer common.

The Ship Inn, Scarborough Road, Langtoft, Driffield
Tel: 01377 267243

The Ship Inn can be found in the centre of the village and started life as a barn before being converted into cottages and then a coaching inn. Today it is the only pub in the village although at one time there were three. The decor is very traditional and features lots of pictures of the village on the walls. Home-cooked food is available here every lunch time and evening. The menu offers a good choice and all the portions are of a good size. The meals are good value for money too - especially the Sunday lunch. In addition to the range of ales there is an extensive wine list. There is accommodation available here, four en-suite letting rooms with colour TV and drinks tray, and the location of the Ship makes this an ideal place to use as a base for walking holidays. This family-run establishment is excellent value for money.

Dating from the 18th century, the **Old Mill Hotel and Restaurant** in Langtoft was formerly the farmhouse attached to the Corn Mill, which can still be seen to the rear. With magnificent views over the Wolds, the rural location makes this a exceptional place to visit. Stephen and Lesley Lai came here just a year ago, and with Stephen's experience in the trade have successfully created a quality establishment offering the best in food and accommodation. The restaurant has earned a name for itself, with the fine cuisine produced by an experienced team of chefs. The menus offer a good selection of unusual dishes and are changed frequently to make best use of seasonal produce. Many regulars drive several miles to get here, and the restaurant can get busy, so booking ahead is advisable. The hotel can offer nine cosy letting rooms all with en-suite facilities. They are well-equipped and come with colour television, direct-dial telephone and drinks tray.

The Old Mill, Mill Lane, Langtoft, Nr. Driffield
Tel: 01377 267284

Six miles north-west of Great Driffield is the popular Sledmere House . It is a magnificent Georgian mansion that has belonged for many years to the Sykes family, its gardens having been landscaped by Capability Brown. On entering the village of **SLEDMERE**, one might be forgiven for thinking that one has been dropped into a masterpiece of classical fantasy. It might be true to say that different generations of the Sykes family had set about creating a decorative playground for themselves - statues of tritons blowing horns herald you through gates, past pillars and even through the doors of the village inn!

There is a wonderful sense of fun around this place - there are humorous friezes by Joseph Rose in the Hall, and lovely little carved parasols above the cresting of a Chinese-style bed. For those of more studious direction, there is a huge library over a hundred feet long. Those of musical tastes may be interested in the large pipe organ, that is played daily between 2pm and 4pm. There is also an Exhibition Centre and a Waggoners Museum, as well as special events throughout the summer.

The curiously named village of **WETWANG** is also deep in the heart of the Wolds and located on a busy road. There is an unusual craft shop here called Oak Rabbit Crafts. This small furniture makers marks every one of its hand-carved products with the symbol of a rabbit.

The Victoria Inn and Restaurant, Main Street, Wetwang, Nr. Driffield Tel: 01377 236677

Home-made meat pies are the particular speciality of the **Victoria Inn and Restaurant** on Main Street, Wetwang. Malcolm and Pat Pickering, the owners, take great care to ensure that both bar food and restaurant meals are freshly cooked to order using the best of local produce. The menus are extensive and items are reasonably priced, and the popularity of the inn with the Wetwang community is self-evident. The restaurant seats up to 40 people and private parties are easily catered for.

Over 100 years old, the Victoria's stone walls, beams and wood panelling combined with pleasant furnishings, create a friendly, comfortable atmosphere in which to relax. Visitors should not be deceived by the small frontage as the pub is actually quite large. The Victoria is a real credit to its owners.

The Star Inn, North Dalton Tel: 01377 217688

The village of **NORTH DALTON** can be found in the heart of the Yorkshire Wolds midway between Pocklington and Driffield. Here, nestling beside the village pond, is **The Star Inn**. This Georgian inn was once a busy staging post on the Minster Way, the route from Beverley to York and today is still popular with travellers who find good refreshment and warm Yorkshire hospitality. The interior is cosy and welcoming with a roaring log fire and characterful rooms.

The candlelit restaurant is relaxed and intimate and the à la carte menu is extensive and reasonably priced. In addition there is a smaller menu of bar snacks which is available. All meals are home-cooked and the food has been Egon Ronay recommended. There is accommodation here too - seven en-suite rooms, some of which overlook the pond. All are equipped with telephone, colour TV, mini-bar and drinks tray. Nicknamed the Inn on the Pond, this is country accommodation at its best.

The Wolds Inn, Huggate, Nr. York Tel: 01377 288217

Hidden gems are few and far between, but one that is waiting to be discovered is the Wolds Inn at HUGGATE. Surrounded by breathtaking countryside, this inn offers the visitor the excellent facilities that country inn are renowned for. The atmosphere that has been created by owners Peter and Patricia is unique and unbeatable. As you enter you will find a characterful lounge bar and dining area to one side and a public bar on the other. The interior features exposed wooden beams and panelled walls throughout and the bar includes pew-style seats and a open log fire. The food is delicious with a good selection of traditional dishes on offer. Behind the bar is an array of well-kept real ales and the pub is recommended by CAMRA. Upstairs there are four en-suite letting rooms.

210

The Wolds Inn is closed all day Monday, except Bank Holidays, and it is essential to book at weekends if you wish to eat. With many pleasant walks in the area the pub is popular with walkers and ramblers. This is an outstanding establishment with great hosts and an even better atmosphere. Once found, you will never forget it.

Pocklington

One of the most attractive features of POCKLINGTON is the succession of open spaces which link together to form an interesting and unique townscape. In addition there are a number of alleyways, many of which are in the final stages of development as shopping precincts.

The town was recorded in the Domesday Book as an extensive Royal Manor and was probably one of only two boroughs in the East Riding of Yorkshire at that time. The settlement was founded in Anglo-Saxon times and the name indicates that it was "Pocela's people" who lived here. It is reputed that the last burning of a witch in England took place in Pocklington.

It has been a market town since the 13th century, but it was the building of the canal in 1815 and the construction of the railway that rapidly increased the prosperity of the area. More recent history has been the building of several airfields in the locality which played an important part in the second World War.

Situated on a section of the wartime aerodrome, the Wolds Gliding Club is well established with excellent facilities. Winch launches and aerial towing are available daily and a free flight often tempts new members to sample this popular leisure activity.

Just 10 yards off the main street in the centre of Pocklington is The Martins restaurant. Arthur Rawlings, the owner, opened the restaurant just two years ago coming here from running a restaurant in nearby Market Weighton

211

and prior to that, running a hotel in York. With this background of over 20 years in the trade it is not surprising that The Martins has been so successful.

A small entrance leads visitors to the magnificent, two level, dining area and a stair lift is available for the elderly or the infirm. Seating up to 50 at one time, the restaurant is very attractive having been well decorated and furnished. The menus offer a good choice, from snacks to full three course meals and the most extensive selection being available in the evening. Vegetarians are well catered for, and senior citizens can take advantage of special meal deals. Children under 12 years can enjoy meals at half price and pre-school children can eat free. The Martins has become particularly known for its excellent carvery which is offered at all times.

The Martins is open 10am to 2pm, Tuesday and Wednesday; 10am to 9pm, Thursday; 10am to 10pm, Friday and Saturday; and 12noon to 7.30pm, Sunday. Closed all day Monday.

The Martins, 5 St. Peter's Square, Market Place,
Pocklington, York Tel 01759 306806

The Feathers Hotel stands proudly overlooking the Market Square of the town. Dating back to the 18th century it has been a post house, a coaching inn and during World

212

War Two, was a hospital. Part of the Pennine Inn chain, the inn has recently been refurbished but retains its traditional character and style. Upstairs the hotel boasts eleven en-suite luxury rooms which are of the highest quality and excellent value for money. Downstairs is split into three different sections. The first is the bar area where locals and visitors mix and where first rate ales are available, including Theakstons Best Bitter, Theakstons XB and Youngers Scotch. The second area is a restaurant seating 40, and the third is a conservatory area which seats 30. The conservatory is an attractive and cosy area to dine, decorated with a floral fabric draped over the wall and ceiling and with a centrepiece of a hanging basket. The hotel is open all day, every day except Sunday and food is served from an extensive set menu and daily specials board. To the rear of the hotel is a large, off road, private car park. This is an ideal spot to use as a touring base in this beautiful part of the country.

The Feathers Hotel, Market Place, Pocklington, York
Tel: 01759 303155

Penny Arcadia, the magical museum of penny-in-the-slot amusement machines, is housed in the Ritz Cinema in the Market Place. 'Museum' is too narrow a word to describe this fun-palace. The entertainment has an imaginative stage presentation lasting about one and a half hours and the cinema also shows the latest releases.

Ashfield Farm lies off the A1079 at Canal Head, near Pocklington. Owned and personally run by Kay and David West, this two acre small-holding was once a working farm and now offers quality bed and breakfast. Kay's knowledge of the area it extensive and could be of great value to visitors. The farmhouse, built at the turn of the century, is a place where you will feel right at home, and you are sure to return again and again. It is ideally situated for exploring the whole of this area.

There are three comfortable letting rooms, all twins, and very cosy. The breakfast will set you up for a long day sight-seeing and, if required, Kay can also provide packed lunches. Ashfield Farm is open all year round and is excellent value for money.

Ashfield Farm, Canal Head, Pocklington, York
Tel: 01759 305238

The Wellington Oak is also located at Canal Head. Renowned throughout the area for its cuisine, this impressive establishment dates back to 1820. Today it is still charming locals and visitors and enticing them to try the excellent food and well-kept ales. The interior is very attractive with a roaring log fire and exposed brickwork adding to the character. The menus are excellent with a varied selection from which to choose. Food is served every lunch time and evening and bookings are advisable on Saturdays and Sundays to avoid disappointment. To accompany your meal, Tetleys is served with a regular guest ale as well.

To the rear of the establishment there is one acre of gardens with a stream running alongside. This is an ideal place to sit on sunny days. There is also a small site which can take five touring caravans. The Wellington Oak is a credit to its owners, and you are sure to want to return.

The Wellington Oak, Canal Head, Pocklington, Nr. York
Tel: 01759 303854

Percy Marlborough Stewart left to the people of Pocklington his collection of water-lilies, one of the finest in Europe, and the Stewart Collection containing illustrations and objects of the many countries of the world which he visited on his hunting expeditions. The gardens and museum can be seen at Burnby Hall Gardens just outside Pocklington.

Situated in eight acres of beautiful gardens, adjacent to Burnby Hall Gardens, are the delightful Lakeside Lodges. When Denise and Tim Slights, the owners, arrived only a year ago, the whole of this area of land was overgrown. They have since designed and built six bungalows and landscaped

215

the surrounding area. The site is now very attractive and the focal points are the three lakes. The main lake is set among mature trees and is well stocked with carp and other coarse fish. Duckwood Lake is man-made, but has also been well stocked with fish. The main lake is open to the public by day ticket and both lakes are open to residents for fishing at no charge. Duckwood has also been made accessible to disabled anglers. The six bungalows are for self-catering holidays and are very well-equipped and comfortably furnished. Each has ample car parking and overlooks Duckwood Lake. They sleep four people with a double bedroom and a twin bedded room and one bungalow has been specially adapted for disabled access and use. Denise and Tim live on the site to provide personal attention. The location of Lakeside Lodges makes them ideal for keen fishermen and visitors who wish to explore this delightful part of East Yorkshire.

Lakeside Lodges, Willow Waters Fishery, Burnby Hall Lane, Pocklington, Nr. York Tel: 01759 306585

Quaint, olde worlde, and characterful, are just some of the adjectives that could be used to describe the wonderful Rambler's Rest Tea Rooms and Restaurant, situated in the tiny hamlet of **MILLINGTON** in the heart of the Yorkshire Wolds. Angela Nesom, the owner, has established an excellent reputation for the establishment in the two years that she has been here. Within, it features stone floors, exposed brick walls and has an old range and fireplace with a roaring log fire. The Rambler's Rest is open Saturday and Sunday in winter months and weekdays on request as well as throughout the summer. It is open from 11.30am onwards and serves snacks and beverages and evening meals. Bookings are however advisable for the evening as the restaurant is only small. The menus for snacks and hot meals offer a good selection and caters to all tastes. All dishes are home-cooked and use only the freshest ingredients.

Rambler's Rest Tea Room and Restaurant, Main Street, Millington, York Tel: 01759 303292/305220

The unspoilt village of **BISHOP WILTON** lies at the foot of Garrowby Hill on the edge of the Yorkshire Wolds. In Saxon times there was a palace here and the village was used as a country retreat by the Bishops of York. It was also the Saxons who began the building of the lovely church which has a fine Romanesque chancel arch and doorway. The unusual mosaic floor made of black and white marble is modelled on one in the Vatican. It depicts birds and scenery, made up of tiny pieces of marble, each no bigger than a fingernail.

In the heart of the village you will come across **The Fleece Inn**, a free house, which is ideal for a quick drink or a bite to eat. The inn can also offer overnight accommodation with four en-suite letting rooms which have all the facilities a visitor might need. The bar area is welcoming and friendly and the hosts, Gwyn and Les Wells, are a charming couple. A good selection of hand-pulled beers is on offer behind the bar and there is a good wine list. The food is of an excellent quality, with a wide choice available every lunch time and evening until 9.30pm, seven days a week. A Sunday lunch is served between 12 noon and 2pm, with a choice of roasts. Other days there are two menus - à la carte and bar meals - and all meals are freshly cooked to order. This is a popular establishment that all will enjoy.

The Fleece Inn, Bishop Wilton, York Tel: 01759 368251

The village of **SUTTON UPON DERWENT** is situated on the east bank of the River Derwent, which serves as the county boundary. It is an equal distance from York and Pocklington.

Situated in an acre of beautifully tended gardens is the impressive **Manor Farmhouse**. Don't let the name of this establishment mislead you though - this is not a working farm but more like a Manor House. The present house is early 18th-century but built on the site of the original Manor House of the DePercy family which dates back to the early 14th century. To the front is the outstanding 12th-century

218

Church of St Michael and All Angels and to the side and rear is open countryside.

This tranquil and characterful establishment offers excellent bed and breakfast facilities in a relaxed and peaceful atmosphere yet very convenient for York. All the rooms are beautifully decorated and feature oak beams, original pine doors and open fireplaces. There is a separate guests' lounge with TV and the hearty breakfasts are served around a large table in the dining room. The three letting rooms - The Goose Room, Church View, and twin that is yet to be named - are cosy, warm and all have en-suite facilities. Packed lunches are available upon request but no evening meals are served as there is an excellent village pub which serves bar meals and has a restaurant, within four minutes walk of the house. Manor Farmhouse is ideally situated to use as a base while visiting York and touring Yorkshire.

Manor Farmhouse, Sutton upon Derwent, York
Tel: 01904 608009

The St Vincent Arms is a 300 year old inn located on the B1228 York to Howden road in the village. Very much a family-run establishment, Phil and Enid Hopwood and their family came here five years ago after 23 years in the greengrocery business. Their son, Adrian, is the chef, Simon is the bar manager and Simon's wife is the head waitress.

The pub is very popular for its fine cuisine and well-kept ales. The menus are extensive and cater to all tastes and pockets so you are sure to find something that will appeal. The whole establishment is very smartly furnished and decorated and the atmosphere is friendly and welcoming. A real credit to the Hopwood family.

The St Vincent Arms, Sutton-upon-Derwent, York
Tel: 01904 608349

HOLME-ON-SPALDING MOOR lies at the foot of the Wolds and is the largest village (in area) in the former East Riding of Yorkshire. The area around the village is very flat, apart from a small hill on which stands the lovely Church of All Saints. The hill is a prominent local landmark and alongside the graveyard is Beacon Field where, in case of invasion, the beacon would be lit.

The village is also the location of Hasholme Carr Farm, home to the 'talking' horses often seen on television adverts. A number of heavy horses can be seen here, as well as a fine collection of horse drawn implements and harness room.

Dating back to the 18th century, the Cross Keys is situated on the edge of Holme-on-Spalding Moor. This historic establishment was once a coaching inn where the teams of coach horses were fed and watered. Susan and Paul Willson took over just a year ago and although this is the first public house they have ever owned they have many years experience in the trade. The food is delicious and the menu features all the traditional pub favourites - the 24oz rib steak is popular dish which should only be attempted by those with a healthy appetite. To complement your meal there is also a good selection of well-kept ales. A traditional roast lunch is served on Sunday.

The inn is open 7 days a week and food is served every lunchtime and evening, except Monday evening. It is open all day in the summer and all day Saturday during the winter season. Children are very welcome and there is good access for the disabled. This is a smashing establishment, well worth a visit.

The Cross Keys, 80 Moore End, Holme-on-Spalding Moor, Nr. York Tel: 01430 860342

The imposing tower of Howden Minster beckons the visitor to this interesting and historic town whose largely unspoilt centre retains the flavour and character of the old East Riding. HOWDEN's growth owed much to William the Conqueror's granting of Howdenshire to the Bishops of Durham. The town then served as a convenient stopping point for the bishops on their way between Durham and London.

The Bishop's Manor House, standing in the beautiful Ashes Playing field, is the remnant of a once much more extensive summer palace built by Bishop Skirlaw in the late 14th century. The building was donated to the town in 1927 and restored by the Monument Historic Buildings Trust in 1984.

The Minster, which dominates the centre of the town, has origins in the 8th century. In 1080 the church, with the rest of the town, passed into the hands of the Bishops of Durham. Sadly, the chancel fell into disrepair and in 1609 it was blocked off from the nave. A great fire in 1929, caused deliberately, finished off the tower and caused the bells to crash to the floor. The nave of the church is still used for worship and the chancel is now cared for by the Department of the Environment.

The Market Place has for hundreds of years been the centre of commercial and social life of the town while retaining much of its 18th and 19th century charm and character. The intricate network of flagged and setted alleys and streets running off it is worth exploring especially following their recent repair and the development of attractive shops.

One notable person to have come from Howden is Barnes Wallis. The town was Britain's largest World War I operational airship station and between 1924 and 1929 the R100 Airship was built here. Barnes Wallis lived in Howden and worked at the airship station where he was responsible for the design of this successful but short-lived flying machine. Nothing remains of the station today but the site is now occupied by the Spaldington Golf Course. Pictures and photographs of the airships can be seen in the clubhouse.

When Anne and Keith Hill arrived at The Station just eighteen months ago the pub was closed down. They have since successfully refurbished and extended the property and made it into a very attractive traditional village inn. Through much hard work and with their great personalities the establishment is now a popular and exciting place to visit. A sporting theme is perpetuated throughout, now doubt the influence of Keith who was a pro-am cricketer with Warwickshire and a keen golf and darts player. His expertise has obviously rubbed off on the regulars as the darts team find it hard to lose, and have won many trophies.

The interior decor is cosy and welcoming with both a lounge bar and public bar. A recently constructed games room is to the rear and is frequently used for darts matches. No food is served but as this is a free house there is a good range of traditional ales including John Smiths and Bass. The pub is open evenings, bank holidays and weekends.

The Station Hotel, 4 Bridgegate, Howden Tel: 01430 431301

South of the Humber

To the south of the Humber estuary there are two towns that attract holidays-makers in their thousands every year.

The popularity of CLEETHORPES grew as a result of the weekend-break requirements of the Humberside masses, with a tradition for the freshest cod and chips in Yorkshire, due to its proximity to neighbouring Grimsby, less than three miles up the coast.

The front is tightly packed with all manner of diversions for the traditional family holiday, and dominated by the pier, which looks out to a broad sweep of the North Sea as it enters the Humber estuary, with the occasional deep-sea trawler and cargo ship heading for Grimsby and the Hull Docks.

GRIMSBY's entertainments are possibly more hidden that most, especially if one is constantly distracted by the all pervasive aroma of the fishing industry, which is king here. The town has its own peculiarly industrial skyline, dominated as it is with the derricks of the cargo handling cranes, lighthouses and masts of the many trawlers that still operate from here, despite the economic handicaps imposed on them through recent fishing quota regulations, which do not appear to have dimmed the spirit of those whose families have carried on the trade here for generations.

The sustaining of Grimsby in relatively modern times has relied, first on the canal system, which helped in the transporting of the fishermen's wares to the rest of the North, then the excellent road system, which now ensures that the many fish-mongers and the mobile outlets that one sees dotted around the north of England (and possibly further) can boast 'Fresh fish from Grimsby'. The huge demand for fish and chips from the east coast resorts, such as Cleethorpes, Mablethorpe and Skegness has also aided the perpetuation of the industry.

Grimsby also, predictably, offers some of the best seafood restaurants in the North so it it worth stopping off, if only to investigate this claim.

The cultural focal point in recent times has been the impressive National Fishing Heritage Centre - no-one can say that the people of Grimsby are not proud of their fishing industry, as a visit to this remarkable centre will prove. The centre comprises a walk-through, theatrical documentary on the history of fishing in the region. It is a sensory experience, enhanced by simulated ships' decks that roll and pitch in an uncomfortably authentic way, and icy blasts of arctic-style gales, in an attempt to simulate the trawlermen's progress through the Arctic fishing grounds. One will also learn about the fishing communities' superstitions, how the skipper knew where to start fishing, how many boats were lost, how much was earned, what their first port of call was when they first arrived home, and so on.

A further attraction is the Perseverance, the last all sail fishing smack to operate from Grimsby, still rigged and floating in a large indoor marina.

The Centre has four galleries that have an ever-changing programme of exhibitions, with visitor participation encouraged throughout, which the Centre describes as a Share and Shiver experience, a gift shop called The Bonded Stores and a café titled The Ice Barrel. There is also a range of music, dance and arts exhibitions and craft markets throughout the summer.

One will leave with a fascination for this dangerous and romantic occupation and those Saturday night fish and chips will never taste the same again!

National Fishing Heritage Centre, Grimsby

The Alexandra Dock is another focus of activity, with a range of water-borne activities, a folk club that operates from the P.S. Lincoln Castle - a finely restored paddle steamer moored there and a jazz festival that takes place in the summer.

There are other musical events of repute that take place, including lunchtime concerts at the historic Town Hall, orchestral and choral concerts of national acclaim and an international singing competition.

Other leisure attractions include an excellent golf course, Peoples' Park, well-equipped Leisure Centre, various activities in the Weelsby and Bradley Woods, charming Victorian and modern shopping streets and malls and, of course, those inns frequented by the fishing and trawlermen, and definitely to be visited by those looking for the real Grimsby that cannot quite be supplied by the tourist industry!

Nearby attractions include the east coast resorts, watersports on offer at Barton Clay Pits, an interesting reclamation project, the 12th century Thornton Abbey, Waltham Mill, with its museum and miniature railway, the 900 year old Alvingham Watermill, the award-winning Elsham Hall Country Park, equipped with craft shops and falconry centre, and the Regency-style Normanby Hall, which is set in 350 acres of magnificent parkland. Details of all these venues are available from the Tourist Information Centre at the Heritage Centre in Grimsby.

Selby and the Vale of York

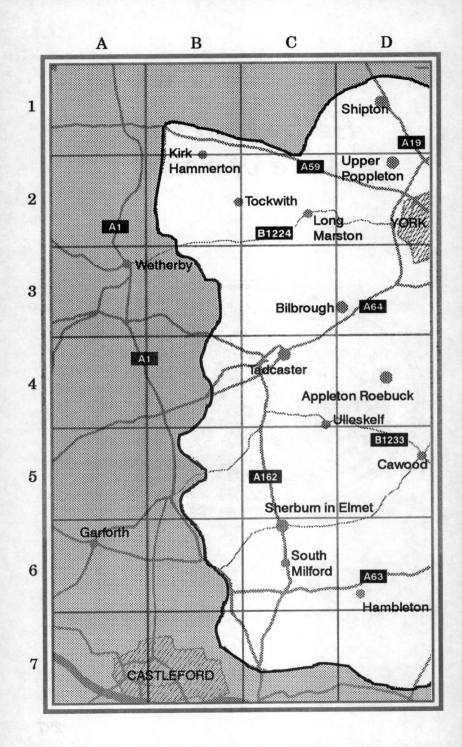

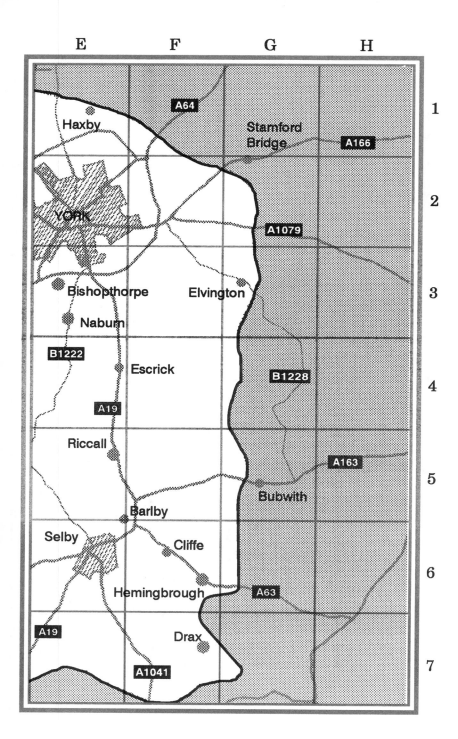

York Minster

Selby and the Vale of York

Lovers of beautiful architecture, archaeology and ancient churches will find no end of such commodities in and around the triangle of Selby, Tadcaster and York. Travelling from Hull to Selby, following the line of the Ouse, one may glimpse the graceful spire of Hemingborough's St Mary's Church, and the tower of the ancient Saxon church at Drax.

This area is famed for its agriculture which makes up most of the flat and highly fertile Vale of York and is ideal for those who wish to explore the countryside on foot and by bicycle.

The Southern Border

The county border to the south of York is marked by the River Aire. Near to where it flows into the River Ouse is DRAX, whose skyline is more dominated by the cooling towers of the power station located there. However, the Church of St Peter and Paul is well worth stopping off for. It has, over the years, been added to and rebuilt, but the original structure is apparent in the shape of the chancel arch and an ancient font was once unearthed in the churchyard that dates from the Saxon period. The church was once connected to an Augustinian Priory nearby, and after this was demolished, several artefacts from the priory, including the finely carved bench-ends, some of the bricks used in the re-built sections and the statues of St Peter and Paul one can see inside. There is a legend that there are as yet undiscovered tunnels below that once led from the Priory and a castle that also once stood here.

A little to the south is the village of **CARLTON** which stands on the River Aire opposite the village of **SNAITH**. Carlton Towers was created during the 1870s by two young English eccentrics, Henry, the 9th Lord Beaumont and Edward Welby Pugin, son of the eminent Victorian architect, A.G. Pugin. They transformed a conventional Jacobean house into an astounding mock medieval fantasy in stone, with turrets, towers, gargoyles and heraldic shields. The splendid and richly-decorated interior was decorated in the manner of medieval banqueting halls by a gifted church architect, John Francis Bentley, and contains a minstrel's gallery and vast Venetian drawing room. Both Beaumont and Pugin died in their forties, bankrupt, and Carlton Towers is now the Yorkshire home of the Duke of Norfolk. It is open to the public in the summer.

Norden Alpines, Hirst Road, Carlton, Nr. Goole
Tel: 01405 861348

On the edge of Carlton, surrounded by the flat countryside of this part of North Yorkshire, is **Norden Alpines**. Set in four acres of grounds, this is a country house bed and breakfast coupled with a plant centre specialising in alpines.

Owned by Norma and Denis Walton, it was Norma who began growing alpines as a hobby 15 years ago. This escalated into a full time project and five years ago the couple moved to the present site, which was previously a ploughed field, built a bungalow and began to create Norden Alpines as it appears today. Most garden centres can now offer a small range of alpine plants, but here you will find over 3,000 varieties. Because of this impressive range, people come from far and wide to add unusual specimens to their collection or just to find some inspiration. The centre is well laid out with all the plants labelled clearly so that you can see them in situ. Even a non-gardener cannot fail to be impressed by the display. The alpines are propagated here as well, not in large numbers, but enough to offer customers a magnificent choice.

In their own home, Norma and Denis are delighted to be able to offer comfortable bed and breakfast accommodation. The rooms all have twin beds and have fabulous views over the gardens and surrounding countryside. There is a comfortable guests' lounge where you can sit quietly after a long day and enjoy your complimentary tea and cake at supper time. Norma is an excellent cook, and the evening meals include many vegetables and fruit grown in their own garden. To the rear there is also a caravan site for five caravans.

Norma's knowledge of alpines is second to none, and her charm as a hostess will make your stay at Norden Alpines one to remember.

Tucked away in the village of **CHAPEL HADDESLEY**, just off the A19, lies the charming **Jug Inn**. The building dates back over 300 years and has been known as the Jug since the mid-18th century. Since then there have been very few structural changes. Though small, this pub has a lot of atmosphere and character, much of it generated by the enthusiasm and warmth of the owners, Syd and Valerie Bolton. There are two splendid small bar areas and a quaint dining area that seats just 12! Be sure to come early to enjoy the wide variety of dishes from the ever changing specials

233

board and taste the real ales that come from breweries all over the country.

Jug Inn, Chapel Haddlesey, Selby Tel: 01757 270307

The Herb and Heather Gardens Centre can be found in the village of WEST HADDESLEY nearby. The gardens comprise over six acres of land in this picturesque village. Here you will find a large variety of high quality plants and the centre specialises in herbs and heathers. The centre boasts over 500 different herbs and houses the National Collection of Santolina.

The Herb and Heather Gardens Centre, Main Road,
West Haddlesey, Nr. Selby Tel: 01757 228279

The Coming of the Railways

Three times Lord Mayor and known as 'The Railway King', it was George Hudson, 1800-1871, who established the impetus for the development of rail at York. The success which has arisen from this can be seen not only in the magnificent station buildings such as the old North Eastern Railway and the Royal York Hotel, but also in the abundance of services available.

Hudson once said 'Mak all t'railways cum t' York' and this has certainly happened.

The city's first railway ran for 15 miles to York Junction on the Leeds and Selby line. Today it takes only 2 hours to travel the 188.5 miles between York and London.

Visitors arriving in York by rail can only marvel at the splendid curve of the station with its triple-arched roof - a fine example of Victorian Railway architecture.

The National Railway Museum is a huge attraction on Leeman Road, and is the world's largest. It covers all railway history, from Gresley's Mallard, Stephenson's Rocket and the Rainhill Trials, to the valiant efforts of the Channel Tunnel builders. The York Model Railway is an equally popular attraction, with almost a third of a mile of track and up to 14 trains running at any one time.

One of the main aims of the centre is to enhance the public's awareness of differing uses of herbs, for culinary, medicinal and fragrant uses, so you can expect to find your visit educational and interesting. The gardens feature heathers and conifers, there is a knot garden and a butterfly garden to enjoy and other areas feature cottage garden plants, meadow and woodland flowers. The centre also has a working nursery and advice on all aspects of gardening is freely available. For a memento of your visit there is a great gift shop and for refreshment there is a small restaurant and tea room.

The magnificent **Owl Hotel and Restaurant** stands on the A63 just three miles outside of Selby in the village of **HAMBLETON**. Very much a family-run hotel, it is a sheer delight for locals and visitors. The establishment dates back to the 1800s and was formerly a country club.

The Owl, Hambleton, Nr. Selby Tel: 01757 228374

On arrival, you will be made to feel right at home with friendly smiles and courteous service. On the ground floor are two dining areas, seating 130 in all. The quality of the food is outstanding with extensive menus offering an excellent choice. Outside, to the rear, there is a terrace and attractive gardens, which can be best enjoyed on sunny days and warm evenings. The accommodation comprises 15 letting rooms

236

which are all en-suite and comfortably furnished. A really special place!

A small hill known as Hambleton Hough supports a plantation of Scots Pine and is a good bird-watching site, particularly in Winter when siskins can be seen. There is also a picnic area and a woodland trail.

The nearby village of **MONK FRYSTON** is charming and has been in existence for over 900 years. It was originally known as simply Fryston, derived from the words 'free stone', probably reflecting the large number of quarries in this area. Selby Abbey was in fact mostly built from stone quarried in this area.

The Swan Hotel, Low Street, South Milford
Tel: 01977 682783

Situated on the main road in the heart of SOUTH MILFORD, is the impressive Swan Hotel. Dating back to the mid-17th century, this was formerly a coaching inn. Full of character the interior features beamed ceilings and exposed brick walls. The owner, Shaun Roberts, made the move from electrician to licensee just two and a half years ago and so far his venture has been highly successful. He has converted all the five letting rooms so that they are en-suite, and each is very comfortable. An overnight stay is very

Bootham Bar, York

Monk Bar, York

reasonably priced too. The Swan serves well-kept real ales and its food is renowned. The atmosphere is welcoming and inviting so you are sure to enjoy a visit. The pub is open seven days a week, all day on Saturday, and food is served every lunch time and evening.

Across the woods and meadows from the village is the 14th-century Steeton Hall Gatehouse. Once owned by the Fairfax family, the gatehouse originally formed part of a medieval castle. A forbear of the famous Cromwellian general is said to have ridden out from here to escape with his sweetheart, a wealthy heiress.

The quaintly-named village of SHERBURN-IN-ELMET is the main western centre of this part of North Yorkshire and was once the eastern capital of the ancient Brigante kingdom of Elmete.

The present All Saints' Church, which lies on a hill to the west, dates from about 1120 and includes Norman pillars and arches. Of interest inside the church are two halves of a Janus cross which was found in the churchway in the 18th century and divided to settle an ownership dispute between the vicar and the churchwarden. The church was used as a secret meeting place for loyal Catholics during the reformation.

Selby to York

The Church of St Mary at HEMINGBOROUGH is prominent, not only for its 190 foot spire, but also for the pale rosy colour of its brickwork which, nestling amidst fields and trees as it does, makes it look extremely attractive indeed. As with Drax, this has been the site of a church since Saxon days, and the nave bears most evidence of this. In 1426, the church became a collegiate under the jurisdiction of the Prior of Durham until the Reformation in Henry VIII's reign. The church was refurbished during this period with the impressive spire that is such a landmark today. St Mary's also possesses the oldest misericord in the country, dating back to 1200, as well as many other fine features.

The town of **SELBY** began as a small Anglo-Saxon settlement of fishermen and farmers, marked by a great oak called the 'Stirhac' which was used as a meeting place.

Selby Abbey

All of this changed in 1069 when a young monk from Auxerre in France called Benedict, sailed up the Ouse following a vision. When three swans flew in formation across the bows of his craft, the monk saw this as a sign of the Holy Trinity and promptly set up a preaching cross under the 'Stirhac'. His community went from strength to strength and was granted land and permission to build a monastery. Unfortunately he fell out with the authorities before the work could begin, and the present church was started by Hugh de Lacy in 1100. To this day the three swans are featured on the town's coat of arms.

240

The beautiful abbey building we can witness today is the product of several centuries of additions to the initial rather heavy Norman style, although one rather quirky feature is that two of the high arches within the church are badly distorted, due to building the great tower too quickly on its soft clay foundations. Sadly, there was a fire in 1905, which caused extensive damage, but its most famous feature, the Washington window, survived. The window depicts the coat of arms of John de Washington, Prior of the Abbey around 1415, and ancestor of George Washington.

Apart from Selby's significance as a trading and religious centre, the Industrial Revolution brought other changes to the town, in the shape of the railway and some of the deepest coal-mines in Britain. The railway station dates from 1834 and is the oldest surviving station in the United Kingdom. The mines produce coal for the giant power stations at Ferrybridge, Eggborough and Drax, which in turn produce power for the national grid, as well as pumping waste heat to the local horticultural centres.

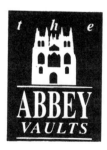

The Abbey Vaults, James Street, Selby Tel: 01757 702857

Set in the centre of Selby and near to the famous Abbey, are the aptly named **Abbey Vaults**. In years gone by this was a tithe barn, part of the Abbey estate, but over the years it was gradually demolished. Remaining stones have been

241

The Vikings of York

In the 9th century, the vikings set about the conquest of England. These were armies from Scandinavia, keen on conquering the richness and splendour of 'Jorvik', home of Kings. This they did, swiftly taking over, rebuilding and populating the city.

In a street called Coppergate, some Vikings who were craftsmen lived, and it was here, between 1976 and 1981, that a series of excavations revealed astounding discoveries.

Findings included the head-high remains of houses and workshops, tools, clothing, shoes, cooking utensils and tiny plant and animal remains. They opened up a whole new picture of the viking kingdom based on York.

Today the 'Jorvik Viking Centre', opened in 1984, provides an imaginative presentation of these remains and an authentic reconstruction of the street. The 'journey' around the centre enables you to become a part of the sights, sounds and smells of the Viking lifestyle. It lasts 13 minutes and ends in the 'Skipper Gallery' which has a rich display of 500 of the 30,000 small objects excavated from the street. The experience is both haunting and thought-provoking.

incorporated into the walls of the pub as it is today. A smashing northern welcome awaits visitors as they enter and the pub is much larger than it initially appears. On one side you will find a tastefully decorated and panelled dining area while the bar area is more cosy with lots of decorative memorabilia. Food is served each lunchtime and every evening except Sunday while behind the bar there is a full range of Mansfield Ales. This is a lively, popular pub and regular entertainment is provided in the form of quizzes and karaoke.

The Olympia Hotel, Barlby Road, Selby Tel: 01757 702459

On the A19, just half a mile outside Selby, is the Olympia Hotel. Having a grand appearance, the building dates back to the early 1830s when it was used as offices and accommodation for the employees of the nearby Olympia Mills - hence the name. It subsequently became an inn and was bought by the brewery on the condition that the rooms were kept to lodge visitors to the mill. In later years it became a coaching inn with stables and it has now reverted to being just an inn, renowned for its well-kept ales and varied accommodation. Present owners, Kevin and Lynda Ewen, have been at the Olympia Hotel for just a year and have so far been very successful. It is very much a locals' pub but visitors are always made to feel very welcome.

Travelling north up the A19 you will shortly come to RICCALL. This village was mentioned in the Domesday Book and still has a Norman Church which stands in the centre of the village.

Old Riccall Mill Restaurant, Landing Lane, Riccall, Nr. York Tel: 01757 248972

Landing Lane is supposedly so-called because it is near to the site where Tostig, King of Norway, landed his fleet in 1066 before he marched on to battle at York. Here you will find the unique Old Riccall Mill Restaurant which is housed in a converted, 19th-century windmill. The present brick tower was constructed in 1811 to replace the mill which had stood on the site since 1290. The mill was converted into a private residence in 1911 and continued as such until 1989 when it was taken over by Spanish-born Manolita Brage and became a restaurant.

Now run with the help of son Martin who is the chef, this is a first class establishment with a pleasant and welcoming atmosphere. The cuisine is a range of Spanish, continental and English and the menu is extensive offering an excellent choice. All dishes are prepared using the freshest ingredients and are cooked to order. Seafood features prominently and vegetarians are also well-catered for. Special Spanish nights are held about once a month and provide a sample of

244

characteristic dishes from the various regions of Spain. Coupled with live music and the opportunity to dance the night away these evenings have become very popular. The restaurant is open daily for lunch and dinner except Monday and Tuesday when it is closed and Sunday when it is open all day. Booking is essential at weekends.

The village of CAWOOD nestles by the River Ouse close to its junction with the Wharfe. Early on in its history, the village belonged the Archbishops of York being the site of one of their palaces. There was also once an important boat-building industry here to complement the village's position as a port, but this is now confined to Selby. The ferry continued to play an important role though, until the bridge was built at the end of the 19th century.

The gatehouse of the Archbishop's palace remains standing, as does a 15th-century building referred to locally as the banqueting hall. Cawood also contains some outstanding examples of buildings with Dutch gables dating back to the end of the 1600s and which are unique to this area.

The Ferry Inn, King Street, Cawood, Nr. Selby
Tel: 01757 268515

The 16th-century Ferry Inn is as pretty as a picture in its setting next to the River Ouse, so step back in time and enjoy

245

this wonderful olde worlde inn. The interior is cosy and traditionally furnished with wooden bench seating, exposed brickwork and open fires. Keep an eye out for the plaque which tells the history of the village. This family-run establishment is renowned for its real ales of which there are at least 8 or 9 at any one time. The bar menu is equally wide ranging with something that will suit everyone. The vegetarian selection is perhaps the most impressive though - the best you are likely to find in any pub. The owners, the Brackenbury family, even offer bed and breakfast accommodation as well. There are three letting rooms which are comfortable and cosy, and packed lunches can be provided. Outside there is an attractive beer garden and terraced area overlooking the river. All in all, this is a wonderful place that should not be missed.

Church Cottage, Escrick, York Tel: 01904 728462

Situated in the village of ESCRICK, and adjacent to the beautiful Church of St Helen, is the Church Cottage Country Guest House. Owned and run by Ron and Nancy Robinson and their son Ian with his wife Alison, this is an old property with a quite unusual history. The then Lord of the Manor had St Helen's Church built in 1856 but unfortunately was not too friendly with the owner of the land adjacent to the church. Subsequently the landowner built a two

246

bedroomed cottage, right next to the church in as ugly a way as possible. It was at that time called Spite Cottage.

Ron and Nancy bought the cottage in 1967 and with thoughtful extensions and refurbishment of outbuildings have successfully turned 'Spite Cottage' into a country guest house of high quality. This is a continuous process, and they plan, in the next few years, to build themselves a home in the two acres of grounds, thereby enlarging the guest house. They will be able to create two extra bedrooms, a resident's lounge and bar as well as increasing the size of the reception area.

Church Cottage is a place many guests fall in love with and return to again and again. All the letting rooms are en-suite, very spacious, warm, have lots of facilities and little personal touches. Each room has a magnificent view over the surrounding countryside. When current refurbishment's are completed they will also be able to offer evening meals for residents and eventually for non-residents as well. Lots of off-road parking is available and Church Cottage is open all year round.

The White Swan Inn and Restaurant, Deighton, Escrick, York Tel: 01904 728287

Standing alongside the main A19 York to Selby road, in the nearby village of DEIGHTON is the White Swan Inn.

In a delightful setting, the inn is very picturesque with its many hanging baskets and flower-filled troughs. The building dates back to the 18th century when it was originally a farmhouse, with a licence to sell alcohol being granted in the mid-19th century.

The White Swan is renowned in the immediate area and beyond for its excellent food and well-kept ales, with lots of variety in both departments. The menu is wide-ranging, with something to suit all palates and pockets. The restaurant area is very cosy and has a real old elm tree in the centre which is a very attractive feature. Behind the bar they serve real ales, and there are usually five to choose from. There are frequent 'special' nights so ring ahead to find out what's going on when you are in the area. You could enjoy a Spanish Wine Evening or perhaps a Whisky Evening!

East of York

The county boundary to the east of York is marked by the River Derwent which flows almost in a straight line, due south, from Stamford Bridge to the River Ouse.

The Jefferson Arms can be found in the centre of the delightful village of **THORGANBY**, twelve miles southeast of York and located near to the River Derwent. This delightful 17th century, traditional country inn offers warm hospitality and a great welcome. Open throughout the day, here you can enjoy good food, fine ales and comfortable accommodation. Run by Gerald Garnham and his daughter Helen, the food really is available from breakfast until late into the evening. The Candlelit Restaurant is also open throughout the day so you can choose your food and then decide whether to enjoy it in the elegant surroundings of the restaurant with its feature inglenook fireplace or the more comfortable ambience of the bar. The food itself sounds delicious, with plenty of continental and traditional English dishes to choose from. All meals are well-priced and come in

248

The Mystery Plays

These plays, once enacted by the City Guilds, are the most famous aspect of York life. Mystery is a derivation of the word 'mastery' and the plays are based on biblical stories. Created as a cycle of 48 they date from the 14th century, are of unknown authorship, and were performed during the European Middle Ages on the Summer feast day of Corpus Christi.

The cycle covers the story of man's fall and redemption, from the creation of angels to the Last Judgement. Certain plays are peculiar to York- the play of Herod's son, of the Transfiguration of Pilate's wife, of Pilate's majordomo, of the high priests' purchase of the field of blood, and of the appearance of the virgin to the Apostle Thomas.

The plays were performed in York, in chronological order, from pageant waggons which proceeded from one selected venue to another.

Today there are half a dozen well-established amateur groups which provide many of the cast for the plays and maintain regular programmes each year.

The original York plays have been preserved in the British Library.

good-sized portions. Other features of the pub are the two conservatories lined with grape vines and an abundance of plants, and outside there is a barbecue area and children's playground. The accommodation comprises 4 en-suite letting rooms, all equipped with colour television and drinks tray. In addition there is a self-contained two-bedroomed cottage which is available for holiday rental. This is a friendly, welcoming establishment which is well worth a visit.

The Jefferson Arms, Main Street, Thorganby, Nr. York
Tel: 01904 448316 Fax: 01904 448837

Also in the village, at the "Steam Gallery" are Maxwell Hemmens Precision Steam Models. The collection is made up of these world famous, hand-built, working models of steam engines, traction engines, locomotives and marine and boat kits. Open to the public daily.

At **ELVINGTON**, due north, is the Yorkshire Air Museum. The museum illustrates the history of aviation in Yorkshire and Humberside - a memorial to the Allied Air Forces who flew from the area in World War II. The museum occupies the original wartime building and has recreated an authentic 1940s atmosphere. Aircraft on display include a rebuilt Halifax and Mosquito and one of the last Lightnings.

Sitting alongside the A1079 York to Market Weighton road, at **KEXBY**, is **Ivy House Farm**, a charming farmhouse which offers the best in farmhouse accommodation. The bed and breakfast is run by Kathleen Daniel and her family and has been for 18 years - the service you will receive is both friendly and expert! This is very much a place where regulars return again and again, especially in the summer months. The whole atmosphere is very homely and guests are well looked after from the moment they arrive. There are three comfortable rooms and views can be enjoyed in every direction. Breakfast is wholesome and hearty and packed lunches can be provided upon request. All in all, this is a lovely place to stay.

Ivy House Farm, Kexby, York Tel: 01904 489368

Since olden times Kexby has been the site of an important river crossing, first by ferry and later by bridge. As a consequence its notability bears no relation to its size. The ferry across the Derwent was mentioned as early as 1315 and the first bridge was built in the early part of the 15th century. A lot of work was carried out on the bridge in 1648-50 and the inscription on it states that it was 'built' in 1650 but it is, nevertheless, the oldest bridge across the Derwent. An attractive modern bridge was built, bypassing the old one, in the 1960s.

The name of the village of STAMFORD BRIDGE is probably known by every schoolchild in England, being noted

251

as the site of the battle of 1066 in which King Harold defeated his half brother, Tostig, who was attempting to regain the Earldom of Northumbria. It was after the battle that Harold then learned of the landing of William of Normandy and went south to fight the Battle of Hastings (which he lost!).

On a rise near the corn mill is a stone commemorating the event with an inscription in English and Danish. Indeed, up until 1878, a Sunday in September was 'feast day' in Stamford Bridge, commemorating the battle. On this day boat-shaped pies were made bearing the impression of the fatal spear, in memory of the Englishman in his boat who slew the Norseman defending the bridge. The day was called Spear Day Feast.

The Cottage Guest House and The Waterside Tea Rooms, 6-8 The Square, Stamford Bridge, Nr. York
Tel: 01759 371115

In the heart of this historic village is The Cottage Guest House and The Waterside Tea Rooms. The two establishments, housed in an 18th century property, front onto the A166 former Roman road and to the rear is the River Derwent. The tea rooms on the ground floor are a real picture and are open seven days a week. The service is friendly and efficient and the standard of the food and beverages available

252

are of an equally high standard. Outside, and next to the river, is a tea garden which is best enjoyed in fine weather. The seven letting rooms of the Cottage Guest House are on the upper floors. The rooms are of a variety of sizes, are spacious and most are en-suite. Some even have four-poster beds.

The tranquil hamlet of LOW CATTON lies on the east bank of the River Derwent. The approach from Kexby is very attractive, being along a narrow road bordered by an avenue of trees and patches of bluebells in the grass verge adding splashes of colour in springtime.

The Church of All Saints is tucked away from the village on a high bank, hidden behind a group of trees. The external appearance is unusual, the building having a sturdy, embattled tower and a chancel that is much higher than the nave. The interior features some fine windows. One, which depicts the Crucifixion, is said to be one of the finest examples of the work of William Morris.

The Gold Cup Inn, Low Catton, York Tel: 01759 371364

Standing in this tiny hamlet, just over a mile from Stamford Bridge, is The Gold Cup. This inn dates back to the early 17th century and, since the arrival of Pat and Ray Hales five years ago, is the place to be seen in the area. The exterior is charming, with creepers growing up the walls and a host of animals, including horses, goats and geese to admire; there is also a large children's play area. Once inside, you enter a different world. Great care has been taken to restore and decorate the interior in a sympathetic manner, in keeping with the age of the structure, with plenty of oak beams and wood panelling. When the new extension was built, beams were used from an old army barracks in Scarborough. All this add to the character and atmosphere of the dining rooms. The emphasis is on the cuisine here - the menu is extensive and a delight to read and making your choice will not be easy. On Thursday and Friday evenings there are special candlelit suppers for two and a splendid Sunday lunch at a remarkable price. The Gold Cup aims to please and provides excellent customer care and value for money.

Situated on the A166 at GATE HELMSLEY is a most attractive establishment called The Duke of York. It is run by Brian and Marie who have created quite a reputation for such a small place. It has received many accolades in the past few years, including Yorkshire Pub of the Year, Yorkshire Pub Food of the Year, Tetley's Master of Mild and Tetley Best Pub in Bloom. Food really is this pub's speciality with a huge variety of meals - there are the regular bar meals and daily specials, an evening à la carte menu, a children's menu, a vegetarian menu, a 'Mature Choice' menu especially for senior citizens and a set 3 course Sunday Lunch as well. But this isn't all! The Duke of York specialises in game and regularly holds Wild Boar evenings. Once a year they also hold a Medieval Night where last year there were 17 different game dishes including South African Water Buffalo, Ostrich and Kangaroo. Don't forget, this is also a pub and you can get a good pint of Tetley's as well. A highly unusual establishment that is well worth going out of your way to find.

The Duke of York, Gate Helmsley, York Tel: 01759 372429

York

At last, we come to the fascinating city of YORK. There is so much to do and see in this wonderful and ancient city, you are sure to find that a one day visit is not enough to cover it fully.

The Romans came here first in AD71, when the Roman governor, Quintus Petilius Cerealis chose it as the best military strong-point for his invasion of Brigantia. He called the new fortress-city Eboracum, and it was soon to become the capital of Lower Britain and a major city within the Roman Empire. The Legions occupied Eboracum until AD410, their headquarters standing on the site where York Minster is today. Parts of their building are evident in the foundations that are on view to the public, and a 31 foot Roman pillar, part of the garrison, can be seen near the south entrance.

The withdrawal of the Romans left the way clear for the invading Anglo-Saxons, who occupied the city and set it up as Eoferwic. The arrival of Christianity also brought learning to the North, and by the 8th century, Eoferwic was the most important centre of learning in this part of Britain. The Vikings invaded in the 9th century - naming the city Jorvik - and remains of their settlement can be viewed at the Jorvik Centre.

The area was in constant turmoil throughout the 11th century, and so troublesome were these Northern lands that William I embarked on a terrible solution to the problem and began the dreaded Harrowing of the North - laying the land barren - driving the Northerners into submission by means of starvation.

York eventually re-established itself as a major centre, which was helped by the birth of William's son, Henry I, at nearby Selby. By the Middle Ages over a hundred crafts were being practised here, bringing about the founding of the many guilds, the wealthiest of which were the Company of Merchant Adventurers, or overseas traders.

York was by now the second largest and most important city in England. The bars, or gates were built at this time, and many kings and queens were frequent visitors. In 1397, a Royal Performance of the York Mystery Plays was staged, an event which has since taken place every four years.

Richard III was the monarch most closely associated with the city. The long standing Wars of the Roses centred on the houses of York and Lancaster, only being resolved through the marriage of Henry VII and Elizabeth of York. The city, however, suffered during the Reformation of Henry VIII, losing its Abbey, priories and friaries; countless treasures were lost. Paradoxically, though, it was the Tudor monarch who did York its greatest favour by setting up the Council of the North, which brought back power to the region.

The Council increased York's importance to such a degree that it became the centre for so many of the battles between the Royalists and the Parliamentarians in the Civil War almost a century later. The turning point of the war happened at the battle of Marston Moor, just to the west of York, after which Prince Rupert was forced to hide within the city walls until the surrender to Sir Thomas Fairfax in 1644.

The York Arms, High Petergate, York Tel: 01904 624508

256

The York Arms, in the heart of the city, lies literally in the shadow of the Minster. Dating back to the 18th century, this was one of the twenty original Coffee Houses in York. Originally called the Chapter Coffee House, it has been known as the York Arms since around 1853. Present owners Barry and Marie Grayson took over the running in 1976 and today are probably the longest serving licensees in the city. The fine interior has lots of character and style and the York Arms can even boast its own ghost, known as the Grey Lady. The inn serves excellent, delicious food and fine ales and a small, first floor terrace overlooks the Minster. There are two letting rooms, one single and one family, and both are spacious and yet very cosy. The whole place is a real gem, with wonderful hosts who have great personalities.

The historical events connected with York are numerous and many are centred around York Minster, the City's cathedral that dominates the skyline from of the town's streets - a splendid vision of great ecclesiastical influence and power.

The origins of the Minster stretch back so far that it has always been in contention with Canterbury itself for ecclesiastical precedence. One should be prepared to spend some time here, as there is a lot to see, from the substantial foundations, right up to the guided tour of the Great Tower which gives breathtaking (not to mention dizzy) views of the city.

The full and proper title of York Minster is 'The Cathedral and Metropolitical Church of St Peter in York. It is a cathedral because it has the 'cathedra' (throne) of the Archbishop of York and can also be called a minster because it was founded in Anglo-Saxon times, when a 'mynster' was a mission centre for evangelism. It is also, of course, a magnificent heritage from the past, containing a wealth of treasures - medieval architecture, stone and wood carvings and 128 windows with some glass being 800 years old.

Sadly, the minster has suffered from three major fires in its long history. The first was caused deliberately by a madman, Jonathan Martin, in 1829. Believing that God wanted him to destroy it, he started a fire with hymn and prayer books. The fire was not discovered until the following morning by which time the east end of the Minster was ablaze.

The second fire occurred only 11 years after the first and was a result of a careless handyman leaving a candle burning. The central vault of the nave was destroyed together with several carved bosses. The third, and most recent fire, took place in July 1984 and was probable caused by lightning. It destroyed the central vault of the south transept and all but two of its carved bosses.

Dean Court Hotel, Duncombe Place, York Tel: 01904 625082

In an unequalled location, in the shadow of York Minster, you will find the Dean Court Hotel. Built in 1850 to provide houses for the clergy of the Minster, it was converted to a hotel after the First World War. Privately owned, and part of the Best Western consortium of independent hotels, the Dean Court has recently undergone a programme of extensive renovation and refurbishment. The restaurant is known locally for the quality of its cuisine, its unique atmosphere and quality of personal service. The menus, which change daily, offer freshly cooked dishes featuring local and seasonal produce. A recent addition to the hotel's facilities is the

Merchant Adventurer's Hall, York

Jorvik Viking Centre, York

Terry's Tearoom. The original tearooms run by Terry's, York's famous chocolate manufacturers, sadly closed in 1978. The Dean Court has since, with the kind permission of Terry's-Suchard, opened its own tearoom to preserve the name and continue the English tradition.

The hotel can offer 40 en-suite rooms, furnished to a high standard with all the facilities you would expect of a high quality hotel. Most rooms are situated at the front and enjoy uninterrupted views of York Minster. A useful feature is that the hotel has its own private car park and although this is located a short distance away a valet will park your car for you should you wish.

The streets surrounding the Minster are fascinating, and the charmingly eccentric lines of the Shambles, Stonegate and Goodramgate, to name but a few, are essential viewing. The streets are also criss-crossed by narrow footpaths - the alleyways, ginnels and snickets or 'snickelways' (a requirement of a snickelway is that it must lead from one place to another). These routes originated as shortcuts to market and they have survived as public rights of way despite being built over, above and around. Incidentally, the narrowest snickelway is Pope's Head Alley, 31 inches wide and over 100 feet deep. Its other name was Introduction Lane, where if one wanted to be introduced, one simply timed the encounter to meet the other party half-way!

The medieval Shambles is probably York's most famous street deriving its name from 'Fleshammels', the street of butchers and slaughter houses. The houses on either side were built so as to keep the street out of direct sunlight. The meat carcasses were hung from hooks outside the houses, many of which can still be seen.

For a taste of traditional British food at its best then pay a visit to one of Russells Restaurants. Both are housed in historic listed buildings, conveniently situated in the heart of the city, and ideal for that special treat while shopping or sight-seeing. Choose either the Victorian elegance of Russells of Stonegate in York's most picturesque street leading to the

Minster or enjoy the rustic atmosphere of Russells of Coppergate, a 16th-century timbered building, formerly a coaching inn.

Russells Restaurant, 26 Coppergate, York Tel: 01904 644330

After a warm personal welcome from the friendly staff you can relax in style and savour the pleasure of the Russells experience - quality food, wine and service - offering true value for money at affordable prices.

Russells Restaurant, 34 Stonegate, York Tel: 01904 641432

First choose from a wide selection of appetising, freshly-prepared starters. Then the highlight of the meal is a visit to the Carving Table with succulent roasts and other main dishes with fresh local vegetables and cool refreshing salads. You will definitely be spoilt for choice! For dessert try their famous bread and butter pudding or any one of the other tempting array of home-made sweets. Finally, for the perfect ending, treat yourself to one of Russells Speciality Liqueur Coffees. Russells Restaurants are open all day serving coffees, lunches, afternoon teas and evening dinner.

The Other Tap and Spile, 15 North Street, York
Tel: 01904 656097

The Other Tap and Spile sits on North Street in the centre of York. It can be found just off Micklegate, five minutes from the Railway Museum, York Station and even closer to the town centre. Built in 1896, the building was formerly used as the Officer's Mess of the Yorkshire Hussars. It later became a public house called The Yorkshire Hussars until it was taken over by the present owners four years ago. Beautifully decorated and furnished throughout, the decor features wooden floors, exposed brickwork and open log fires - very cosy and full of character. Real ales are the real speciality here and there are always plenty to choose from. The blackboard in this pub doesn't offer food - but a changing list of real ales with their strength and price per pint. Food is served as well though, with a reasonably priced selection of bar meals. The whole establishment is a real credit to its owners.

Another of the old inns of York is the Royal Oak in Goodramgate. The inn is traditional, cosy and welcoming after the hustle and bustle of the busy streets. Renowned throughout the city, the pub has a reputation for the quality of its food. The menus are extensive and adventurous and there is not a chip, or French fry, to be seen - they have even won awards for catering excellence. All bread is home-baked and the soups and pies are also home-made. The portions of all the meals are of a good size and very reasonably priced. Food is served all day until about 7.30pm. The beers are of an equally high standard as the food, and there is also the usual selection of wines and spirits. There are three separate rooms - a public bar, side snug cum children's room and a cosy back lounge. The pub also features wonderful murals by a local artist.

The Royal Oak, Goodramgate, York Tel: 01904 653856

The Jorvik Centre, on Coppergate, is one of the many prides of York, a fascinating experience for museum-goers of all ages. Visitors are required to step aboard a time-car and travel back through representations of real-life Viking Age Britain. You can witness a bustling market, full of Danes bartering for chickens, corn and other essential provisions and wares, dark smoky houses (no central heating in those days!), and a busy wharf, when goods were transported along the Ouse and Foss and deposited here from other regions. All have been recreated in accurate detail, complete with authentic sights, sounds and smells to the minutest detail, and this centre is a great favourite with adults and children alike.

The ARC (Archaeological Research Centre) is located in a beautifully restored church close to the Shambles, and is an award-winning hands-on exploration of archaeology for visitors of all ages. Here one can meet practising archaeologists who will advise you on how to sort and identify genuine finds and to try out ancient crafts. For the more technically minded, there are a series of inter-active computer displays which demonstrate the value of modern technology in uncovering the past - a fascinating educational experience. The ARC must be visited by all those who value the part archaeology has played in presenting the history of this oldest of places.

Those interested in the history of York and its mysteries will no doubt feel compelled to go on the Original Ghostwalk of York, which starts at the King's Arms pub on Ouse Bridge, and takes place at 8pm every night. It is not for the faint-hearted - for the most part, York's history is full of torture and intrigue. There are, predictably, many haunting and mysterious stories connected with York and these are related against a backdrop of memorable scenery. For those with a romantic and curious nature, this is a must.

It is very difficult to date the building which houses The Hole in the Wall on High Petergate, just inside the city walls and not far from the Minster. It is known that it has in the past been a monk's wine shop and also the city jail, of which a wall and windowsill can be seen to this day, giving the pub its name. Owned by the Mansfield Brewery, the Hole in the Wall is a real credit to them. Expertly refurbished and decorated, it retains its traditional charm with all the modern facilities that are necessary. The atmosphere is friendly and the management and staff will ensure that your visit is a pleasant one. Food is available every lunch time and evening, and the menu offers a good selection of bar meals and the real ales are well-kept. The location of the Hole in the Wall makes this a good place to try while sightseeing.

The Hole in the Wall, 10 High Petergate, York
Tel: 01904 620931 / 634468

One of the most historic buildings in York is the **Judge's Lodgings Hotel**. This early Georgian Grade I listed building was built in 1710 as a private residence by a Dr Winteringham. Nearly a century later, in 1806, it became the official residence of the assize court judges from which the hotel gained its name. In 1979 it was converted into a hotel and provides high quality accommodation in this ancient city. Present owners, Philip and Maureen Brown were the managers for 14 years before buying the property themselves and continue to provide excellent service. Throughout, the hotel is tastefully and appropriately decorated and furnished, retaining much of the historic character. The dining room is elegant and well-suited to candlelit dining. There is a wide selection of food available but tables are limited and bookings are advisable. The popular Judge's Bar is housed in the original wine cellars and offers an extensive range of food, complemented by traditional ales. Special features of the

York- City of 140 ghosts

York has the reputation of being the most haunted city in Europe and there are said to be 140 ghosts within its walls. Guided haunted walks are available during most summer evenings, and provide an insight into the number of 'haunted' buildings. As you stroll around the haunts you'll hear traditional tales, spine chilling stories and true accounts of ghostly goings on, and who knows what you may see!

The 'Grey Lady' of the Theatre Royal makes regular appearances and it is believed that she ensures a successful performance if seen.

In Holy Trinity Church, Thomas Percy's headless body is seen looking for its head, and in The Anglers' Arms there is the ghost of a Victorian child.

Other sightings include a procession of Roman soldiers, apparently marching on the level of the old Roman road, and a portrait of a Stuart nobleman coming to life in St Mary's Abbey.

The most terrifying of all is probably the story of the canine 'Barguist' which roams the alleyways of the city. The huge black dog with glowing red eyes, supposedly in search of human prey, is rarely seen. Interestingly, similar black dogs have been sighted in other parts of Britain and nearly always near ancient ruins or on prehistoric routes.

Continuing with dogs, apparently The Olde Starre Inn can be upsetting to canine visitors. There have been several accounts of dogs behaving quite strangely here - one even ran into a wall for no reason and knocked itself out. Whatever it is that causes the phenomenon, it is not visible to humans, but it may be related to the two black cats that have been seen here.

house are the magnificent, sweeping, wooden spiral staircase and the original decorated ceilings and cornices. The 12 bedrooms are equally fine in their decoration and furnishing. One contains an enormous four-poster bed - ideal for a romantic break.

The Judge's Lodging Hotel, 9 Lendal, York
Tel: 01904 638733 Fax: 01904 679947

Railway enthusiasts will be similarly drawn to the National Railway Museum on Leeman Road (voted Museum of the Year in 1991), where two hundred years of technical and social changes brought about by the invention of railways and their contribution to the civilisation are celebrated. Here you can see the history of Britain's railways, from Stephenson's Rocket, right through to the Channel Tunnel and beyond. There is an impressive collection of locomotives, historic carriages and displays which demonstrate the workings of the railway system. An absorbing place for boys - and girls - of all ages!

Seekers of information on anything to do with railways can also use the extensive reference library here, with a reading room attached (booking may be necessary for this). After all this if you're seeking refreshment try a break in the Brief Encounter Restaurant in the South Hall, themed on the classic movie.

The black and white timbered Merchant Adventurers' Hall on Fossgate is another magnet for tourists, who are drawn by the history that is associated with this powerful guild. It comprises the Great Hall where all their affairs were transacted, a hospital or almshouse and their own chapel of worship. The guild controlled the trade in all "goods bought and sold foreign", and indeed, is still in operation today. The building with its beautiful and complex timbered roof exhibits the many colourful banners of York's Medieval guilds. In a similar vein, there is also the Merchant Taylors' Hall on Aldwalk, originally constructed by the Confraternity of St John the Baptist.

The Corner Pin, 17 Tanner Row, Rougier Street, York
Tel: 01904 629946

The Corner Pin sits cosily in Tanner Row just two minutes walk from the Lendal Bridge. Attractive in appearance it dates back to the 15th century and has in its time been called the Unicorn. The interior is just as appealing, featuring low, beamed ceilings and loads of character. Good real ales are served - Old Bailey's, Riding and Mansfield Bitter - and all are kept in excellent condition. Food is available every lunch time and evening and the pub is open all day (except Sunday). The menu is varied and delicious and is supplemented by daily specials. Meals can be enjoyed in the main bar area or in a separate conservatory or out in the terraced garden. You will not be disappointed with the inn's character, fine ales and delicious food, and a warm welcome is assured.

The York Museum of Automata holds an appeal for children and adults alike. The definition of automata is 'man-made objects that imitate the movement of living things through a mechanism that is concealed, so as to make them appear to move spontaneously'. The Museum traces the history of automata, from the simple articulated figurines from ancient civilisations, through to the displays of modern robotics. The Automata Shop provides one with an opportunity to buy contemporary pieces, music boxes, mechanical toys and craft kits suitable for all ages.

The York Castle Museum is a goldmine of nostalgic memorabilia and reconstructions not to be missed. It was opened in 1938, based on the collections of Dr John Kirk, a country doctor from Pickering, who acquired the objects to represent a way of life that was fast disappearing. Today, the Museum has extended to fill the former Female and Debtor's prisons that used to be here. Amongst the collections of memorabilia, the period reconstructions are perhaps the most fascinating, from the Jacobean and Georgian Dining rooms, through to an authentic representation of Victorian Kirkgate.

Those interested in York's Roman heritage may wish to view the Roman Bath Inn, where one can see the remains of the steam baths used by the occupants of the garrison here, or the Roman Corner Tower, located behind the Merchant Adventurers' Hall. Parts of the stone walls built by the Romans to surround their fort are most evident at this point, where it rises to a height of 16 ft.

The medieval bars, or gates, stand at the old four corners of the city, and were reconstructed in the middle ages from the old Norman fortifications. These edifices are impressive enough, but standing back seem small in comparison with the mass of York Minster that stands within their protection.

On the banks of the River Ouse overlooking the ancient city, is the outstanding **Lady Anne Middleton's Hotel**. This Quality Hotel, owned and personally-run by Andy and Kâthe Clarke was, perhaps surprisingly, created only 22 years ago. The focal point of the complex of buildings is Skeldergate House, built in 1659 by Dame Anne Middleton, wife of Peter Middleton, a Sheriff of York. Over the years, Andy and Kâthe have bought the surrounding land and buildings; two small cottages, two town houses, an old organ factory and a disused sawmill. The buildings have since been restored and carefully converted to their present functions providing a wide range of facilities for the business traveller and holiday maker.

Lady Anne Middleton's Hotel, Skeldergate, York
Tel: 01904 611570 Fax: 01904 613043

Skeldergate House contains 22 en-suite bedrooms that are all pleasantly furnished and well-equipped. To the rear runs the old Roman terraced wall which has been exposed and now forms the rear wall of a small garden area which leads to Cromwell House. Here there are a further 18 bedrooms and the spacious Sawmill restaurant. The Conservatory, constructed of reclaimed timbers from the original Sawmill, is a lounge and dining area, physically linking Skeldergate House and Cromwell House.

pleasant walled garden. The adjacent former blacksmith's shop has been converted into a self-catering cottage called, appropriately, Blacksmith's Cottage. The cottage sleeps up to six people and is very characterful and cosy.

The Blacksmith's Arms, Naburn, Nr. York Tel: 01904 623464

At ACASTER MALBIS the River Ouse, on its way south to join the Humber, takes a long sweeping bend. Here, with views both up and down stream, stands The Ship Inn, a 17th-century hostelry which has probably always played a part in the history of this area.

The Ship Inn, Acaster Malbis, York Tel: 01904 703888

To say that the inn is character-filled is an understatement - there is an air of history dating back to a time when the river traffic was more sinister than the present pleasure-boats.

Inside, much of the decor is traditional, with stone flagged floors in some areas, roaring fires, and plenty of maritime memorabilia. The superb conservatory can seat up to eighty at any one time, and is suitable for private parties and functions. The food is of a very high standard with a good selection on both the bar menu and à la carte menu which changes regularly. Behind the bar, traditional Yorkshire hand-pulled beers - Tetley's and Taylor's - are on tap. Also available here is overnight accommodation, with eight en-suite letting rooms. One has a four-poster bed and all are tastefully furnished and very comfortable.

Run by the same people who own The Ship Inn, Paul and Elaine Eckhart, is Castle Line boat company in the centre of the city of York. The company has two river launches which offer lunch time, supper and dinner cruises from York.

The Manor, Acaster Malbis, York Tel: 01904 706723

In the heart of this beautiful village is the outstanding Country Guest House, The Manor. Set in over five acres of beautiful parkland, the house dates back in parts to the 1700s. There have of course been many changes over the

276

centuries, the most recent of which is the addition of a new dining room. The emphasis on any stay here is on peace, relaxation and being well looked after. The owners are Susan and Doro Viscovich, and their home is an absolute delight.

There are ten letting bedrooms, all spacious and characterful and with en-suite facilities. The 'Manor Bistro' is open to residents and non-residents each evening, and serves a good variety of fresh, home-cooked meals with a selection of wines and beers to suit all tastes. Outside in the extensive grounds, there is a small lake which is stocked for coarse fishing, and the remains of a 15th-century chapel. This wonderful place, with equally wonderful hosts, should not be missed.

Compared to the many diversions of York, nearby TADCASTER would appear to have less to offer - but it does have the memorable distinction of being one of the foremost brewing centres in Yorkshire.

The quarrying of stone in this area dates back to Roman times when the settlement was called Calcaria, which means simply "limestone". In medieval days the quarried limestone was the main means of prosperity but by 1341, the brewing industry already had a firm foot-hold, with two breweries being recorded as in existence. They located in Tadcaster because of the quality of the water obtained from the River Wharfe. Today there are three companies - John Smiths, Samuel Smiths and Bass Charringtons - with breweries in the town, forming the backbone of the town's economy and dominating the skyline.

Facing the famous and oldest brewery in Yorkshire, Samuel Smiths, on the High Street is the very impressive Claire's Pantry and Tearooms. The building dates back to the 17th century and has, in its time, been a pub and a dentist's surgery. With partly flagstoned floors and the original fireplaces it is now a charming and cosy tea rooms. Owned and run by Claire Brewer the rooms are open during the day to serve the most delicious snacks and light meals along with tea and coffee. The imaginative menu also tempts you to try the wonderful cakes, fancy slices and puddings - they just melt in the mouth. All the food is home-cooked by Claire - 'just the way Mother used to'. A visit here is most definitely a treat.

Claire's Pantry and Tearooms, 18 High Street, Tadcaster
Tel: 01937 834004

Situated in the picturesque village of BILBROUGH, midway between Tadcaster and York is The Three Hares.

The Three Hares, Main Street, Bilbrough, Nr. York
Tel: 01937 832128

Nun Monkton Church

Beningbrough Hall

Converted from a small-holding and blacksmith's shop, which now serves as one of the restaurants, the pub retains much of its original character. Run by Peter and Sheila Whitehead, the reputation of the Three Hares for serving fine food extends throughout the local area and beyond. The menu is certainly impressive - offering a wide selection of fine cuisine, all freshly cooked and using many locally-sourced ingredients. Although the establishment is food oriented you will also find two traditional, real ales on tap and a superb wine list. Wine is Peter's hobby and many of the wines listed can be purchased. Because the Three Hares is so popular, bookings for the restaurants are recommended at weekends.

The battle of Marston Moor took place on 4th July 1644, half a mile north of the crossroads in the village of LONG MARSTON, between Oliver Cromwell and Prince Rupert. This was one of the most crucial encounters of the Civil War and its anniversary is commemorated annually by the Order of the Sealed Knot. There have even been reports of phantom soldiers being seen around the time of the battle each summer by travellers on the road which runs across the battlefield.

Overlooking Marston Moor, where Prince Rupert was defeated by Oliver Cromwell, is Gill House Farm. Legend has it that the owner of the farmhouse at the time of the battle was a Mrs Gill, and she was cooking dinner when a cannon ball smashed through the window! Whether or not this tale is true, a variety of 'battle' memorabilia has been collected from the surrounding moorland during the intervening years and is now on display.

A warm and friendly establishment, farmhouse bed and breakfast accommodation is available here today, courtesy of Amber and Philip Barnitt. Gill House Farm is still a working farm with 500 acres of land and numerous cattle, sheep and horses - not to mention the working sheep dogs! The farmhouse itself is very spacious and has been beautifully decorated and furnished and there are four letting rooms. A hearty Yorkshire breakfast is served each morning and

280

packed lunches, laundry and baby sitting services are available.

Gill House Farm, Tockwith Road, Long Marston, York
Tel: 01904 738379 Mobile: 0850 511140

Between here and Beningbrough Hall, one may happen upon the picturesque village of NUN MONKTON, worthy of being pictured on a chocolate box, with its distinctive red-roofed cottages that nestle around a village green and duckpond.

The Alice Hawthorn is a famous and historic public house. The building is thought to date back to 1700 and the pub is named after a famous racehorse of the 1840s. In a career that spanned four years the horse, Alice Hawthorn, won 51 races from 69 outings. Previously called the Blue Bell, the name was adopted in 1900. 'The Alice' later played an important role during the Second World War when it became home from home for many Canadian air crews. Even today many ex-servicemen return here to relive the past.

Today, the Alice Hawthorn is a popular establishment welcoming many regular visitors from near and far. The inn can boast a number of awards for its fine ales and outstanding cuisine. Many of the beers are hand-pulled and a choice of four is usually available. The menu features hearty, traditional pub fayre, with a number of local

281

specialities. The small intimate dining room is separate from the main bar areas and it is advisable to book on summer weekends. All in all, this is a great place with lots of character and style - well worth a special visit.

The Alice Hawthorn, Nun Monkton, York Tel: 01423 330303

The village also contains the beautiful and ancient buildings of Red House Preparatory School and the famous Church, built from the former remains of the old Priory.

The Priory was founded in the 12th century, as the home of Benedictine nuns. Partially demolished during the Dissolution, fortunately what was salvaged presents us today with a very attractive building, rebuilt in stages due to the poverty of the local community, who were unable to complete their project all at once, lacking the larger income of the great Cistercian priories. Among the prioresses of Nun Monkton were two members of the distinguished local family, the Slingsbys whose chief memorial is Red House across the river at **MOOR MONKTON**.

Red House was the hiding place for Sir Henry Slingsby at various stages of the Civil War, who despite his best efforts was spotted by Parliamentarians and led off to his execution on the 8th of June 1658. It is said that the present adventuresome occupants of the school now here still fill their leisure hours in search for the secret room the unfortunate Slingsby was forced to hide in. The school has in fact gone to great lengths to preserve the house in its original state.

Continuing to the north of York, the village of **WIGGINTON** can be found on the B1363. In the village is the **Jacobean Lodge Hotel**. This is a wonderfully hidden place and dating back to the 17th century it has many delights in store for the visitor. Throughout, the hotel is very olde worlde in atmosphere and it is packed with lots of bygone memorabilia and brasses. The building is a converted farmhouse, originally called Plainville Hall and is set in a picturesque one and a half acre garden. Owners, Brian and Elaine Gwinnett are proud of their reputation for serving good food at very reasonable prices. The restaurant is open each night, while bar meals are available every lunch time and evening. The hotel is particularly renowned for its Sunday lunches. Guests can enjoy the open log fires, a friendly relaxed atmosphere and spacious bedrooms. There are fourteen, all en-suite and some with four poster beds. All rooms also feature a colour TV and drinks tray.

Jacobean Lodge Hotel, Plainville Lane, Wigginton, York
Tel: 01904 762749

On the main street of the adjacent village of **HAXBY** is **The Cottage Inn** This was once a private house, home to the parents of present owner Joyce Carr. In 1980 it was extended and refurbished to create The Cottage Inn. Once inside you will feel very welcome, and here you can enjoy a drink or some delicious home-cooked food. This is a free house, so you can expect some good real ales, usually John Smith's, Tetley's and Theakston's. Food is served every lunch time and evenings except for Sunday night. There is a good variety on the menu with extra daily specials.

The Cottage Inn, 115 The Village, Haxby, York
Tel: 01904 763949

Between Knaresborough and York, one can find Beningbrough Hall, a delightful 18th-century house, with 7 acres of gardens, wilderness play area (which should keep restless children occupied for a good while), pike ponds and scenic walks. The hall has a fully working Victorian laundry which makes one feel extremely grateful for 20th-century technology! Another item of interest is the permanent exhibition of 18th-century portraits on loan from the National Portrait Gallery. There are often other exhibitions that take place here for which there is usually an additional charge.

CHAPTER SIX

Harrogate to the Durham border

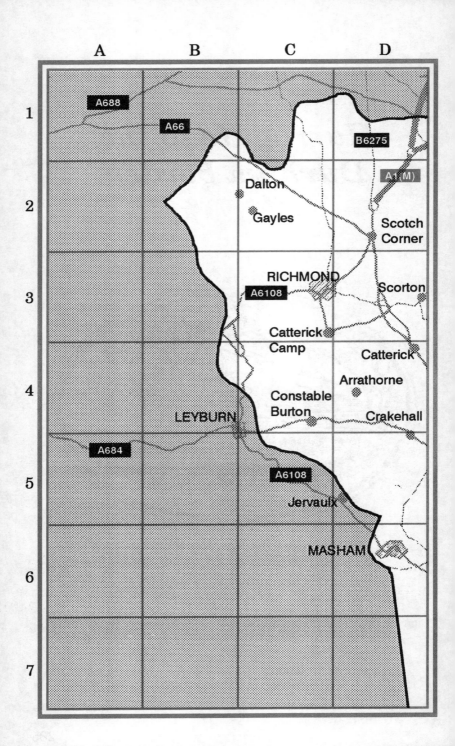

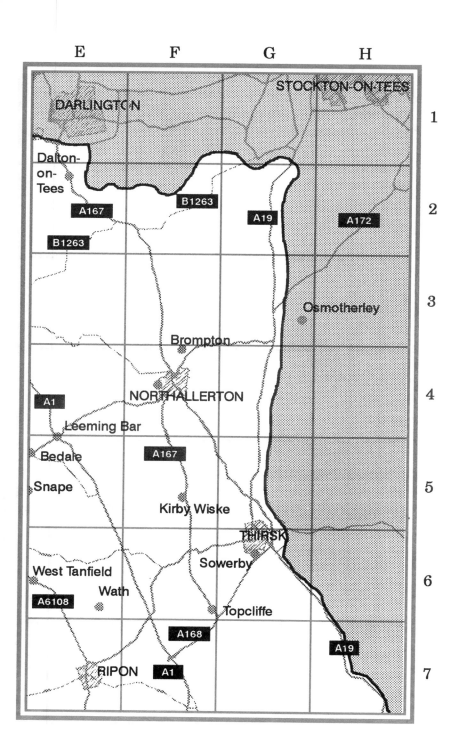

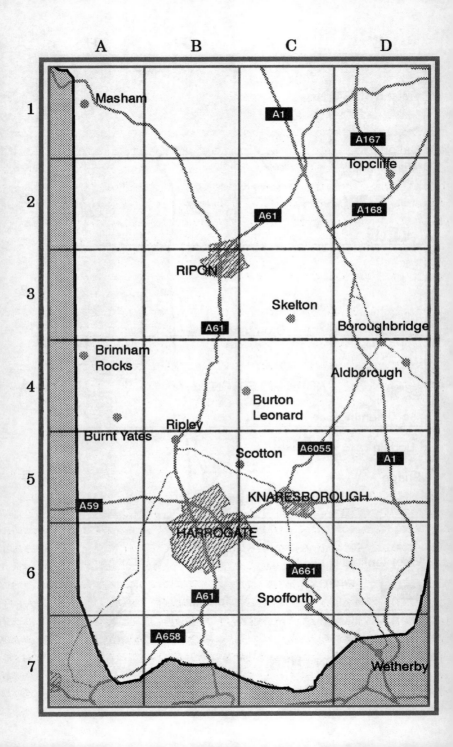

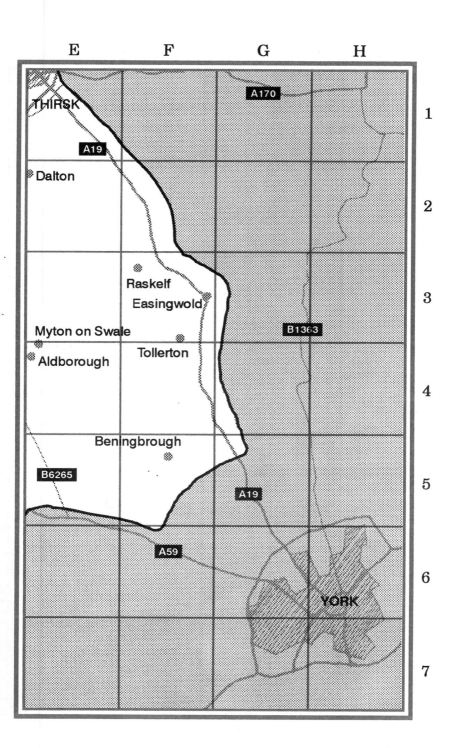

Knaresborough

Fountains Court, Harrogate

dwelling hewn out of the solid rock over some sixteen years by a father and his son. On the banks of the River Nidd there is also the infamous St Robert's Cave which is an ancient hermitage. St Robert was the son of a Mayor of York who, at the time of his death in 1218, was so beloved that the people of Knaresborough would not allow the monks of Fountains Abbey to bury him, instead keeping his bones and finally interning him in a place near the altar in the chapel of Our Lady of the Crag. It is guarded by the statue of a larger than life-size figure of a knight, in the act of drawing a sword.

In the tradition of this town's reputation for exceptional and odd characters is Blind Jack of Knaresborough. Jack Metcalfe was born in 1717, and lost his sight at the age of six, but went on to achieve fame as a roadmaker. He was a remarkable person who never allowed his blindness to bar him from any normal activities - he rode, climbed trees, swam, and was often employed to guide travellers through the wild Forest of Knaresborough. He was a talented fiddle player and one of his more roguish exploits was his elopement with Dolly Benson, the daughter of the inn-keeper of the Royal Oak in Harrogate, on the night before she was due to marry another man. His most memorable achievement however, was the laying of roads over the surrounding bogs and marshes which he achieved by laying a foundation of bundles of heather down, a feat which had never been done before.

Spofforth Castle, a couple of miles south of the town on the A661, is another place of note, an historic building whose sight stirs the imagination, despite its ruined state. The powerful Percy family originally founded the castle which, among other events that took place here, is said to have been the birthplace of Harry Hotspur. Its crumbling walls and wind-blown chambers and passageways, hewn out of the solid rock, hold an eerie fascination for all who come here. The ruins are now in the care of English Heritage.

Nearby Plumpton Rocks, between Spofforth and Knaresborough, is an idyllic lake surrounded by dramatic

Ripley Castle has been home to the Ingilby family for over 600 years. Set in an outstanding Capability Brown landscape with lakes, a deer park and an avenue of tall beeches that the attractive towers only just seem to peek over, the castle is open to the public. Its tranquillity belies the events that happened here after Marston Moor, when Cromwell, exhausted after his day's slaughter, camped his Roundheads here and chose to take sojourn in the castle.

Newby Hall

The Ingilbys, however, were Royalist and his intrusion was met with as much ill-will as possible, offering no food or bed. Jane Ingilby, dubbed 'Trooper Jane', due to her fighting skills, was the house's only occupant and having forced the self-styled Lord Protector of England to sleep on a sofa with two pistols pointing at his head declared the next morning, "It was well that he behaved in so peaceable a manner; had it been otherwise, he would not have left the house alive". Cromwell, his pride damaged by being bettered by a woman, ordered the immediate executions of his Royalist prisoners, within earshot of the castle, causing the musket-ball holes in the church walls. Forced to listen to Cromwell's revenge, 'Trooper Jane' may have had reason to regret staying her hand the previous evening.

Ripley Castle has held its share of secrets over the years, too. A priest-hole was discovered in 1963 behind the wainscoting in the Knight's Chamber where Catholic priests were hidden to prevent them from suffering terrible reprisals. Despite this hiding place, Francis Ingilby, the priest of the family in Elizabethan days, was arrested and hung, drawn and quartered at York in 1586.

The Guy Fawkes Arms, Main Street, Scotton, Knaresborough Tel: 01423 862598

The village of **SCOTTON**, between Ripley and Knaresborough, was once the home of the mother of Guy Fawkes, and in the centre of the village you will find the delightful establishment **The Guy Fawkes Arms**. Taking its name from the infamous Guy Fawkes who used to make frequent visits to Scotton to visit his mother, it is believed to be the only pub in the country with the name. This is very much a family establishment, owned and run by Chris Hall, his wife Doreen, and their son and daughter Jason and Sarah. Together they have created a local reputation for their
300

good food and warm and friendly atmosphere. It is popular with locals but is also ideally placed for tourists and visitors passing through the area. The interior is cosy and traditionally decorated featuring exposed beams, stone flagged floors and open log fires in the lounge area. There is a separate dining area where you can enjoy home-cooked food from the regular menu, which is supplemented with daily specials. Snacks are also available from the bar. A friendly establishment where all visitors are made to feel right at home.

The small villages and hamlets surrounding Ripley are a tonic for any city-weary visitor, and HAMPSTHWAITE is particularly so. Here one can see St Thomas à Becket's Church, where Peter Barker, "Blind Peter", a character in the tradition of Jack Metcalfe, is buried. Despite his blindness, Barker was a skilled cabinet-maker, glazier and musician; by the font is a mysterious portrait of a bearded man, painted by the local vicar's daughter, which may well be Blind Peter himself.

Raventofts Head House, Watergate Road, Bishop Thornton, Nr. Harrogate Tel: 01767 620279

The parish of BISHOP THORNTON, to the north, has always been a dispersed settlement with no main village. Its natural boundaries are streams which in the past provided

301

power for corn, woollen, fulling, flax and silk mills. Raventofts Hall is haunted by a headless nun who walks the orchard at night.

Raventofts Head House can be found just outside the village and this traditional Yorkshire farmhouse enjoys splendid views over the surrounding countryside. Travelling up the drive from the main road you will find yourself in the large farmyard where undercover parking is available. The three letting rooms are in the main farmhouse and are furnished attractively and simply. The guests' lounge and dining area are cosy and again traditionally styled. The breakfasts are hearty enough to set you up for a day's sightseeing and evening meals can be provided by prior arrangement. This is a relaxed, informal establishment which is sure to be enjoyed by all.

Boroughbridge to Thirsk

On the western side of Boroughbridge is Newby Hall, a small but beautiful Adam house, adorned with tapestries, pictures and antique furniture, with gardens that sweep down majestically to the banks of the Ure. Its architectural history is prestigious indeed. The original Hall was designed by Sir Christopher Wren, and in 1766, two extra wings were added by Robert Adam, one of which was intended to house the current owner, William Weddell's collection of statuary. Weddell also commissioned Adam to buy the beautiful Gobelin tapestries which have made Newby Hall world-famous.

BOROUGHBRIDGE is an historic town dating from the reign of William the Conqueror. Once a main thoroughfare for both the Celts of Brigantia and later the Romans it was the bridge, from which the town takes it name, over the river that formed an important link between Edinburgh and London. Busy throughout the coaching days with traffic passing from the West Riding to the North, Boroughbridge has now returned to its former unassuming role of a wayside village with a by-pass (A19) that takes most of the 20th century traffic from its streets.

The great Devil's Arrows, three massive bronze-age monoliths, stand like guardians close to the new road and form Yorkshire's most famous ancient monument. Thought to date from about 2000BC, the tallest is 30 feet high. The monoliths stand in a line running north-south and are fashioned from millstone grit which has been curiously fluted by weathering.

On the eastern side of Boroughbridge is the ancient Roman town of Isurium Brigantum, or ALDBOROUGH, as it is known today. It was once the home of the 9th Legion, who wrested it from the Celtic Brigantian tribe.

The modern-day focal point is the tall maypole on the village green, around which traditional dances take place each May. At one end of the green is a raised platform which is all that remains of the Old Court House. An inscription on it recalls that up to 150 years ago the election of members of Parliament was announced here. Below are some well-preserved stocks that are, in fact, only replicas of the originals.

There is a small museum in Aldborough, which houses relics of the town's Roman past. This was once a thriving Roman city of vital strategic importance and close by to the museum are some of the original walls and pavements of that city.

The Church of St Andrew in Aldborough was built in 1330 on the site of a Norman church that was burnt down by the Scots in 1318. This in turn was built on the site of the ancient Temple of Mercury. Modern archaeologists no doubt reel in horror at the fact that parts of the present church were built with stones from the Temple's walls. One ancient relic, however, that is still preserved in the Church's grounds is the Anglo-Saxon sun-dial called the Ulph-stone.

Its bridge is perhaps most famous by association with the murder of the rebel Earl of Hereford by one of Edward II's

303

loyalist forces, which took place during a battle on the bridge itself. At the death of their leader the rebels fled in disarray.

Two miles from Aldborough, one may decide to visit the village of **MYTON IN SWALE**, which was once the site of one of the strangest battles ever fought on British soil.

In 1319, Berwick-on-Tweed had fallen into the hands of the Scots, and the English under Edward II, 'The Hammer of the Scots' as he was dubbed, had held them under siege in retaliation. Robert Bruce, by means of a diversion decided to mount an attack on York, the plan being to capture Queen Isabella. News of the plan reached York before him and the Queen was moved from the city. The Scots probably would have withdrawn, their plan thwarted, save for an attack, mounted by William de Melton, Archbishop of York, aimed at teaching them a lesson.

An army of priests and tradesmen was hurriedly assembled, and the rabble marched on up the Swale valley to meet with the Scottish forces. The untrained volunteers, though thousands strong, were no match for the battle-hardened Scots, and were slaughtered, priests and all in a tragically uneven foray.

June and Richard Burkill are waiting to welcome you to their beautiful home, **Bungalow Farm**, set in an eight acre small-holding surrounded by delightful countryside at nearby **TOLLERTON**. Their modern bungalow-style house offers the very best bed and breakfast accommodation in this part of Yorkshire. The four en-suite bedrooms are decorated and furnished to a very high standard, are spacious and comfortable, and the rest of the house meets the same exacting standards. June is a great cook and you are sure to enjoy a hearty cooked breakfast and evening meal which is available by prior arrangement.

To the rear of the house you'll find their three milking cows, geese, chickens and a small number of pigs. This is not your normal muddy farm though, quite unexpectedly, but ideal for visitors, it is kept very clean and neat. Bungalow Farm can be found on the edge of the village of Tollerton.

Fountains Abbey

The Bungalow Farm, Warehills Lane, Tollerton, York
Tel: 01347 838732

EASINGWOLD is the first market town reached by visitors travelling north from York and is a perfect introduction to the area of Hambleton. The market place, tucked away behind the main road is a real delight - the ideal place to browse without the bustle of traffic. Here visitors can see several reminders of the past including the impressive market cross and, nearby, the outline of the old bull-baiting ring set in the cobbles.

Easingwold stood in the midst of the Forest of Galtres, a Norman hunting preserve, and the distinctive name is still used locally. During the 18th century Easingwold developed as a prosperous coaching centre and by 1776 posting services were coming through the town. It is full of character and well worth exploring.

In the centre of Easingwold is situated **The Angel** public house. Dating back to the 17th century, the black and white building overlooks the old market square of the town. In the pleasant and cosy atmosphere, enhanced by brick fireplaces and original oak beams, festooned with gleaming horse brasses and old sporting prints, Barry Hooper offers a warm welcome. This popular, friendly pub serves fine ales, with featured guest beers, as well as home-cooked food, in the fine Yorkshire tradition. Open all day there is also a daily specials board that is well worth reading.

The Angel, Market Place, Easingwold Tel: 01347 821605

The Station Hotel in Easingwold was built in 1892 to accommodate the users of the Easingwold Railway. The Railway was completed the previous year, 1891, and ran for just two miles to the main line station at Alne. The line became known for being the shortest standard gauge railway in the country! The line was operated by one small locomotive, nicknamed the Coffee Pot, pulling mixed passenger and goods loads back and forth every day of the week except Sundays. The line finally closed to passengers in 1948 and the goods service stopped in 1957. Today, you would never guess that the railway once ran past the hotel as there has been so much re-building since it closed.

The impressive hotel has only recently been taken over by Bob and Lynda Lancaster and Steve and Christine Parkinson, and already they have made their mark. Throughout the hotel you will find lots of memorabilia, much of it relating to the railway. The à la carte restaurant has rapidly gained a reputation for its good value and imaginative range of food, prepared using fresh produce from local suppliers. The food is complemented by a comprehensive list of wines, including several which are made from grapes which are organically grown. The bar retains many original Victorian fittings and is open to non-residents, serving as a popular focus for the local community. On offer is a range of real ales including guest beers from all over Britain. Steve and Bob have been brewing beer for many years and have just opened a Micro-brewery to the rear of the premises producing about 20 barrels a week. Visitors are welcome to come and see it in operation. The hotel can also offer five letting rooms, all en-suite, and spacious and comfortable.

The Station Hotel, Knott Lane, Raskelf Road, Easingwold
Tel: 01347 822635

On country roads, some eight miles west of Boroughbridge, is the old village of RASKELF mentioned in the Domesday book, and renowned for its 15th-century church which boasts one of the few wooden towers remaining in the country.

In this tiny village, just to the north of Easingwold, is Old Farmhouse, an award-winning friendly country hotel owned and run by Bill and Jenny Frost. The house was originally the farmhouse for Village Farm and although not now connected with the farm it still retains its original character while at the same time offering every modern comfort to ensure an enjoyable stay. There are ten rooms in total, all with en-suite bathroom, hospitality tray, colour TV and direct dial telephone. There are two comfortable lounges, and a large dining room featuring locally hand made chairs. The main rooms have open fires to make those chilly evenings more agreeable. The food is of an excellent quality too - four course evening meals with plenty of choice are prepared by Jenny, with fresh local produce wherever possible. The restaurant is open to non-residents and it is best to book ahead to ensure a table. To complement the meal the extensive wine list is unusual in that some wines are bought at auction, ensuring some excellent wines at reasonable prices.

Old Farmhouse, Raskelf Tel: 01347 821971
Fax: 01347 822392

The Three Tuns in the centre of the village is not only the hub of the local community, but a welcoming establishment for visitors and tourists. The lively hosts are Sue and Tony Scarborough who run The Three Tuns with their daughter Sally. You can be assured that from the moment you step through the door you will be welcomed and made to feel right at home. Formerly called The Peacock Inn this is an historic establishment that dates back hundreds of years.

James Herriot Country

The 'Herriot Country' of the Dales includes all of Swaledale and Wensleydale with its tributary valleys of Raydale, Bishopsdale, Walden and Coverdale. It is an area of fells and hillsides, stone walls, farms and friendly villages, and a superb setting for the location filming of the BBC series 'All Creatures Great and Small', based on James Herriot's books, which illustrated for the world the unique beauty of the Yorkshire Dales.

It was Herriot's special gift to be able to communicate the magic of the area and yet no amount of reading or television comes near the experience of visiting 'Herriot Country' in person - walking along the paths and tracks, sitting on a high top to gaze over the valley below, and enjoying the clear air and tranquility which is so much a part of the scenery.

A drive through this picturesque and historic country is the perfect way to obtain an impression of what has been recorded in books and on TV. Why not spend a day visiting places such as Askrigg, the 'Darrowby' of the TV series, with Cringley House which featured as the well loved Skeldale House.

Food is available each lunchtime and evening, and Sue is in charge of the kitchen. The meals are wholesome and delicious and the portions are hearty and plentiful. The same menu is on offer in both the bar and the dining area and you will find a good range of well-priced dishes. A new dining area has been created to the rear which seats up to 40 so bookings are not required. To complement your meal the bar can offer a good selection of well-kept, hand-pulled ales. Sue and Tony regularly host Charity and Fund-raising events.

The Three Tuns, Raskelf, York Tel: 01347 821335

A warm, hearty Yorkshire welcome awaits all visitors to Raskelf Farm, situated just a mile from the A19. Run by Anne and Basil Elsworth and their family, you are assured of a memorable stay from the moment you arrive to be welcomed with a cup of tea and something home-made! Set within a 520 acre working arable farm, the Georgian Farmhouse where the letting rooms are located is a real picture. The three letting rooms are very spacious and beautifully furnished and an impressive guests' lounge and separate breakfast room are set aside for your private use. Anne's breakfasts are quite impressive, certain to set you up for a day's sightseeing and although no evening meals are available, the local pub is just a few minutes away and can offer excellent food and drink. Visitors to Raskelf Farm are welcome to wander over the farmland and enjoy the surrounding countryside, with magnificent views towards the White Horse and the Hambleton Hills. A great establishment run by lovely people, which serves as an ideal touring base.

Raskelf Farm, Raskelf, Easingwold, York Tel: 01347 821315

On the old A19, adjacent to the new road at **BIRDFORTH**, is the magnificent **Gables Restaurant**, owned and personally run by Malcolm and Margaret Wride.

The Gables, Birdforth, Nr. Easingwold Tel: 01845 501495

The building dates back to 1877 when it was built as the village school, continuing as such until 1961 when it closed down. It then remained empty and was derelict until bought by Malcolm and Margaret in 1988. It was then completely refurbished and now is a classy and stylish establishment. Malcolm is the chef and he offers an impressive and extensive menu which will cater to every discerning palate. Some of the dishes that might appeal are the fresh Lobster Bisque, Escargots Bourguignonne or perhaps Palm Hearts cooked in a Marsala Sauce from the vegetarian menu. There is plenty of choice, and the option of a table d'hôte or à la carte menu. While Malcolm cooks, Margaret tends to the needs of the customers at the front of house and together they make a great team.

Nearby **TOPCLIFFE** is probably better known to tourists as the venue for the famous annual gypsy fairs. The village is set in one of the most beautiful locations, where the sparkling Swale rushes past charming churches, an old inn and a series of huddled cottages, sheltered by the east bank or "cliff". No wonder the gypsies chose this as the most suitable place to congregate!

The church dates back to the 14th century, the Topcliffe family brasses being its greatest treasure, although a visit to nearby Maiden Bower reminds us that it was the powerful Percy family that shaped this land before the Topcliffes resided here. The castle that once stood proudly on its brow was constructed soon after the Battle of Hastings, the precursor to such strongholds as Wressle, Spofforth and Leconfield.

In the village, a short distance from the river, is **The Angel Inn**, a delightful 17th-century former coaching inn. The Angel is owned and managed by Tony and Trish Ardron who have carried out many improvements since taking over in 1986, more than doubling the original size. There are now three bar areas all full of character and traditionally decorated, featuring horse brasses, exposed beams and open log fires. A separate restaurant serves an impressive range of

313

English and Continental dishes with all the pub favourites as well. There is a games rooms and, to the rear, an attractive beer garden with barbecue patio and wishing well. The pub doubles as hotel, offering 15 tastefully decorated letting rooms, all of which are en-suite, with satellite television, mini-bar and direct-dial telephones. There is also private river fishing available to guests.

The Angel Inn, Long Street, Topcliffe, Thirsk
Tel: 01845 577237

Our next stop is the town of THIRSK, famous as the home of veterinary surgeon Alf Wight, better known as James Herriot, who sadly died in early 1995.

The history of this market town dates back to the Domesday book, when William the Conqueror gave the manor of Thirsk to one of his barons, Robert de Mowbray. Thirsk is also well known for its racecourse. There are eight race-days a year which are well attended especially by visitors wishing to sample an intrinsic part of Yorkshire life. On travelling through the areas between the Dales and the North Yorkshire Moors, one is constantly reminded of the great tradition of horse-breeding that the county is famous for, and the tradition runs deep. Even the long flat straight stretch of main railway line between York and Darlington is known as the 'racecourse'.

314

Ripon to Bedale

The cathedral town of RIPON has a tapestry of rich historical tradition mostly missed by those rushing through to attend the famous race-meetings, or taking the children to the Lightwater Valley Theme Park.

The town's history goes back to AD886, when its charter was granted by Alfred the Great, and the people of Ripon are proud of their traditions - every night at 9pm a hornblower, in tricorn hat and full regalia, still sets the watch by sounding the ancient horn at each corner of the market cross and in front of the Mayor's house - as has been practised for centuries. This tradition is also considered the oldest form of burglar insurance in the world - householders paid a premium and if any break-ins occurred after the setting of the watch, the Wakeman was obliged to re-imburse them for their loss. The 13th-century dwelling that the Wakeman owned is still standing in the Market-place, but the title of Wakeman has since changed to that of Mayor.

The greatest pride and joy is, of course, the imposing Cathedral of St Peter and St Wilfrid, known as the Cathedral of the Dales. It may not be as graceful nor as extensive as York Minster, but its very solidity, a mixture of Saxon and Perpendicular architecture, commands the attention. There is something very characteristic of Yorkshire in its austerity and the grey millstone grit from which it is made. It appears to have almost monolithic proportions when viewed from the narrow little streets of the town and is probably best viewed 'broadside on' from across the River Skell, especially at night, when it is illuminated.

The markets in Ripon take place on Thursdays and Saturdays, heralded by the ringing of the Corn Bell and there are 12 race days a year that take place on the Garden Racecourse, which is considered to be one of the most beautifully landscaped in the country.

Ripley Castle

Many people would prefer to opt for a day's visit to the elegant Water Gardens of STUDLEY ROYAL, rather than the noisier amusements of Lightwater Valley, situated not far away. These are one of the last surviving examples of a Georgian green garden, its classical temples, follies, views and lakes are a delight to see. It is a National Trust property, along with the even more famous nearby FOUNTAINS ABBEY, the pride of all the ecclesiastical ruins of Yorkshire and a designated World Heritage Site.

Fountains was one of the wealthiest of the Cistercian houses and is arguably one of the most beautiful, as well as the largest in Britain. Founded in 1132, with the help of Archbishop Thurstan of York, the first buildings housed just 12 monks of the order, and over the centuries its size increased, even spreading across the River Skell itself, reaching its peak in the 15th century with the grandiose designs of Abbot Marmaduke Huby, whose beautiful tower still stands as a reminder of just how rich and powerful Fountains became. In fact the Abbey was run on such business-like lines that at its height, as well as owning extensive lands throughout Yorkshire, it had an income of about a thousand pounds a year, then a very substantial sum indeed.

The Dissolution hit the Abbey as it did all the powerful religious houses. The abbot was hanged, the monks scattered, and its treasures taken off or destroyed. The stonework, however, was left largely intact, possibly due to its remote location. In 1579, Sir Stephen Proctor pulled down some out-buildings, in order to construct Fountains Hall, which still stands in the Abbey's grounds.

North of Ripon, on a minor road off the A61, is the stately home of Norton Conyers, owned by the Graham family since 1624. The house's main claim to fame is the visit of Charlotte Brontë, who heard the story of "Mad Mary", supposedly a Lady Graham, while she was resident. Apparently Lady Graham had been locked up in an attic room, now tantalisingly inaccessible to the public, and Charlotte eventually based the character of Mrs Rochester in her novel "Jane Eyre" on her. Visitors to the hall will also see the famous painting of Sir Bellingham Graham on his bay horse, as Master of the Quorn Hunt. It is rumoured that ownership of the painting was once decided on the throwing of a pair of dice.

On the B6108, to the north, is the village of **WEST TANFIELD**, where the once powerful Marmion family dream on in the alabaster splendour of their tombs, which reside in the church there, guarded by the forbidding presence of the Marmion Tower.

Heading out of West Tanfield on the Masham Road will bring you to Glebe Buildings, the workshop of **Frank Jobling**. Frank, a fine craftsman, is a wonderful character and will happily chat to visitors enthusiastically about his work, making garden furniture, bird tables and nesting boxes. He is delighted to let visitors to the workshop watch him as he works, using pine, iroko, elm, mahogany and other hardwoods for his solidly constructed, built-to-last garden seat and picnic tables. Frank has been at Glebe Buildings for 16 years now, and can turn his hand to the individual requirements of all his customers, whether it's for a private garden or a busy pub.

Frank Jobling, Masham Road, West Tanfield, Nr. Ripon
Tel: 01677 470481

The town of MASHAM lies beside the River Ure and is a very picturesque place with old buildings and narrow roads. The heart of the town is wonderfully spacious with a great market place which is partly cobbled. The ancient church of St Mary stands at one corner, the school founded in 1760 at another and at its centre is the market cross amid trees and flowers.

Masham is home to Theakston's Brewery, famed for its Old Peculier brew. The brothers Thomas and Robert first practised their craft 150 years ago and the brewery is now a major employer of the town. Adjoining the brewery is a new visitor centre where you can learn about the process of brewing and the cooperage. Interestingly, the name of the famous brew commemorates the fact that Masham was a 'peculier' from Roger de Mowbray's time, when the Archbishop of York freed it to have its own 'Peculier Court' - an ecclesiastical body with wide powers.

Mad Hatters Tea Rooms, Masham Tel: 01765 689129

On Masham's attractive market place you will find the Mad Hatter Tea Rooms, a delightful establishment serving delicious Yorkshire teas and light meals. The tearooms have been run since 1990 by Margaret and Brian Boshier and inside, they have successfully managed to create an atmosphere which is welcoming and full of traditional character. The menu offers a choice of eight different teas, several blends of coffee and a number of old-fashioned soft drinks including sarsaparilla and dandelion and burdock. There is also a wide range of mouthwatering cakes, scones and snacks including Welsh rarebit and open sandwiches. Open daily except Thursdays. Margaret and Brian also have two spacious en-suite letting rooms available which overlook the market square.

Only a couple of miles southwest of Masham is the mysterious Druid's Temple. This is, however, not a meeting place constructed by pagan worshippers but rather a charming folly, built in the 1820's by William Danby of the nearby Swinton Estate. His project was intended to provide work for local unemployed people, and could be compared to a rather more complete, if scaled down, version of Stonehenge - it is considered one of the best druidical follies in the country.

Colsterdale is one of the lesser known dales, but the visitor who takes time to drive or walk along its quiet roads and pleasant pathways will be both delighted and surprised. Although only short compared with others, this is a gem set in an area of small, family farms and interesting villages.

Pasture House stands alongside the little road that leads, eventually, to a dead end at the head of the dale. It was formerly owned by Leeds City Council who had plans to use the reservoir. The discovery of porous rocks or, as the locals have it "a plug hole", in the valley floor prevented this happening and the house was bought by Gerry and Avril Scott.

There are wonderful views from every window in the house and guests staying in any season will be enchanted by the scenery. A silent, proud memorial to the Leeds "Pals" Regiment - decimated at the Somme in World War I - stands on the opposite hillside.

Pasture House is centrally heated, has excellent facilities and offers evening meals, bed and breakfast. All bedrooms have colour televisions, hot and cold water and tea-making

320

facilities. There is fishing (fly only) and pony trekking within 3 miles of the house and, of course, incomparable walking in the area. Gerry Scott won the Grand National in 1960 on Merryman II and a collection of photographs of the event provides an "ice-breaking" talking point in the entrance hall.

Pasture House

Pasture House, Colsterdale, Healey, Masham
Tel: 01765 689149

For those desiring more sedate pleasures, the tranquillity of **KIRKBY MALZEARD**, accessible via country roads, may be more to your taste. Here is a village which holds many interesting secrets, starting with the Anglo-Norman church of St Andrew, noted for the abundant evidence of witchcraft that is connected with it. The north-eastern corner of the churchyard was favoured by practitioners of the black arts for conducting their strange rituals and charms.

One place not to be missed while in this area is The Thorp Perrow Arboretum which is situated on the Well road near the village of **SNAPE**. Founded in 1927, this unique private collection of rare and exotic trees was the creation of one man, Colonel Sir Leonard Ropner, the present owner's father. Sir Leonard travelled all over the world collecting rare and unusual species for Thorp Perrow, and today the hundreds of trees he enthusiastically collected are in their prime. The arboretum was initially Sir Leonard's private hobby and visitors were not encouraged; however, after he sadly died in 1977, his son, Sir John Ropner, took the decision to open the 85-acre arboretum to the public and it is now gradually becoming known by visitors from all over the world. This tranquil and peaceful haven is set within 1000 acres of parkland and is home to some of the largest and rarest trees and shrubs in England. Enthusiasts and casual visitors alike come to admire the specimen trees and to enjoy the woodland tree trails, grassy glades, spectacular wild flowers and beautiful lakeside walks. Special attractions include the Milbank Pinetum (a collection of conifers planted from 1840 to 1870), an attractive rustic picnic area, and the formal gardens in front of the great house. Catalogues of the collection, maps of the tree trails and fascinating archive material on the origins of the arboretum are available in the recently-opened information centre and tearoom.

The Fox and Hounds, Carthorpe, Bedale Tel: 01845 567433

The Fox and Hounds, in the tiny quiet village of **CARTHORPE**, recommended by all the local B&B's and hotels for its food, is a very popular establishment run by Howard and Bernadette Fitzgerald. Dating back to the early 18th century, the building was originally a farmhouse, later an alehouse, then a coaching inn, a blacksmiths and today, a pub of great quality. The interior of the inn is particularly

Walking in the Dales

For all capabilities, the Yorkshire Dales provide the perfect setting for walking, with at least 1000 miles of public footpaths and ancient tracks, waterfalls, wild flowers, upland pastures and bridleways.

The Pennine Way, Britain's first Long Distance Footpath, is 270 miles in length and particularly inviting to all ramblers. If you are particularly fit and would wish to brave the wild weather with a strong will and a backpack then it can be done. Otherwise, confine yourself to a short length, stopping off at pubs, youth hostels or guesthouses on the way.

The Pennine Way is full of contrasting and beautiful scenery - limestone pavements, potholes such as Gaping Gill, waterfalls like Hardraw Force, which boasts 96 feet of shimmering water, not to mention 'The Three Peaks' - Pen-y-ghent, Whernside and Ingleborough.

The Cleveland Way at 93 miles long is another popular footpath. Its most dramatic section is across the crests of the Cleveland Hills. The Wolds Way, only opened in 1982, offers 72 miles of pleasant low-level walking across the plains of Humberside.

Walkers are advised to always remember that the Country Code is there to maintain the beauty and safety of these areas, and actions such as keeping to paths, closing gates and not leaving litter are vital if the countryside of Yorkshire is to remain so striking and so popular, within Britain and beyond.

attractive - the restaurant area retains the old forge as a feature, and throughout are many old smithy tools. The bar area is also full of character and features an open fire and walls covered with antique prints. The food is outstanding, prepared by Howard and his daughter Helen and the set menu is complemented by an extensive specials board. The food is delicious, with good-sized portions, and very reasonably priced. Full credit has to go to the owners who create the great atmosphere and food that their customers drive miles to enjoy.

Just out of the village is an area known as Howe Hill. This is said to have been a Celtic settlement and three skeletons were found here, a man, woman and child, as well as some pottery and some jewellery, now in the Victoria and Albert Museum.

Tatton Lodge, Londonderry, Nr. Northallerton
Tel/Fax: 01677 422222

Situated in three acres of grounds, mid-way between the old and new A1, at **LONDONDERRY**, is the very impressive **Tatton Lodge**. Formerly a farmhouse, then an alehouse, and then an inn, it is now a private house that offers first class bed and breakfast accommodation. Owned and personally run by Denise and Jim Bleasdale, their love of horses is very apparent from the moment you arrive. Jim was a flat race jockey for over 20 years and Denise is also a keen horse-woman, and you can see some of their horses in the adjoining pastures. There are six letting rooms in all, and three are housed in recently-converted stables, the others are in the main house. All rooms are of an excellent quality and the ones in the main house enjoy magnificent views towards the North Yorkshire Moors. This is a really outstanding establishment where you can enjoy the first class facilities and be really pampered.

Jervaulx Abbey

West from Northallerton, dominating this area, is the town of BEDALE which holds many places of interest for the curious traveller. This little market town is described as the ideal base for exploring the Yorkshire Dales and the Moors, and indeed, situated as it is on the B684, connecting the two expanses, and conveniently close to the A1, it well deserves its claim. It has a curving main street, dominated by the parish church at its north end. Tourists can also seek out the

325

Thorp Perrow Arboretum

18th-century Leech House (so called because it was once used by the local apothecary to store his leeches).

Bedale developed around the point where the Saxon track from Ripon joined the route from Northallerton to Wensleydale. Traders met here and in 1251 Henry III granted a charter for a weekly market which still flourishes today. The market cross stands at the top of Elmgate, a narrow street leading from the river to the market place.

As commercial activity developed, water power was harnessed from the Bedale Beck for the processing of wool. Skinners and tanners worked down by the ford and the town was a lively hub of cottage industry.

The beautiful parish church of St Gregory, with its strongly fortified tower, was recorded in the Domesday Book and incorporates architectural styles from 1000-1500. Just inside the churchyard is an old building dated 1674 which served as a school in the 18th century. Across the road is Bedale Hall, housing the library and local museum. Its north front is an excellent example of the Georgian architecture which gives the town its special character. Visitors can enjoy lovely walks along the river and in the market place there are several inns and attractive cafés.

To the west of Bedale one will find Jervaulx Abbey, one of the great Cistercian sister houses to Fountains Abbey. The name Jervaulx is a French derivation of Yore, or Ure, Vale, just as Rievaulx is of Rye Vale. Jervaulx eventually amassed enough wealth to own half of the Ure Valley, but its glory was shattered during the Dissolution. Despite its ruination, Jervaulx's haunting, ivy-clad walls have been described as "romantick in decay". Its grounds have been transformed into one of the most beautiful of gardens, the shattered walls providing interesting backdrops for its sculptured trees and colourful plants and shrubs.

Connoisseurs of ice cream might not be able to resist making a quick detour one mile southeast of this ancient Abbey where one will find High Jervaulx Farm, home of the celebrated Brymor Real Dairy Ice Cream. The company was founded in 1984 by Brian and Brenda Moore in the village of Weeton on the edge of Wharfedale. The new ice cream was such an instant success with the public that the company soon began to outgrow its original production facility; however, restrictive planning regulations meant that instead of being able to expand on the existing site, new premises had to be found in a different location. This was finally achieved and in February 1992, Brian and Brenda finished installing their new production equipment and moved their herd of pedigree Guernsey cows to their new home at High Jervaulx Farm. The Moores and their staff now make ice cream, frozen yoghurt, sorbets and special diabetic desserts in over thirty different flavours using fresh whole Guernsey milk, double cream and the finest natural Italian fruit flavours. In their 'Big Country' range, they also use nuts and other special ingredients imported from the USA and Canada. Visitors are welcome to tour the farm, meet the animals, and view the ice cream production process. They are also able to purchase delicious cones, sundaes and ice cream gateaux (which can be specially decorated 'while-you-wait') from the helpful and knowledgeable staff. Altogether, a fascinating and mouthwatering place to visit.

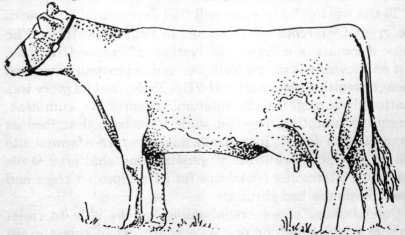

Brymor Ice Cream Parlour, High Jervaulx Farm,
Nr. Masham Tel: 01677 60377

Two miles northwest of Bedale, on the A684 Leyburn road, is the delightful village of LITTLE CRAKEHALL. Here you will find Crakehall Water Mill, a recently-restored 17th-century corn mill containing machinery dating from the 18th and 19th centuries.

Today, stoneground wholemeal flour is again produced by two pairs of millstones driven by a breast-shot water wheel powered by Crakehall Beck. Visitors can view the fascinating interior, buy the flour, or simply enjoy a delicious home-made tea in the grounds.

Little Holtby, Leeming Bar, Northallerton Tel: 01609 748762

Little Holtby at LEEMING BAR provides excellent overnight accommodation both for through travellers and for those looking for a touring base in the beautiful Vale of York. This fully refurbished farmhouse is situated just off the main A1, two miles north of Leeming services. The house has lovely gardens and provides spectacular views across rolling countryside towards Pen Hill. Owner Dorothy Hodgson always provides her guests with a warm welcome and superb Yorkshire hospitality. She has four beautifully decorated guest rooms available, three with en-suite facilities and the fourth with its own private bathroom. All are immaculately furnished and appointed to a good modern standard.

Particularly attractive are the wooden floors and furniture throughout the establishment. Children are welcome.

Northallerton and Richmond

All those interested in fine furniture, paintings and porcelain should make a point of finding Sion Hill Hall near the village of **KIRBY WISKE** six miles south of Northallerton. This fine neo-Georgian mansion was designed in the style of Lutyens by the famous York architect Walter Brierley. Completed in 1913, it is one of the last country houses to be built before the Great War ended the construction of such servant-intensive houses. Its main function is to house the collection of artifacts which was acquired over a period of sixty years, by Herbert W Mawer. The Mawer Collection can be viewed Wednesdays to Sundays between March and October and by pre-arranged groups at other times. In the grounds are a Bird of Prey Centre, a visitors' centre, tea rooms and a gift shop. The Bird of Prey Centre is open all year round, with daily flying displays.

Sion Hill Hall, Kirby Wiske, Thirsk Tel: 01845 587206

NORTHALLERTON has had the dubious distinction of being famous for its strong ale. There's certainly no shortage of inns in the area, which was, it is said, one of the favourite haunts of Charles Dickens, who was known to frequent the Old Fleece Inn, a truly Dickensian place, with great oak beams and old-world atmosphere.

Northallerton is the county town of the North Riding, and is an important market and shopping centre. There are many old buildings of interest, including an ancient Grammar school, medieval church and a 15th century almshouse. It is an important rail and road junction, and its market days draw the most prosperous farmers in all Yorkshire. The hotels and inns are well-booked at this time, as casual visitors should be warned.

The Black Bull, 101 High Street, Northallerton
Tel: 01609 773565

The Black Bull stands proudly on the main street of this popular market town. Dating back to the early 18th century it was originally called The Blacksmiths. It has been run by Iain McCosh for the past two years, although he can boast 15 years experience in the trade. This is a typical, market town inn that provides the best in accommodation, food and ale. The cosy restaurant can seat up to 70 people and booking is not usually required. The food is traditional home-cooked fare, with good sized portions that are very reasonably priced. The ales are well-kept with a good variety kept on tap

- the regulars are John Smith's and Marston Pedigree. The upstairs of the establishment is being modified at the time of writing and by early 1995 there will be bed and breakfast accommodation available in five en-suite rooms, all individually styled and attractively furnished. The location of the Black Bull, in the heart of North Yorkshire, makes this an ideal touring base.

James Herroit's Surgery, Thirsk

Those looking for truly exceptional guest house accommodation in this area should make a point of seeking out **Porch House** in the heart of the town. This historic Grade II listed residence is probably North Yorkshire's oldest surviving private house to remain in continuous use. The land on which the building stands was purchased by Richard Metcalfe (cousin of Mary Queen of Scots) in 1584, and soon after he built an early vernacular crook beam house which now comprises the southern part of the building. The original house had a thatched roof and was constructed of cobbles

332

Millgate, Richmond

bound with dung and chaff. These primitive walls were almost four feet thick and when they were replaced by one foot thick walls some years later, the original 'tunnel' doorway became the porch that can be seen today.

James I and Charles I stayed at Porch House. Charles I was held under open arrest, his eventual release through the Porch signalled the end of Absolute Monarchy and heralded the beginning of Constitutional Monarchy - still in existence.

In the years that followed, the house was re-built with a timber frame and then in the 18th century the brick-built north end was added and the entire building re-roofed with pantiles.

Porch House, High Street, Northallerton Tel: 01609 779831

The guest house is owned by Jackie Smith and David Summers who have been careful to preserve the character and charm of the building. Jackie and David extend a royal welcome to their guests while also providing them with the best in Yorkshire hospitality. The atmosphere is cosy and welcoming and the whole establishment is appointed to a very high standard. All the bedrooms have en-suite facilities and are equipped with drinks tray and colour television. All in all, this a unique guest house, ideal for a touring base or overnight stop.

334

The most interesting event in the history of the adjacent town of BROMPTON is the battle of The Standard which took place on the 22nd August 1138. On this day King David and the Scots were defeated by King Stephen and the English, a mile or so outside the village. It was said that thousands of Scots were slain and buried in a spot which has since been known as Scot Pit Lane. Land nearby is known as Red Hills because of the blood which flowed, and the nearby farm is known as Standard Hill.

The Duke of Wellington, Welbury, Northallerton
Tel: 01609 882464

At WELBURY, to the north, the village inn, The Duke of Wellington, is run by Geoff and Val Thompson and their daughters Claire and Louise. Both Geoff and Val are true locals, coming from the farming community, and this is their first joint venture. From the exterior of the inn it is evident that it has been converted from a row of small thatched cottages and this has added considerably to its charm and character.

Geoff and Val have modernised and extended the building since their arrival six years ago, adding a restaurant. They can offer an excellent range of food which can be enjoyed in either the restaurant or the bar area but at weekends bookings are advisable for the restaurant. The Duke of

335

In the footsteps of the Romans

The Roman Causeways of the Dales are some of the few remainders of Roman occupation in Britain. There is a well preserved stretch of road , 1.25 miles long and 16ft across, on the edge of Wheeldale Moor, called Wade's Causeway. This is just one of the stone-flagged causeways which are such prominent features of the moors, ruuning through woods, villages and alongside roads. Over 150 miles have been traced in total and yet this is only a small proportion of what once existed.

Wade's Causeway was constructed by a Roman Army almost 2000 years ago. The structure consists of a raised centre, called an agger, to help drainage. However it is not as it was in Roman times, since the top layer of small pebbles, or gravel, has long since vanished. The road was rediscovered in 1914 and our ancestors would have us believe it was built by a giant called Wade to provide a route between his castles at Mulgrave and Pickering.

It has been found almost impossible to date many such causeways, although it seems likely that many originated in medieval times. Their function was concerned with links between monasteries such as Whitby and Byland and also to collect and export wool and fish. It would have been the monasteries that actually provided the stone flags.

The industrial growth of the North increased the demand for these tracks and nowadays the National Park Authority restores the stone flags which have been so hollowed by centuries of use. This way, tracks such as Wade's Causeway can be enjoyed by walkers in the Dales and admired as a remarkable piece of early engineering.

Wellington is a typical village pub with traditional, hand-pulled ales complementing the bar food. The atmosphere is rural and interesting - very different from that of city establishments. Geoff and Val can also offer a one-bedroomed holiday cottage for self-catering holidays. Ring for full details and availability.

CATTERICK is famous for two things - its racecourse and its RAF and Army garrison. It has always been a soldiers' town, as far back as Roman times, known in those days as Cataractonium. Visitors to the town will no doubt on their journeys see a road named, rather incongruously, Trafalgar. The connections with Nelson and the town of Catterick are not immediately obvious, but are explained by the fact that Alexander Scott, a vicar of Catterick in 1816, was at Nelson's side when he died at the famous battle.

Another connection may be that Lady Tyrconnel, the Admiral's sister-in law, lived at nearby Kiplin Hall, a Jacobean country home famous for its beautiful interior plasterwork and medieval fishponds. The hall contains many memories of Nelson and Lady Hamilton and on display in the Blue Room is a folding library chair from the Admiral's cabin on the Victory.

Catterick village is the site of a Roman settlement, located on the highway between London and Hadrian's Wall and near to where Paulinus, Bishop of York and creator of its first minster, baptised 10,000 Christians in the River Swale. The church retains a black marble font and screenwork from the 15th century.

Before continuing to Richmond, a short diversion south along country lanes will lead to ARRATHORNE. Here, situated between Bedale and Richmond, you could enjoy a stay at the country hotel, Elmfield House, which is owned and run by Edith and Jim Lillie. This handsome traditionally-furnished building is set within its own secluded grounds and enjoys magnificent views over the surrounding countryside. The hotel has a solarium, games room, a spacious lounge with residents' bar, and a pleasant dining room where guests can enjoy delicious home-cooked meals. A recent addition is a conservatory at the rear of the premises which overlooks the gardens. There are nine spacious bedrooms, all with en-suite facilities and the two bedrooms on the ground floor are also suitable for disabled guests.

Elmfield House, Arrathorne, Bedale Tel: 01677 450558

RICHMOND is yet another place with a rich and fascinating history. The former county of Richmondshire (which locals still refer to) of which this town was the capital, once occupied a third of the North Riding. Alan Rufus, the first Earl of Richmond, built the original castle here in 1071. The site, 100 feet up on a rocky promontory, with the River Swale passing below, is imposing indeed, and well-chosen. The keep rises to 109 feet in height with walls 11 feet thick, while the other side is afforded an impregnable defence by means of the cliff and the river.

With such an inspiring setting, it is hardly surprising that there is a legend that King Arthur himself is buried here, reputedly in a cave beneath the castle. The story goes that a simple potter called Thompson stumbled across an underground passage which led to a chamber where he discovered the King and his knights lying in an enchanted sleep, surrounded by priceless treasures. A voice warned him not to disturb the sleepers and he fled, predictably, unable to locate the passage again.

On Frenchgate, near one of the original gates to the old walled town, you will find The Frenchgate Hotel. Once a Georgian gentleman's town house, the building is protected as being of historical and architectural interest. Now a comfortable hotel it can offer a total of thirteen bedrooms which are a mixture of doubles, twins and singles. Seven of the rooms include en-suite facilities. The rest of the house is delightful with some parts dating from the 16th century and others from the 18th century. Many original features have been retained, all complemented by the fine decor. Much of the woodwork, in particular the fire-surround and the doors, was created by Robert Thompson, the famous local craftsman who carved a mouse on every piece of his work.

The Frenchgate Hotel, 59-61 Frenchgate, Richmond Tel: 01748 822087 Fax: 01748 823596

The Frenchgate Hotel has an excellent reputation for the standard of its cuisine. Meals are served in the elegant Georgian dining room from an extensive à la carte menu. In the summer months a table d'hôte menu is also on offer. All dishes are cooked freshly to order and are followed by a delicious selection of hand-made desserts. To complement your meal there is a good range of wines on the wine list.

This hotel is without doubt one of the best in Richmond and the high standards have been recognised by AA and RAC two star classification. This establishment is a real credit to its owners.

The Regimental Museum of the Green Howards, the North Riding's infantry regiment, is based in the old Trinity Church in the centre of the cobbled market square. The regiment dates back to 1688, when it was founded, and the displays and collections illustrate its history with war relics, weapons, uniforms, medals and regimental silver. Also housed in the museum is the town's silver.

Easby Abbey, situated outside the town's boundaries, on a minor road off the B6271, is a low-built monastic ruin which looks down to the River Swale. Founded in 1155. Its order of monks were of more modest leanings than the Cistercians, and the building certainly possesses none of the grandiose lines of Rievaulx and Fountains, although the riverside setting is typically in common. The Abbey can be reached by a pleasant riverside walk which is well sign-posted.

The Yorkshire Dales

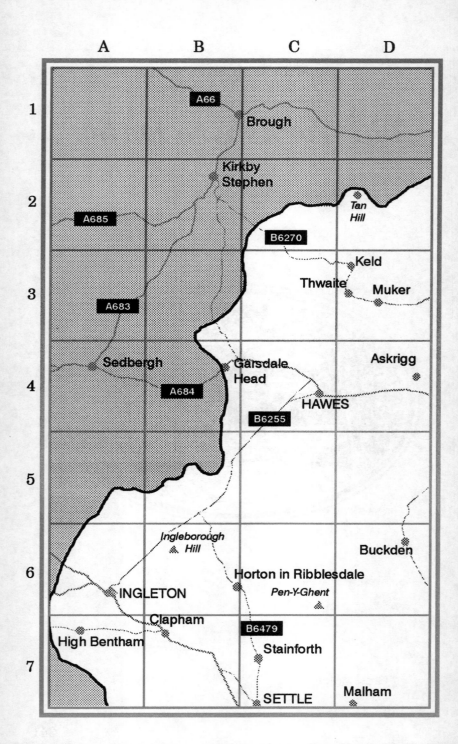

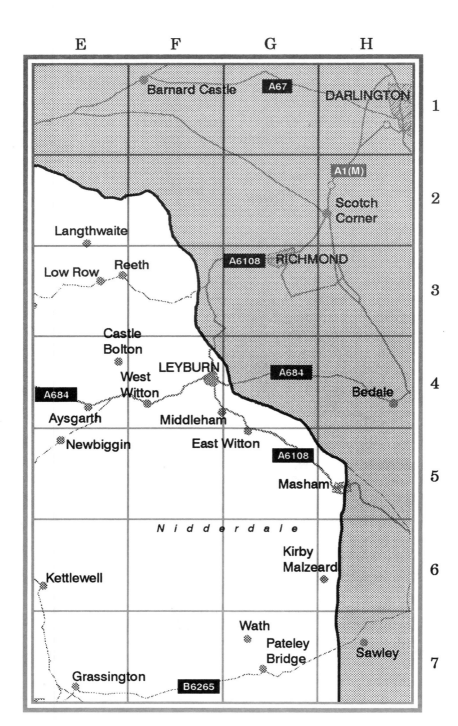

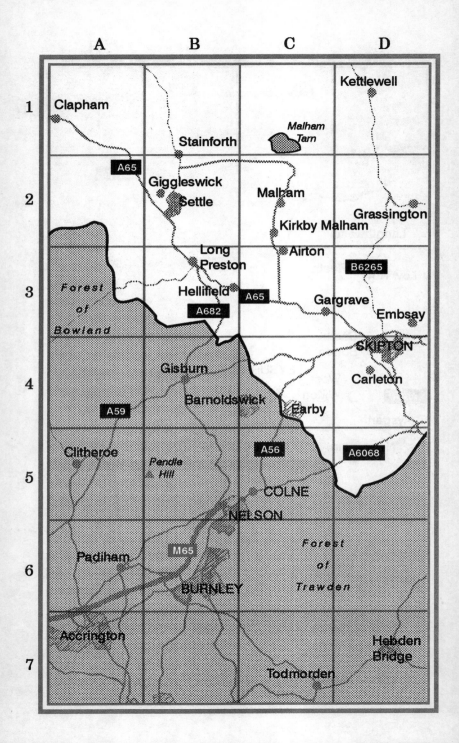

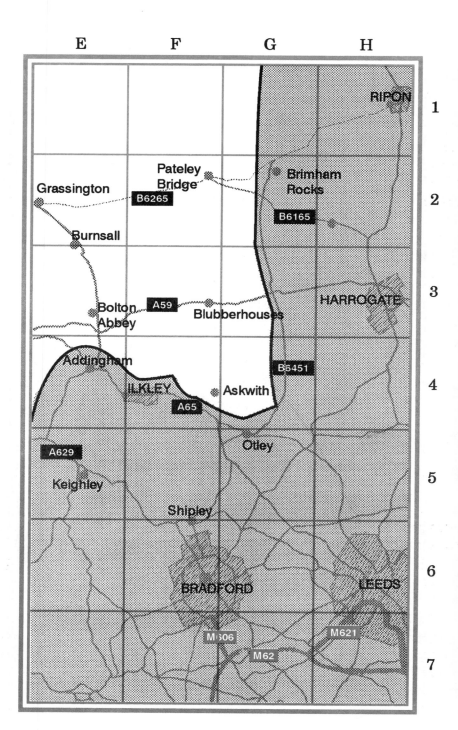

Bolton Abbey

The Yorkshire Dales

The huge expanse of the Yorkshire Dales, one of the favourite haunts of the redoubtable traveller Wainwright, in fact stretches over the three counties of Lancashire, Yorkshire and Cumbria. The main attraction of the area has to be the natural wonders of its caves, waterfalls and outstanding geological features including such natural glories as Malham Cove, Hardraw Force, Fountains Fell, the cryptically named Lovely Seat, not to mention Rogan's Seat, Middle Tongue and the villages of Muker and Crackpot, for yourselves. With such evocative names how can the inquisitive fail to be drawn to investigate.

Swaledale

Lying to the east of Richmond is Swaledale which offers the visitor spectacular landscapes, its steeper slopes largely carved by glaciers and their lakes. As the waters retreated, the (now disappeared) mass of silver birch trees provided deer forests hunted in by the Normans. A relative of the Conqueror, Walter de Gaunt, was married to the daughter of Earl Alan, who built Richmond Castle and owned the whole of Swaledale; de Gaunt gave the land for Grinton church to be built which for 400 years was the Dale's only Christian burial place - the old road leading to it is still called Corpse Way. Lead mining was another important feature of Swaledale's history from Roman and Norman to Victorian times.

Approaching Upper Swaledale from Richmond, there is a wealth of sights and villages to explore. Start at the village of

MARRICK which is chiefly noted for its abbey, a stern looking Benedictine nunnery founded by Roger de Aske. This is an area of soft wooded hillsides and lush riverside meadows, but as the dale climbs towards **GRINTON** the lower dale gives way to the wilder scenery of its western section.

The village of **REETH**, considered the capital of Upper Swaledale, is poised at the juncture of the Swale and its main tributary, Arkle Beck. The town was noted in the Domesday Book, while everything else in the area was written off as untaxable "waste land". Until the end of the 19th century a total of four fairs were held here annually, as well as a weekly market. Today the annual agricultural show in September, held on the sprawling village green, is still a magnet for farmers from the entire length of the dale and beyond. Along the top of the green is High Row, with its inns and shops and outstanding Georgian architecture, reflecting the affluence of the town in the 17th century when the trade in wool and lead was booming.

Arkleside Hotel, Reeth, Richmond Tel: 01748 884200

The charming **Arkleside Hotel** is a 17th-century country house which was converted to a hotel in the Edwardian era. Set in beautiful Swaledale with breathtaking views it is the perfect setting in which to relax and step back in time.

348

The present owners, Dorothy and Richard, have done much to bring the establishment up to the standard of a modern top-class hotel. The eight individually-decorated bedrooms are beautifully appointed and equipped with televisions and courtesy trays. There is also a charming drawing room, a conservatory bar, and a restaurant serving an excellent five-course dinner menu which features traditional Yorkshire recipes, fresh fish and locally produced cheese. Open February to December. Unsuitable for children under 10.

Hackney House, Reeth, Richmond Tel: 01748 884302

Hackney House in Reeth is a guesthouse which offers the very best in old-fashioned hospitality. Proprietor, Lorraine Plant, is continuing the tradition of good food and first-rate accommodation that was started in 1943. The house was built around the turn of the century on the site of former artisans' cottages and is situated in the heart of the village on the northern side of the B6270 Swaledale road. Inside, the atmosphere is homely and relaxing; all the letting rooms are comfortable, well-appointed and are equipped to a good modern standard with colour TVs. Lorraine is renowned as a warm and friendly host and many of her guests return to Hackney House again and again. She is also known for

Drystone Walls

Many drystone walls date back over several centuries and have become an important element of our history, landscape and heritage, blending beautifully with their surroundings. It is however crucial that they be constantly repaired and maintained. The walls have great practical as well as scenic value, helping to confine the sheep which live on the dales. Their mortarless construction remains a fascinating feature and the clumsy, irregular shapes actually require skilful selection and placement - a mark of true craftsmanship.

The walls are constructed by packing small stones on top of a firm foundation and tying these with 'troughs'- stones spanning the width of the wall. At about five feet in height they are finished with top stones, often set on end for greater stability.

The walls originated from a new demand for scientific management of the land by enclosure, following the agricultural revolution of the 18th and 19th centuries. Arrow-straight dividing walls sprung up high in the hillsides. The enclosures are easily recognised by their geometric shapes. Often the positions and shapes were first mapped out on paper, creating difficulties for the wallers, who then had to skilfully build walls along steep slopes.

providing splendid Yorkshire breakfasts and, by arrangement, evening meals.

While in Reeth, you can visit the Swaledale Folk Museum, once the old Methodist Sunday School, and now the home for exhibits of local farming methods, crafts, and mining skills, as well as displays on local pastimes, the impact of Wesleyan Methodism and the exodus of the population to the industrial areas of the southern Pennines when the mines closed. Climbing the valley, travelling west, the terrain becomes more forbidding by the mile, sparsely populated by gritstone cottages, little changed since the days when the Norsemen gave the places their names.

Taking a detour up the wild, remote dale of **ARKENGARTHDALE**, one can see the ridge at Langthwaite which featured in the title sequence of the TV series of "All Creatures Great And Small". There are villages here that were established long before mining dominated the area, with such wonderful Nordic names as Booze, Arkle Town, Eskeleth and Whaw. The mines still scar the hillsides here, the ruins of smelting and crushing mills scattered here and there. Most of the mines were owned by Charles Bathurst, Lord of the Manor in the 18th century, and namesake of the village of **CB**, the only placename in Britain to be made up of initials.

A quarter of a mile beyond Arkle Town, the narrow Arkengarthdale road leads to the tiny hamlet at **LANGTHWAITE**. Here you will find the 17th-century inn, the **Red Lion**, which stands beside the old drovers' route to Tan Hill. Rowena Hutchinson became the licensee in 1979 after the inn had been in her family for fifteen years. Today, it is still full of genuine character with timber beams, pew-style seating, and to the rear, an intimate snug area where children are welcome at lunch times. Rowena provides an excellent pint of traditional ale and a range of first-rate bar meals all year round. Keep an eye out for the photographs of the leading characters from the Herriot series which were taken in the bar.

*The Red Lion Inn, Langthwaite, Arkengarthdale, Richmond
Tel: 01748 884218*

Three miles from Reeth is the village of **HEALAUGH**, Norse for "high forest clearing", with Low Row just beyond and its inn where weary travellers could stop for rest and refreshment after carrying their burdens along the Corpse Way.

Swaledale Pottery, Low Row, Swaledale Tel: 01748 86377

A few yards from Ye Olde Punch Bowl Inn is one of **LOW ROW**'s interesting enterprises, the **Swaledale Pottery,**
352

which has been run since 1976 by Juliet and Martin Bearpark. Here, they produce a range of attractive hand-thrown domestic stoneware in a variety of glazes and styles. All items are dishwasher and microwave proof, and being handmade, each has its own subtle individuality. Visitors are welcome to browse around their showroom which is situated on the main B6270 Richmond to Kirkby Stephen road and is open daily except Sundays. As well as producing pottery for the showroom, Martin undertakes special orders and large commissions. Items from the Swaledale Pottery are also available at the Pot Shop in Reeth.

Travelling along the B6270 you may well be drawn to the signposts for CRACKPOT through curiosity and decide to take a detour. Its main attraction is the sad and lonely ruin of Crackpot Hall, which was abandoned in the 1950s due to subsidence caused by local mining activity.

Although only the wonderful prospect over the river indicates its former glory, it is well worth a visit to view the wonderful position it occupies, at the head of a sweeping valley. The mines nearby have also long been abandoned, although the blacksmith's forge still remains largely intact behind the crumbling walls.

The nearby village of GUNNERSIDE, meaning "Gunnar's Pasture", was once the land where a Viking chief guarded his livestock. Later, it became known as the "Klondyke of Swaledale", although it was the centre of the boom of lead-mining rather than gold, and the Old Gang Mines were the most famous in Yorkshire. The paths and ways here are mainly those trodden by the many successions of miners, travelling to their work. The valley's sides are still scarred with mine-workings, but these are now an established part of their character, and by no means detract from the grandeur of the gorge and the expanse of Melbeck's Moor that leads from it. In the village, one can visit tearooms that offer such delights as "Lead Miners' Bait", and the delicious Gunnerside cheese-cake, made from a recipe handed down from the mining days.

An old stone bridge leads into the village of **MUKER**, which consists of a collection of grey stone cottages and a church, dating back to the reign of Elizabeth I, built by the parishioners to bring an end to the tedious journey along the Corpse way to the mother church at Grinton. Local family names, such as Harker, Alderson and Fawcett feature prominently on the gravestones, as they do among the villagers still living here today.

Again, local specialities are on offer in the tea-rooms such as Swaledale Curd Tart, Yorkshire Rarebit and Deep Apple Pie with Wensleydale Cheese. The main crafts revolve around the wool provided by the hardy Swaledale sheep, in great demand by carpet manufacturers and for jumpers worn by the fell walkers and climbers.

Swaledale Woollens, Muker, Swaledale Tel: 01748 86251

One place to visit here is the local enterprise of Swaledale Woollens, which was established in 1974 to revitalise the local cottage industry of hand-knitting and crocheting woollen items using fibre from the famous Swaledale breed of sheep. In the decades leading up to the Second World War, many generations of miners' and farmers' families supplemented their incomes by producing and selling knitted and crocheted items such as sweaters, cardigans and socks. However, this practice was steadily

354

dying out until Swaledale Woollens set up their base in the 1970s.

Today, their cottage shop provides a thriving centre for the collection, display and sale of hand-knitted woollen garments and cloth. (There is also stock of various natural yarns on cone or in packs for those who do their own hand or machine knitting.) Visitors are welcome to call in at the centre to view the fascinating exhibition on the Swaledale sheep, a breed which is renowned for its hardiness, its excellent mothering qualities and for its tendency to remain on a given area of open hillside, thus making shepherding easier. A wide selection of locally designed and produced sweaters, cardigans and other items is on sale at the centre which is open daily. An efficient mail order service is also available.

Further on, the tiny village of THWAITE stands amid the panoramic scenery of Kisdon Hill, Great Shunnor, High Seat and Lovely Seat, and is the last stop for the stout-hearted climbers looking for a challenge. The name is of ancient origin, as are most in this region, coming from the Nordic "thveit", meaning a clearing in the wood, although the woodlands that once provided shelter and fuel for the Viking settlers have long since gone.

From the mountainous scenery of Thwaite, the scene changes completely on arriving at KELD. This is a place where the rushing sound of water is ever present, the word "Keld" meaning "a spring" in Nordic. The little cluster of stone buildings here stand at the earliest stages of the River Swale. For lovers of green woodlands and breathtaking waterfalls Keld is definitely the place to go. It gives an impression of a place apart, untouched by the modern age. It occupies a hollow in the hills and is surrounded by inhospitable and barren moorland. This truly can be defined as a hidden place, although it is today something of a crossroads for long distance walkers.

You should definitely take time to walk the short distance to one or more of Keld's forces, or waterfalls. Wain Wath Force can be found alongside the Birkdale road, and Catrake

Force, with its stepped formation, can be reached from the cottages on the left at the bottom of the street in the village. Following a rough lane at the bottom end of the street, this soon becomes a lovely woodland walk, from which there is a short detour to Kisdon Force, which is confined to a narrow channel through which the young river thunders.

The Tan Hill Inn stands 1732 feet above sea level and is noted as the highest inn in England. It occupies one of the remotest sites in the county, four miles north of Keld on the northernmost border of North Yorkshire. Alec and Margaret Baines have managed to bring some extra comfort to the inn since they acquired it in 1986. Inside, it features exposed beams, stone-flagged floors and a welcoming fire which burns every day of the year.

An excellent pint of hand-pulled Theakston's is served (in winter it has been known to freeze in the pipes) along with a fine selection of bar food. There are also seven comfortable and well-appointed en-suite bedrooms available. Open all year.

Tan Hill Inn, Tan Hill, Keld, Richmond Tel: 01833 628246

Travel back through Thwaite and continue south for a drive through Buttertubs Pass, one of the highest and most forbidding mountain passes in the country. The Buttertubs themselves are an outstanding natural feature and are well

Waterfalls, Keld

known to walkers and travellers. They are a series of closely packed vertical potholes, not linked by a series of passages as potholes usually are, but freestanding, bearing only a slight resemblance to the objects after which they are named.

Wensleydale

After Buttertubs, a snake-like road leads through the mountains down to Hawes and Upper Wensleydale. **HAWES** is not a particularly old town, springing up as it did after the railways arrived in the 1870s. There was an older town here once though, as one can see in some of the street names indicating ancient trades, such as Dyer's Garth, Hatter's Yard, Printer's Square and Cooper's Garth. Hawes is now the commercial and market centre of Wensleydale with a good range of shops and accommodation.

For more information on these old local trades, take a trip to the Dales Countryside Museum, based in the old railway station, which tells the story of how man's activities have helped to shape the Dales' landscape, with historical information on domestic life, the lead-mining industry, hand-knitting and other local trades. Hawes is also renowned for its rope-making industry, and at the Hawes Ropeworks, one can still see the trade being practised, with the experienced ropers twisting cotton and man-made fibres to make halters, picture cords, dog leads and clothes-lines.

Hawes' streets are usually inhabited at any time of the year by the stout-hearted walkers travelling the Pennine Way which south of here makes its way across the sparsely populated Langstroth Chase, through the middle of the Dales to Malham, Todmorden and across Howarth and Saddleworth Moor to Kinder Scout in the Peak District.

Hawes' greatest attraction, though, has to be the nearby Hardraw Force, at 98 feet the highest unbroken waterfall in England that is above ground. Access can be gained through the Green Dragon Inn for a small fee. It is located in an amphitheatre-like surround of limestone crags, where Hardraw Beck plunges over the edge in a breath-taking cascade, behind which, due to an under-cut in the cliff, walkers can gain access to the back of the waterfall, as both Turner and Wordsworth did. An adventure not to be missed!

Another impressive waterfall, Cotter Force, is located three miles out of Hawes, following the Sedburgh road and accessible through fields. The stream passes through the tiny hidden village of Cotterdale, before it transforms into a magnificent display of giant steps of limestone over which the water drops gracefully, overshadowed by leaning boughs of trees.

Wensleydale is richer, kindlier and more verdant than Upper Swaledale, as the quality of its ewes-milk cheese would suggest. It is the only one of Yorkshire's dales not to be named after the river that flows through it, but rather after the town of Wensley, where the lucrative trade in the cheese began in the 13th century before the Plague wiped out its population. Before this, the dale was known by the ancient name of Yore Dale, after the River Yore or Ure that flowed through it. It was the monks of the affluent nearby Jervaulx Abbey who started the trade in the cheese, although the farming communities took over when its popularity became apparent.

Wensleydale is also the home of the greatest concentration of waterfalls in the dales, and travelling along the B684, five miles from Hawes, is the market town of ASKRIGG, and the natural feature of Mill Gill Force.

Once an important market town, before Hawes grew in prominence, Askrigg is now better known as the main location for "All Creatures Great and Small", in which it is called Darrowby. The house opposite the ancient church serves as 'Skeldale House', and the King's Arms as the 'Drover's Arms'.

Across the river lies BAINBRIDGE, once known to the Romans as Virosidum, where they built a succession of forts on Brough Hill (now an overgrown grassy hummock located

Wensleydale Cheese

It is widely believed that the medieval Abbots of Jervaulx were responsible for introducing the manufacture of cheese to Wensleydale over 700 years ago. Initially handed down by word of mouth over the generations it is only recently that the recipe has been made into written record.

The cheese was at first made from Ewes' milk but by the 17th century the milk of shorthorn cows was used as sheep became more important for wool and mutton. Nowadays, though, thousands of gallons of cows' milk are handled each day - a huge increase from the 200 gallons of the 19th century.

Each year hundreds of tons of traditional Wensleydale cheese are made and despite the advances of modern technology and improvements of the process, the cheese is still soft, mild and milky, appealing to a wide market.

Originally a Summer occupation, mainly a task handed to the farmer's wife, the first Wensleydale cheese factory was established by Edward Chapman in 1897, at Gale Beck in Hawes. This example was later followed by Alfred Rowntree and Kit Calvert. Today, the factories are open to the public and have become popular visitor attractions.

on private land). In Norman times, this was a hunting forest, and the Forest Horn is still sounded at 9pm each evening between Holyrood (September 27th) and Shrove Tuesday - an ancient custom introduced to guide travellers though the forest.

Semer Water, lying to the south, is an isolated lake in a lovely location, steeped in myth. It is said that a town lies beneath its depths, cast under water by a curse. A poor traveller once sought shelter here, but was turned away by the affluent inhabitants. The next day, he stood on the hill above the town and laid this curse and a great flood engulfed the town completely. A curious postscript to this tale is that during a drought the level of the lake dropped to reveal the remains of a Bronze Age town, thereby proving the truth behind the legend.

Travelling back along the A684 you will reach AYSGARTH, famous for its pottery and the spectacular Aysgarth Falls. Here, the river thunders through a rocky gorge and drops some 200 feet over three huge slabs of limestone, the falls being divided into Upper, Middle and Lower Falls, particularly exhilarating after a heavy rainfall. Nearby stands Yore Mill, in its time a corn mill, flax mill and wool-spinning and stocking-making factory. Now it houses the Yorkshire Carriage Museum, with its comprehensive collection of horse-carriages, farm carts, fire engines, hearses and even a haunted cab!

North of Aysgarth is CASTLE BOLTON, known predictably enough for its castle. It was built in 1379 by Richard le Scrope, Lord Chancellor of England to Richard II, and a personal friend of Chaucer, who is said to have used him as a model for the Knight's Tale. Today a luxurious fortified manor house, still occupied a direct descendant of the first Lord Scrope, it remains impressive with its gaunt towers and huge Guest Room, which serves as the Castle Tea-room. Its halls and galleries are remarkably well-preserved, some of the private apartments having been the home of Mary Queen of Scots between 1568-69. The view from the battlements is awesome, if rather exposed to the full force of the winds.

One and a half miles southwest of **WEST BURTON**, on the B6160 Kettlewell Road, is the tiny hamlet of **NEWBIGGIN IN BISHOPDALE**. A great place to stay the night is at **Newbiggin House**, a delightful bed and breakfast establishment run by Mr and Mrs Proctor. This handsome creeper-clad residence was constructed of local stone in 1924 and today provides charming and peaceful accommodation for visitors to the area. The Proctors have two comfortable letting bedrooms available (one twin, one single) and provide Yorkshire breakfasts that are second to none. They also own a self-catering holiday cottage, rated as three key, commended. Newbiggin House Cottage adjoins the main house, can sleep two people and overlooks the attractive garden.

Newbiggin House, Newbiggin-in-Bishopdale, Leyburn
Tel: 01969 663583

The village of **WEST WITTON** is known for its annual feast of St Bartholomew, patron saint of the Parish Church, which takes place on August 24th each year. An effigy of "Owd Bartie" is carried through the village, though it is unlikely that the origins of the festival are anything other than pagan. The effigy is eventually burned at Grassgill End at the culmination of three days of festivities.

Travelling through the quiet, pretty village of Wensley, one will eventually come to LEYBURN, the main market and trading centre of the middle dale, as its wide cobbled market places, bordered by high, affluent -looking buildings, would seem to suggest. Its name is a corruption of Le Bourne, as it is called in the Domesday Book, or "Stream by the Clearing", and the nearby area of escarpment known as the Shawl was occupied as far back as prehistoric days.

The town has many famous connections, one of which is the fact that Lord Nelson's surgeon, Peter Goldsmith, once lived in the Secret Garden House in Grove Square. Another can be discovered on a visit to the War Memorial, where one will see the name of flight lieutenant Alan Broadley DSO, DFC, DFM, the famous "F" for Freddie, of Dam Buster fame. Much of the imposing architecture dates from the 1700s, and such buildings as the Grove Hotel, the Sandpiper Inn and Sanderson's Paint shop are worth investigation.

The Shawl lies to the west of the town, a mile-long limestone scarp along which runs a footpath with panoramic views. One legend says that it gained its name from the fact that Mary Queen of Scots dropped her shawl here during her flight from Bolton Castle, though a more likely explanation is that the name is a corruption of the one given to the ancient settlement here. Spring is probably the best time to visit the town, for it is at this time that both the Swaledale and Wensleydale Festivals take place, as well as the prestigious Dales Music Festival.

Historic MIDDLEHAM is entered via a fascinating castellated bridge, similar to those one would normally see spanning a castle's moat. The famous castle here was once the stronghold of the powerful "Kingmaker" Neville family, and favourite home of Richard III. However, on the death of Richard at Bosworth Field, the great castle fell into to decay, much of its stone being used to create buildings for the town below. The recent discovery of the Middleham Jewel near the ruins, which was sold for £1.3 million, brought new interest in the castle and its history.

Middleham itself has two market places, some splendid Georgian and Victorian buildings, and a profusion of racing stables, for which the town is renowned. There is also an old stepped cross in the main market, known as the Swine Cross, which once bore the White Boar emblem of Richard III, hence the name. The lovely parish church is outside the town, with an inscription over the door that tells us the church was built by Thomas, Lord of Aylesbury. This spot is quiet and idyllic, with sheep grazing in the graveyard on the brow of the hill that sweeps down to the Coverdale valley.

Old School Arts Workshop, Top Cross, Middleham, Leyburn
Tel: 01969 623056

A short distance from the cobbled village centre, you will find a fascinating establishment, the **Old School Arts Workshop**. This former village school was constructed in 1869 in elaborate Victorian Gothic style and has an unusual central tower topped with a castellated parapet and a raised bell arch. Following the school's closure in 1977, the building (which is now Grade II listed) was allowed to fall into disrepair until it was purchased in 1981 by Peter and Judith Hibbard. They restored and converted it into a modern study centre which today offers courses in sculpture, painting and

364

related arts. Visitors are invited to look around the gallery exhibitions and book shop, and to visit the workshop's pleasant sculpture garden.

Millers House Hotel, Middleham, Wensleydale
Tel: 01969 622630 Fax: 01969 623570

An ideal place to stay in Middleham is the impressive hotel and restaurant, Millers House Hotel, which is owned and personally-run by Judith and Crossley Sunderland. This handsome Georgian residence was built in 1726 in a sheltered position just off the cobbled market square. Inside, it has been extensively furnished to bring it up to the standards of a modern first-class hotel. There are seven luxuriously appointed guest rooms, all with en-suite bathroom, each named after one of the Yorkshire Dales; the Wensleydale room has a four-poster bed and a magnificent antique bathtub, and the Wharfedale room has beamed ceilings and magnificent views over the surrounding countryside. On chilly evenings your bed may even be warmed by an old stone 'hot water bottle'. The hotel restaurant has been awarded the AA 'Red Rosette' for the high standard of its cuisine. The menu is changed regularly and offers a mouth-watering range of English and continental dishes, including such delights as Gazpacho soup, 'Magret duck breast with pears, fennel and pernod', and a delicious selection of desserts including the delightfully named 'Orange Boodle'. Middleham is a major racehorse training centre (three Grand National winners have come from here) and the hotel offers special breaks for enthusiasts which include tours of local stables and visits to the races.

The owners go out of their way to ensure your stay is a happy one, with many thoughtful touches including a comprehensive information pack in each bedroom. The quality of this establishment has been recognised by the local Tourist Board who named Millers House as Hotel of the Year (Runner Up) 1994.

The Black Swan Hotel, Market Place, Middleham, Leyburn
Tel: 01969 622221

In a superb position overlooking the town square, a highly recommended establishment is the Black Swan Hotel, a handsome Grade II listed building which retains much of its original 17th-century character. Proprietors Sue and George Munday have seven beautifully decorated guest rooms available, all with private bathrooms and first-rate modern facilities; two also have four-poster beds. All rooms have direct-dial telephones and remote control colour TVs. Top quality meals, which are Egon Ronay recommended, are served in the bar and main dining room. The house specialities include steaks and 'tipsy' casseroles. To the rear there is also an attractive beer garden which backs onto Middleham Castle.

PATELEY BRIDGE, considered one of the prettiest of dales towns, is perfectly situated as a base to explore the reaches of Upper Nidderdale. Considering its size, it is remarkably well-connected by roads which have in fact been here since the monastic orders established trade routes through the town for transporting their goods. A street market whose charter was granted in the 14th century has, however, been abandoned for some time, although the sheep fairs and agricultural shows still take place here.

The Nidderdale Museum is based in Pateley Bridge, a fascinating record of local folk history, stored in one of the original Victorian work-houses, built in 1863. This museum was winner of the National Heritage Museum of the Year, and gives an insight into the daily life of folk in this picturesque dale.

The town is filled with quaint, pretty buildings, such as the 17th-century Apothecary's House and Sweet Shop. The oldest building is St Mary's Church, a lovely ruin dating from 1320, with spectacular views. Another fabulous vista can be obtained from the aptly named Panorama Walk, the main medieval route from Ripon to Skipton. St Cuthbert's Church was built to replace St Mary's, and is based further down the town. It houses the original bell from Fountains Abbey, rescued after the Dissolution.

Built in 1670, Harefield Hall was a remote country residence until the late 1950s when it was converted into a delightful hotel. Set in 22 acres of woodland, the large rambling building just waits to be discovered. The decor is what you would expect of a private country house with large pieces of furniture and walls decorated with sporting and fishing prints. There are 21 en-suite bedrooms in all and the claim is that no two rooms are alike. There is a large dining area set aside for guests' use and where the breakfasts and evening meals are served. The cuisine is traditional English and French with Chicken Sinatra being the house speciality.

There are excellent leisure facilities which can be used by guests without charge. In addition, the surrounding countryside provides a range of hill and flat walks and seasoned walkers may prefer to stay in the chalet style accommodation. Private fishing is available nearby.

Harefield Hall Hotel, Pateley Bridge Tel: 01423 711429

An interesting curiosity of the area is the Brimham Rocks, some three miles from the town. These strange rock formations rise to heights of over 20 feet above the open moorland. The huge outcrops of dark millstone grit were carved out millions of years ago by glacial action, and were given fanciful names by Victorian visitors, such as Dancing Bear, Oyster Shell and Indian's Turban.

Eileen Payne offers guests a warm and friendly welcome to her old and historic farmhouse, **North Pasture Farm**, which shelters under the famous Brimham Rocks. Originally it was part of the Manor of Brimham and along with other properties in the area belonged to Fountains Abbey. The present building was rebuilt by a Michael Inman whose initials and the date of 1657 appear above the doorway; the Inman family were ancestors of the shipping family of Liverpool who carried the same name.

By the end of the 17th century the Kirkley family were tenants, and continued in residence for more than 250 years.

Malham Cove

During this time, one notable visitor was John Wesley who once came to preach in the room that now serves as the dining room.

The farm itself is still worked, extending to 135 acres, and is ideally placed for guests to visit many local places of scenic and historic interest. The farmhouse is centrally heated and contains many interesting architectural features like the fine six light mullion window. The bedrooms are all en-suite, beamed and mullioned and full of character. Guests have their own dining room with individual tables and a separate TV Lounge for their sole use. Meals are home-cooked, a five course evening dinner is available if pre-booked. North Pasture Farm enjoys a three crown status and has recently been awarded a Highly Commended rating by the English Tourist Board.

North Pasture Farm, Brimham Rocks, Summerbridge, Harrogate Tel: 01423 711470

Wharfedale and Malhamdale

Visitors to this area with a sense of adventure should not miss out on a trip to the Stump Cross Caverns, a spectacular cave system discovered in 1853. This labyrinth of limestone caves are rich in stalactites and stalagmites. Only the upper level is available to tourists, the lower levels being the more hazardous domain of the potholers. Nicknamed "Hell", due to the conditions down there, explorers still have not entirely charted the extent of the system.

Further west is GRASSINGTON, known as the capital of Upper Wharfedale. In many ways this is a typical dales village, with the ubiquitous market square. Historically important Wharfedale roads meet here and the monastic route from Malham to Fountains passed through, so it easy to appreciate why it developed.

Rooted in Celtic history the village was mentioned in the Domesday book, later being a centre for the lead-mining industry. The present Grassington is an Anglian settlement which passed through various families before descending to the Dukes of Devonshire. Its heyday arrived when lead mining grew in importance in the 17th century and this is reflected in the many houses that date from this time.

Today Grassington is the main residential and commercial centre of Wharfedale, with the greatest concentration of amenities in the area.

Robert Bunney, The Square, Grassington Tel: 01756 752576

In the centre of the village, overlooking the market square, is the establishment of Robert Bunney. This is a high class

371

men's outfitters which has an emphasis on town and country wear. Here you will find an excellent selection of suits, jackets, trousers, coats, knitwear and shoes. The range is hard to beat and it can be viewed in the tastefully furnished and relaxed surroundings. The shop specialises in tweed suits and jackets.

Established in 1965 and still run by the same family, Robert Bunney's maintains a high standard of quality and service on which their reputation was built.

The Country Gardener can be found on the main road into Grassington not far from The Square. This traditional, long-established business has recently redesigned and refurbished the outside areas to form a garden centre. In addition there is now a gift shop stocking an unusual range of countryware including dried flowers, candle, lace products and folk art. The garden centre stocks a large variety of plants and shrubs together with sundry gardening-related items from which many gardening gifts can be found. This family-run business is worth a visit.

The Country Gardener, Station Road, Grassington
Tel: 01756 752272

Situated in the heart of the lovely and unspoilt village of Grassington, **Number Forty Seven** Restaurant offers food and accommodation of the highest standard. David and

372

Sarah Whitefield and their family have transformed this delightful 17th-century cottage into a charming and friendly restaurant. There is a wonderful stone feature fireplace, dating from about 1620, in the dining room and the decor is very much in keeping with the period of the establishment. The food is delicious and their specialities include game dishes, when in season. There is certainly something to meet everyone's tastes. With accommodation of five bedrooms this is an ideal base from which to enjoy the Yorkshire Dales.

Number Forty Seven, Main Street, Grassington
Tel: 01756 752069

On the northern edge of Grassington, make a point of calling in at the fascinating workshops and showroom which are the home of Kents Traditional Furniture. Since moving here in 1986, the firm has won a rural development award for the refurbishment of their premises which stand in a superb position overlooking Grassington and the Wharfedale valley. Founders Janet and Paul Kent and a dozen skilled craftspeople currently produce a range of traditional hand-crafted solid oak furniture which is shipped to all parts of the country. Each piece is made from carefully selected fully-seasoned oak and carries the firm's famous signature, a hand-carved White Rose which is discreetly added as a final seal of approval. Visitors interested in finding out more about traditional methods of furniture making are welcome to call in at the Moor Lane showrooms which are open seven days a week. A small showroom is also at 65 Main Street, just above the market square. Open days are also organised which include tours of the workshop and inspection of the beautiful finished pieces of furniture.

Kents Traditional Furniture, Moor Lane, Grassington
Tel: 01756 753045

Across the river from Grassington is THRESHFIELD. The heart of the village is the Park, a small green with the original village stocks and a few treesm with a number of 17th-century houses clustered around it. In the village is the delightful bed and breakfast establishment of Franor House.

Owned and run by Frank and Norma Cahill, retired teachers, you can be sure of a warm and friendly welcome. All the three comfortable bedrooms have either en-suite or private bathrooms and are decorated in a traditional style. This remains very much a family house with the guests all sitting together round a large antique table for meals in a dining room that overlooks the garden through patio style doors. The Cahills have a mine of information on the local area and have a wealth of books that can help you make the most of your visit.

One of Wharfedale's outstanding landscape feature is Kilnsey Crag, a gigantic limestone outcrop that reaches 170 feet. A remarkable 40 foot overhang is popular with rock-climbers, providing them with a stiff challenge.

*Franor House, 3 Wharfeside Avenue, Threshfield, Skipton
Tel: 01756 752115*

Near to the village, Kilnsey Park has been developed as a visitor centre orientated about freshwater fish. There are specially designed trout-fishing lakes and a trout-feeding pond. A Riverlife Museum displays a variety of British freshwater fish in aquariums.

The lovely Upper Wharfedale village of KETTLEWELL provides an ideal base for exploring the dramatic beauty of the Dales whether by car or on foot. It lies five miles north of Grassington on the B6160 Wharfedale road midway between Skipton and Wensleydale. Those looking for superb bed and breakfast accommodation or a first-rate self-catering holiday cottage in this wonderful part of the country should make a point of finding Fold Farm on the eastern edge of the village.

Fold Farm is a typical Dales hill sheep farm covering 350 acres of unspoilt upland to the south of Kettlewell Beck. Mrs Barbara Lambert offers delightful bed and breakfast accommodation at the main farmhouse, of a Tourist Board 2 Crown Highly Commended standard. This unique residence

Turner in the Dales

One of Britain's greatest artists, J. M. W. Turner, covered much of the Dales in only four tours. In 1797, 1816, and 1817 he travelled through Teesdale, Swaledale and Wensleydale, producing haunting watercolours which were to contribute to his fame.

He aimed to experience nature at its most vivid and thus he would paint in any weather condition, often sitting beneath an umbrella, cold and wet. The result was always an exciting one.

In 1816 Turner travelled through the North of England for three weeks on horseback, and filled three sketchbooks with over 400 drawings of castles, rivers, abbeys, towns and villages.

Throughout Wensleydale and Swaledale there are a series of seats kindly donated by the Wensleydale Tourist Association known as Turner Trail Seats. These enable visitors to the region to sample some of the natural beauty that so inspired Turner - in Askrigg, Wycliffe and Grinton and at the spectacular Hardraw Force, to name but a few locations. Most sites are accessible by footpath or road and will no doubt reward even the less artistic visitor.

A fully illustrated account of Turner's tour of 1816 is given by David Hill in his book "In Turner's Footsteps through the Hills and Dales of Northern England".

is believed to be a late medieval timber-framed 'open hall' and is thus one of the most important houses in Upper Wharfedale. Parts of the building date back to the 15th century, in particular the oak structure which comprises the main hall. There is evidence to show that this was encased in stone in the 17th century, and then was subsequently refenestrated in the 19th century. The modern interior is full of ancient character with exposed stone walls, original timber beams and stone-mullioned windows. There is also an unusual spiral stone staircase which leads to the beautifully decorated letting bedrooms on the first floor. The wonderful historic atmosphere of the house coupled with the Lambert's excellent hospitality makes this a very special place to stay.

Fold Farm, Kettlewell, Skipton Tel: 01756 760886

The Lamberts have also converted some of the farm's original stone-built outbuildings into five superbly equipped holiday cottages which sleep from two to six people and which are now English Tourist Board four key commended. All the cottages have beamed ceilings and open fires (coal and logs can be purchased at the farm). Every comfort has been thought of, even down to dishwashers. The sitting areas all have colour televisions and carefully chosen furnishings, and the bathroom facilities are similarly well appointed.

Fold Farm is open all year round and offers a range of special off-season breaks. It is tucked away next to the village stream and behind the church. The facilities in the village are good and three pubs are within walking distance. For accurate directions, telephone Barbara or Clifford Lambert. The establishment has an excellent reputation and around 90% of visitors come back again. What better recommendation could there be?

Carrying on up the B6160 into the heart of Upper Wharfedale you will shortly reach the small Dales village of **BUCKDEN**. In a dramatic position facing the village green with the 2,300 foot Buckden Pike as a backdrop, you will find the **Buck Inn**, an impressive Georgian coaching inn which is renowned for its good food and accommodation. The present owners, the Hayton family, have done much to enhance the inn's original interior in recent years. The bar has a genuine traditional atmosphere, and a fine residents' restaurant has been created in the courtyard where local wool auctions were once held. The inn also offers fifteen beautifully-decorated bedrooms which are all equipped with en-suite facilities, colour televisions and direct-dial telephones.

Buck Inn, Buckden Tel: 01756 760228

The scenery of Wharfedale changes noticeably at **BURNSALL**. Above the village are the distinctive limestone uplands with gleaming scars and hillsides criss-crossed with white walls. To the south the valley becomes more wooded and less dramatic.

The picturesque village of Burnsall, beside the River Wharfe dates back over a thousand years. **Valley View Guest House**, on the main street, used to be the village smithy and joiners shop - now tastefully converted, this guest house offers the very best in bed and breakfast accommodation with three comfortable and individual bedrooms, one of which is a family room. This is very much a family place and Carol Fitton, your host, has worked hard to ensure that the atmosphere is pleasant and relaxed. A delightful place to stay in the heart of an ancient and historic village and within easy reach of some wonderful countryside.

Valley View Guest House, Burnsall, Skipton
Tel: 01756 720314

The peaceful village of **APPLETREEWICK**, further south, is overlooked by the craggy expanse of Simon's Seat, while Burnsall Fell rises beyond to some 1661 feet. Its single street, situated on the side of the hill, appears as if to be sliding down towards the valley bottom. The lead mines on the northern slopes were the property of the monks of Bolton Abbey. This was also the home of William Craven, almost legendary Lord Mayor of London, who returned to spend much of his amassed wealth on improvements and additions to the town's fine old buildings. The cottage where he was born was largely furnished by the similarly legendary Robert Thompson of Kilburn.

A little further on, downriver from Appletreewick, is the stately ruin of Barden Tower, a residence of Lord Henry Clifford, owner of Skipton Castle. It was built in the 15th century, but allowed to fall into decay, and despite repair in 1657 it is once more a ruin. Nearby is the attractive Barden Bridge, a 17th century arch, now designated as an ancient monument.

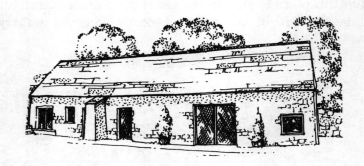

Howgill Lodge, Barden, Nr. Skipton Tel: 01756 720655

If you were to try the walk from Bolton Abbey, up the 'valley of desolation', on to Simon's Seat and down into Howgill, then an ideal place to stop for lunch is at **Howgill Lodge** where there is a small restaurant which serves traditional grills, salads and afternoon teas. If you are also looking for an excellent bed and breakfast establishment in the area then you need look no further either. The accommodation is located in a converted 17th century barn which was completely renovated by Bernard and a team of willing helpers in 1986. Today, not only do the guest rooms enjoy panoramic views, but they are also equipped with en-suite facilities, colour television and tea/coffee facilities. Ann

380

and Bernard are North Yorkshire born and bred, and as well as excellent accommodation, they offer their guests superb local hospitality. Situated just off the B6160 between Bolton Bridge and Grassington, it is advisable to telephone the owners, Ann and Bernard Foster, for directions. Further on down river, the wide river bed suddenly narrows into a confined channel of black rocks, where its waters thunder through. This is known as The Strid, so-called because heroic types down the ages have attempted to leap its width as a test of bravery - or foolhardiness. Some way on, the spectral ruins of Bolton Priory come into view. This was, in fact a 12th century Priory, sister to Fountains Abbey. Its sad, graceful arches make the perfect subject for atmospheric photographs, and a wonderful backdrop to the many diversions the nearby river has to offer. Confusingly, the village has acquired the name Bolton Abbey despite the fact that the ruins are of a Priory.

Devonshire Arms, Cracoe, Near Skipton Tel: 01756 730237

Midway between Skipton and Grassington, in the village of CRACOE, is the Devonshire Arms. The pub dates back to the 17th century and the main Fell Bar, which was the first part of the inn to be built in 1604, retains many of the original beams. The owners, Jill and John Holden, have worked hard to gain their reputation for fine food, good beer

381

and warm and friendly atmosphere - they like nothing better than to take time to chat to their guests. As well as serving bar type meals in the 'Snug' and more formal meals in the oak-panelled Dales dining room, there are also several pleasant and attractive bedrooms. With a charming garden, used during the summer, this is a lovely place from which to explore the surrounding countryside.

Six miles west of Grassington lies an area of geological interest around **MALHAM**. There is much spectacular scenery in this area, as the many sightseers who come here will testify. There are old mine workings below Pike Daw Hill and Langscar Gate, under which run a complex system of tunnels and caverns, indicated by the remains of a lonely smelt mill. At Langscar are also the traces of an important Iron Age settlement, the lynchets, or cultivation terraces of these early settlers are still to be seen flanking the hillsides of Malham Beck, their drystone walls indicating a primitive land husbandry long since gone.

It is the ancient glacial grandeur of Malham Cove itself that gives the greatest feeling of the past. The way to the Cove is from the Langcliffe road beyond the last buildings of Malham village, down a path alongside the beck that leads through a scattering of trees; as one walks on through the trees the 300 foot limestone amphitheatre emerges into view in the most dramatic fashion. This is the most spectacular section of the mid-Craven fault and, as recently as the 1700s, a massive waterfall cascaded over its edge, higher than Niagara Falls! These days the water disappears through potholes at the top called water-sinks, and reappears through the cavern mouth at Aire Head near the village. A steep path leads to the limestone 'pavement' at the top, with its distinctive 'clints' and 'grykes', where water has carved a distinctive natural sculpture through the weaknesses in the limestone.

From here it is not too far to reach the equally inspiring Gordale Scar, a huge gorge carved by glacial melt water. An impressive waterfall leaps in two stages from a fissure in its

382

Pen-y-ghent

Castle Bolton

face. Further on is another waterfall known as Janet's Foss, beside which is a cave which Janet, a friendly fairy, is reputed to inhabit. Three miles north of the scar is Malham Tarn, a glacial lake, and Malham Tarn House, where such famous names as Ruskin, Darwin and Charles Kingsley (author of 'The Water Babies') received inspiration.

Ribblesdale

Due east is the Dales town of SETTLE through which runs the famous Settle-Carlisle Railway, a proudly preserved memento of the glorious age of steam, the line flanked by charming little signal boxes and stations that are a real tourist magnet. This attractive railway was, however, built in the midst of great controversy and even greater cost in both money and lives, earning it the dubious title of "the line that should never have been built". There is a churchyard at St Leonard's in Chapel-le-Dale where over 100 of the workers and miners, who laboured under the most adverse conditions, lie buried. Today, the trains still thunder over the 21 viaducts, through 14 tunnels and over the numerous bridges they gave their lives for.

The town itself is dominated by one of these huge viaducts as well as the Castleberg cliff, and is worth spending some time in. Settle's architecture is very distinctive, in the main being Victorian sandstone buildings that all look as if they are born of the railway culture. Buildings of note include the arcaded Shambles, originally butcher's slaughter houses, the French-style Town Hall, the Victorian Music Hall, and the oldest building, Preston's Folly, described as an extravaganza of mullioned windows and Tudor masonry, and so-called because the man who created this anomalous fancy impoverished himself in the process! Apart from the grander structures on the main streets, there are charming little side streets with Georgian and Jacobean cottages criss-crossed with quirky little alleyways and ginnels and hidden

384

courtyards and workshops of a time gone by. In Chapel Street is the Museum of North Craven Life, which gives a historical, topographical and geological background to the area.

The features of the surrounding countryside are equally interesting. The fascinating Victoria Cave, for example, has yielded finds of Roman relics, Stone Age artifacts and even 120,000 year old mammoth bones. Other places include the erratic Ebbing and Flowing Well, the lovely Catrigg Force near Stainforth, numerous unusual geological features and caves (including the grimly titled Dead Man's Cave) and the fascinating Celtic Wall, a defensive structure probably constructed by a local Celtic tribe to help deter invaders.

Wonderful scenery, two National parks and a host of places steeped in history - these are all part of a Yorkshire holiday. Now a new attraction has been added, bringing the work of Dales craftsmen into one centre at Watershed Mill in Settle.

On the banks of the River Ribble, this 1820s cotton mill has been converted by owners Lynne Ridgway and David Wilkinson into the Dalesmade Centre, a prestigious retail showcase devoted entirely to products made in the Dales, and winner of the 1992 White Rose Award for "The best newcomer to Tourism". Past an imposing entrance with the centre's logo depicted in glowing coloured glass, the retail space is artistically arranged around a fountain bubbling over pebbles from the nearby riverbank. The displays are sited to lead the eye from one area to the next with lush plants and natural wood adding to the atmosphere.

Products range from paintings and prints to designer knitwear, jams to jewellery and greetings cards to oak dressers, offering a wide choice of gifts for friends and family or an item of lasting value for your home. Craft demonstrations are an added feature, with regular exhibitions showing the skills needed to create many of the products on display. During the spring and summer months events are held including Craft Demonstrations, Farm Week, Wool Week, Art Activity Week and Charity Week, all part of the unique attractions of Watershed Mill. In addition to the shopping section there is an Arts Activity Area, originally designed for children, who can dabble with paints and clay and let their imaginations run riot while the family browse at leisure.

Finally there is Hector's Restaurant, named after the original mill owner. Here the flowery tables and leafy murals reflect the conservatory ambience, and you will find delicious home cooked food and a varied selection of coffees, teas and fruit infusions. Yorkshire specials are the highlights of the week.

There is ample free parking for cars and coaches and easy level access for disabled people. Information on events and workshops during your holiday is always available from the helpful staff.

WATERSHED MILL

Watershed Mill Arts, Settle Tel: 01729 825111

Two miles north of Settle, the B6479 Ribblesdale road reaches the delightful village of STAINFORTH. Look out here for the stone packhorse bridge which is said to have been built by the monks of Sawley Abbey in the 14th century. Standing adjacent to the bridge you will find the Craven Heifer Hotel which is run by Christina Tillotson and her sister Belinda Nixon. Built over 200 years ago as a stopping place for packhorse traffic between North Lancashire and the northeast of England, this charming establishment offers good food and traditional ales in a relaxed and intimate atmosphere. There are also three comfortable letting bedrooms available, all equipped with colour televisions, hot and cold washbasins and tea-making facilities. One room, known as the "Lovers' Room", has a few extra special touches and is ideal for that romantic weekend away.

The Craven Heifer, Stainforth, Settle Tel: 01729 822599

The road from Settle to Hawes follows the River Ribble for 10 miles, to its source at RIBBLEHEAD. HORTON IN RIBBLESDALE lies about mid-way between the two and is an ideal point from which to explore the limestone landscapes and green hills of upper Ribblesdale. To the east the view is dominated by Pen-y-ghent, 2273 feet high, which is one of the 'Three Peaks' of the area. Horton is a popular stopping off point for walkers on the Pennine Way and well as Three Peaks challengers.

The Three Peaks Challenge is the demanding 22 mile hike over the summits of Pen-y-ghent, Whernside and Ingleborough. Its completion within twelve hours qualifies for membership of The Three Peaks of Yorkshire Club based at the Pen-y-ghent Café in Horton.

Situated in the beautiful valley of the River Ribble, in the village of Horton in Ribblesdale, stands the Crown Hotel.

The Swaledale Sheep

The Swaledale sheep are the most common on the Yorkshire uplands, the ram having even been adopted as the emblem of the Yorkshire Dales National Park. They are an extremely hardy breed, recognisable by their black face, white muzzle and grey speckled legs.

The sheep were introduced to the Moors in the 1920s, taking over from the Scottish blackface although a few examples of this breed remain. Each flock knows its own territory - they are said to be 'heafed' to the moor and it is apparently a hereditary knowledge - and yet the matter is confused by the lack of fences which makes intermingling inevitable.

The sheep are marked to determine the ownership. Colour near the shoulder or on the loin, ear notching and ear tags are common methods. They have to cope with extremely wild weather - so typical of these heights - though it is acknowledged that the motor car is a greater threat than the weather.

Their hardiness is typical of the warm, durable wool which they provide which in turn has helped the revival of the hand-knitting industry in the area.

This is one of the few hotels in the Yorkshire Dales National Park which actually stands on the Pennine Way and it is also surrounded by the Three Peaks. This charming building dates back to the 17th century and, for the past 25 years, the hotel has been in the very capable hands of Norma and Richard Hargreaves. With two cosy residents' lounges, comfortable bedrooms and a cosy bar there is a warm welcome awaiting all guests. This is just the place to stay while visiting the nearby sights and enjoying the surrounding countryside with many walks starting on the hotel's own doorstep.

The Crown Hotel
Horton-in-Ribblesdale.

The Crown Hotel, Horton-in-Ribblesdale, Near Settle
Tel: 01729 860209

High on the slopes of Ingleborough, two miles from the village of Horton-in-Ribblesdale and near to the Ribblesdale Viaduct lies South House Farm. This has been a working farm for over 200 years and the present owner, Margaret Kenyon, offers excellent bed and breakfast accommodation and evening meals by arrangement, with an accent on traditional Yorkshire hospitality. This is an isolated location but the views, in all directions, are magnificent. The house overlooks the infant River Ribble and the Settle-Carlisle railway in the valley below. This is also an ideal location for

389

exploring the surrounding area of Wharfedale, Wensleydale and Littondale and the towns of Settle, Skipton and Malham.

South House Farm, Horton-in-Ribblesdale, Settle
Tel: 01729 860271

Situated in the middle of the three peaks of Whernside, Ingleborough and Pen-y-ghent, is the Station Inn, in the shadow of the famous Ribblehead viaduct.

The Station Inn, Near Ingleton Tel: 015242 41274

The owners, Keith and Pauline Coates, maintain a railway theme inside the cosy bar, with paintings, drawings and photographs adorning the walls. The bar is stocked with fine ales and a good selection of malt whiskies and the open log-burning fires and convivial atmosphere welcome the thirsty traveller. The inn also has a snug dining room were you can enjoy a wide variety of home cooked meals including the house speciality of a giant Yorkshire pudding. With five bedrooms, three of which are double rooms with en-suite bathrooms, a bunkhouse and a bunk cottage this is a wonderful place to stop while discovering the magnificent scenery of the surrounding area.

The whole of this area has been designated as being of Special Scientific Interest, mainly due to the need to conserve the swiftly eroding hillsides and paths. This is an ancient landscape, well worth the efforts to preserve its relic ash woodlands, primitive earthworks and rare birdlife such as Peregrine Falcon, Ring Ouzel and Golden Plover. There are also a great many caves in the area, which add to the sense of romance and adventure one feels in this place.

For those that are interested in the origins of names, Pen-y-ghent means "Hill of the Winds" and Ingleborough originally meant "Fire Mountain", the reason being that its flat top was used by the Brigantian tribesmen for their signal beacons. It was here that they were held under siege by the Roman legions, this being the highest Iron Age fortress in Britain and a coveted vantage point.

INGLETON, the 'Beacon Town' of the Dales, is an idyllic location for all lovers of the great outdoors, with its pretty waterfalls and grottoes. Here the tributaries Twiss and Doe fall in a succession of cascades to converge as the lovely River Greta, surrounded by sylvan glens.

The town is dominated by the viaduct that spans the river, with typical dales architecture and a cosy little parish church, built in the squat squarish style so common to these once isolated, hidden places. While here, one should not miss out on a trip down the magnificent Ingleborough Cave, with its maze of underground formations, streams and illuminated pools. There is even a picnic area, should one fancy a subterranean snack! Above ground, the four miles of waterfalls called collectively the Ingleton Falls, and which include Pecca Twin Falls, Holly Bush Spout, Thornton Force, Beezley Upper and Lower Falls and Baxengill Gorge, amongst others, should only be attempted with the aid of a pair of stout walking shoes.

Situated in the village of Ingleton are the delightfully secluded **Pinecroft Lodges**. This five acre site has five pine log cabins, all imported from Finland, which owners Robin and Dorothy Hainsworth let out for family holidays and weekend breaks. Overlooked by Ingleborough Hill, the cabins are beautifully furnished with pine furniture and contain fully equipped kitchens and bathrooms. They really are a home from home. Pinecroft Lodges is in a perfect position from which to enjoy the magnificent scenery of the surrounding area. Robin and Dorothy have also recently added a 48 bed bunkhouse on the site. This is a perfect setting for those who want to relax and enjoy the natural world.

Pinecroft Lodges, Ingleton Tel: 015242 41462

Also located in this popular Yorkshire village is **Thorngarth House**, a spacious Victorian mansion offering all the delights and comforts of a country house. Owned and run by Ann Holt, who has earned an excellent reputation for fine cuisine, however long or short your visit you will certainly feel at home. The comfortable guest lounge offers superb views of Ingleborough and the surrounding countryside with the cosy atmosphere provided by a log burning fire. The food here is delicious, with a mouthwatering evening menu and an afternoon tea that is the house speciality. Each bedroom is individually decorated and comfortably furnished. This is a delightful hotel which offers a discreet and professional service to all guests, all in a perfect setting.

Thorngarth Country House Hotel, Ingleton
Tel: 015242 41295

Lying at the end of the one way system, **The Wheatsheaf** is only 100 yards from Ingleton centre. The pub is approximately 250 years old and inside the open fire, low oak beams and brasses certainly provide a welcoming atmosphere. Recently acquired by John and Jeannie Bennett they have embarked on a planned programme of renovation, including making all the bedrooms en-suite, creating a large beer garden and children's play area and revamping the previously unused restaurant to provide gourmet-style pub grub.

On the southwestern fringe of the Dales National Park is the village of **CLAPHAM**, a community which for many centuries has been a stopping place for travellers en route between West Yorkshire and the Lake District. Standing on the old A65 midway between Settle and Ingleton, the village has a great deal to offer the visitor including access to the three peaks circular walk and to Clapham's famous Ingleborough Cave, a spectacular show-cave which forms part of the Gaping Gill underground river system. More recently, Clapham has become noted for being the home of the Dalesman magazine.

The Wheatsheaf, 22 High Street, Ingleton Tel: 015242 41275

Situated in the centre of the village, the **New Inn Hotel** has been providing hospitality for travellers and locals for over 200 years. This impressive free house and hotel is run by resident proprietors Keith and Barbara Mannion, two charming hosts who take great pride in providing their customers with the very best in food, drink and accommodation. There are two bars at the New Inn, both with open fires and a cosy traditional atmosphere. Here, customers can enjoy a pint of hand-pulled ale or choose from the excellent range of bar meals which are served every lunchtime and evening.

There is also a first-class restaurant for those wanting a choice of more elaborate dishes. Keith and Barbara have thirteen comfortable letting bedrooms available, all equipped with en-suite bathrooms, colour television, tea and coffee

394

making facilities and telephones. Guests can also make use of a private lounge which is located on the first floor. The New Inn is English Tourist Board three-crown commended and provides an ideal base for exploring the many attractions of the surrounding area. Children welcome.

New Inn, Clapham, Nr. Settle Tel: 01524 251203

A great sense of history pervades all of the journeys around this region, as one travels the roads from Ingleton. **AUSTWICK** is an ancient place of stone cottages and crofts, dry-stone walls, abandoned quarries and patchwork hills. Its name originally meant "Eastern Settlement", as it was known to the Nordic settlers who made it their home. The largely 17th century buildings, with their elaborately decorated stone lintels, flank what remains of the village green, where the ancient cross stands as a reminder of when this was the head of a dozen neighbouring manors.

The most peculiar feature of the area has to be the Norber Erratics, eerie black boulders which stand on limestone pedestals which, despite their contrived appearance, are in fact a completely natural feature. They are known as "erratics" because they are anomalous - the grey silurian slate they are composed of usually occurs beneath limestone rather than on top of it. The mystery of their existence is explained by the fact that these huge rocks were originally

395

deposited by glacial action at the end of the last Ice Age. Another distinctive feature is the Clapper Bridges, medieval structures made from large slabs of rock that span the becks hereabouts, with such eccentric titles as 'Pant', 'Flascoe' and 'Wash Dubs'.

Nearby GIGGLESWICK sports several interesting places, including the 15th century church of St Alkelda and the well-known Giggleswick Public School with an observatory that was used by the Astronomer Royal in 1927 to observe an eclipse of the Sun. The green-domed school chapel is a conspicuous landmark, well worth a photograph or two. From Giggleswick Scar, the views across the Ribble Valley to the distinctive promontory of Pen-y-ghent are truly awe-inspiring.

Skipton

Following the A65 towards Skipton and you will pass through the impressive Coniston Estate which lies in a beautiful position on the banks of the River Aire at CONISTON GOLD.

Coniston Estate, Coniston Cold, Nr Gargrave
Tel: 01756 748136

Skipton Castle

Within the grounds of this splendid privately-run estate there is a magnificent twenty-four acre lake stocked with 2 to 14 pound rainbow and brown trout. Visiting fly fisherman can fish here by the day, or if they prefer, they can try for wild brown trout on the nearby two-and-a-half mile stretch of the River Aire. The estate also offers clay pigeon shooting facilities for individuals and groups of all levels of experience. Those preferring their fish and game ready-caught should make a point of calling in at the wonderful estate shop where an unrivalled selection of fish (fresh, frozen and smoked), shellfish, venison and game is always available.

Visitors are also invited to call in at the estate's delightful tearoom and restaurant which serves delicious morning coffees, lunches, afternoon and high teas between 10am and 6pm, seven days a week.

A visit to the Craven area would not be complete without a trip to **SKIPTON**, the 'Gateway of the Dales'. Its origins can be traced to the 7th century, when Anglian farmers christened it 'Sheeptown', for reasons which do not need explanation.

The Normans built the first castle here in the twelfth century, and established the markets and fairs here, which have carried on ever since, in the wide cobbled market place. The hungry traveller will find much to tempt here; J Stanforth's Pork Pie Establishment sells its delicious pies straight from the oven and Whitaker's 100 year old Chocolate Emporium has a huge selection of mouth-watering chocolate confections on the ground floor and a friendly tea-shop on the first level. On market days all sorts of local delicacies are on offer, including smoked Wensleydale Cheese and there is a wide assortment of restaurants and cafés.

A wonderful place to eat in Skipton, especially for lovers of top quality fish and seafood, is **Eastwoods Fish Restaurant** in Keighley Road. The restaurant can be found a short distance south of the town centre in a superb position on the brow of Pinder Bridge across the Leeds-Liverpool Canal. Inside, the atmosphere is pleasant and welcoming with old beamed ceilings and walls lined with interesting boating memorabilia, and window seats with views over the adjacent canal.

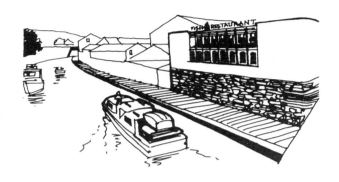

Eastwoods Fish Restaurant, Keighley Road, Skipton
Tel: 01756 795458

Proprietors Mr and Mrs Sumner continue the extremely successful policy, developed over the last 20 years, of serving top quality fish at surprisingly reasonable prices. As well as delicious fish and chips, their menu also includes a wide choice of more exotic fish dishes such as halibut, trout and salmon, many of them cooked in mouth-watering sauces. There is also a good selection of non-fish dishes such as gammon and Cumberland sausage, a number of specially prepared vegetarian dishes, a special children's menu and a good range of starters and desserts. The restaurant is also fully licensed and stocks an unexpectedly varied list of wines and beers. A good value set lunch is served on weekdays and there is also a take-away facility next door. All in all, the quality of the food, the generous portions and excellent value make this an outstanding place to enjoy traditional English cooking at its best. Open for lunch, teas and suppers, every day except on Sunday when the shop and restaurant are open from 4pm.

Feeling well-fed and rested, one may decide to take a trip to the Craven Museum, which boasts Britain's oldest piece of cloth, a Viking tombstone and Georgian and Victorian relics.

The Parish Church of the Holy Trinity is another fascinating place to visit, built originally in the 12th century and replaced in the 1300s. There is a wealth of interest inside, topped by a beautiful oak roof, constructed originally in the 15th century. It is possible to spend much time discovering the centuries of artefacts in this place, and the various tombs and memorials are just as interesting and include the many tombs of the Clifford family whose home was Skipton Castle. Many of the tombs were defaced by Cromwell and his men, but defiantly and lovingly restored at a later date. If taking a rest in Skipton, take time to explore this church - your efforts will be well rewarded.

C & H Brown, 4-8 Newmarket Street, Skipton
Tel: 01756 792437

C & H Brown is a double fronted shop on Newmarket Street, just off the bottom of the High Street, established for over 20 years. Recently extended, the shop offers a complete range of matching accessories - shoes, handbags, gloves, belts and hats. Ladies shoes are stocked in sizes from 2 to 9 and silk and satin shoes can be dyed to match any outfit from a choice of over 500 shades. They can also offer a hat matching service. Gentlemen's shoes are by Grenson, Loake, Bally and Rombah Wallace.

The upstairs showroom is an Aladdin's cave of leatherware, purses, wallets, writing cases, jewel boxes, briefcases and much more. A selection of fashion jewellery completes the ensemble. This traditional, family-run establishment offers a personal service for every customer.

The Craven Court Shopping Centre in the heart of Skipton is a covered side street with the period feel of a Victorian shopping arcade. Here, on a balcony overlooking a courtyard, is Hemingway's, The Tea Shop. Owned and personally run by Tim and Anne Hemingway, this is an delightful establishment where all the traditional values of good, efficient service are upheld.

Hemingway's, The Tea Shop, 10-11a Craven Court, Skipton
Tel: 01756 798035

Here you will find a variety of snacks and drinks to refresh you after a hard day of shopping. To start there is a wide range of speciality teas and coffees both to take away and for consumption on the premises. The tea is predominantly by Taylor's of Harrogate and most of the coffee is ground on the premises. In cold months the hot chocolate is ideal, served with marshmallows, roman orange or brandy cream. The establishment is licensed and there is a good selection of affordable wines. To accompany your drink there is an excellent selection of home-baked pastries and cakes - the strawberry tarts are very popular, or you could try the chocolate fudge cake or the fresh meringues. This is also the only place in the area selling locally made English muffins and crumpets. For a savoury snack there are hot beef sandwiches and another Hemingway's speciality, toasted cheese and bacon muffins. The home-made soups are made fresh daily, and other hot dishes include such delights as salmon and broccoli crepes, haddock bake and various vegetarian options. Hand-made preserves, fudges and haggis can be purchased here - an ideal and unusual gift. A further feature is the resident pianist who plays most days, enhancing the atmosphere. A great place!

Based in Skipton, or in canal terms, on the Springs Junction of the Leeds and Liverpool Canal, are **Pennine Cruisers**. Here you can hire a traditionally styled narrowboat for a day or for a cruise of a week or weekend. The boats available for daily hire can seat up to ten people and are ideal for exploring the seventeen mile lock-free pound of the canal between Gargrave and Bingley. Here you can enjoy the hospitality of the many waterside pubs and observe the outstanding beauty of the varied wildlife. The boats are equipped with cooking facilities and a toilet and are available for hire all year round. For extended cruising, there is a range of eight boats, varying in size from the Flasby (4 berth at 35 feet) to the Grassington (8 berth at 59 feet). Narrowboat holidays are ideal for the whole family or for a group of friends. Discover a whole new outlook on Yorkshire - even the most familiar places look completely different from the water! All boats are well equipped with shower, toilet, full cooking and food storage facilities and even central heating for colder evenings. If you haven't sampled this type of holiday, you will be surprised at how much room there is on a narrowboat, designed for ease of access through the day converting to full size berths with quilts and fresh linen (provided), at night. The hire fee includes all heating and fuel charges, instruction in boat handling and licences to cruise several hundred miles of the canal network. Ring for availability.

Pennine Cruisers, The Boat Shop, 19 Coach Street, Skipton
Tel: 01756 795478

Skipton Castle, home of the Cliffords, was started here in 1090 and the powerful stone structure we see today was devised in 1310 by Robert de Clifford, the 1st Earl of Skipton. The Cliffords were a fighting breed and throughout the middle ages wherever there was trouble you would often as not find a Clifford.

Skipton Castle is lauded as one of the most complete and well preserved medieval castles in England. Despite the heroic nature of its owners, time has been kind to it - the Royalist forces who sought refuge here fared better than most and when Major General Lambert was ordered by Cromwell to 'slight' or make the castle untenable, he wrote back to the Lord Protector that the labourers in charge of the operation "come late, go early, and stand idle while they are here", thereby preserving a monument that gives a great deal of pleasure to visitors today.

In the picturesque Pennine village of LOW BRADLEY, to the south of Skipton, lies The Slaters Arms. This 18th-century public house is family-run and very much a locals' pub; during the summer months you will find the cricket team meeting in the snug. The lounge bar is cosy and friendly with low beamed ceilings and a fine stone fireplace with a roaring log fire. For warmer weather, there is an attractive patio garden at the rear of the pub with plenty of seating and views over the surrounding countryside. To accompany your hand-pulled pint of real ale there is an interesting menu of bar snacks, featuring all traditional dishes, including steak and kidney pie and game. Some dishes are available in a variety of sizes depending on your appetite. A delightful place to stop which welcomes all.

The Slaters Arms, Low Bradley, Near Skipton
Tel: 01535 632179

West Yorkshire

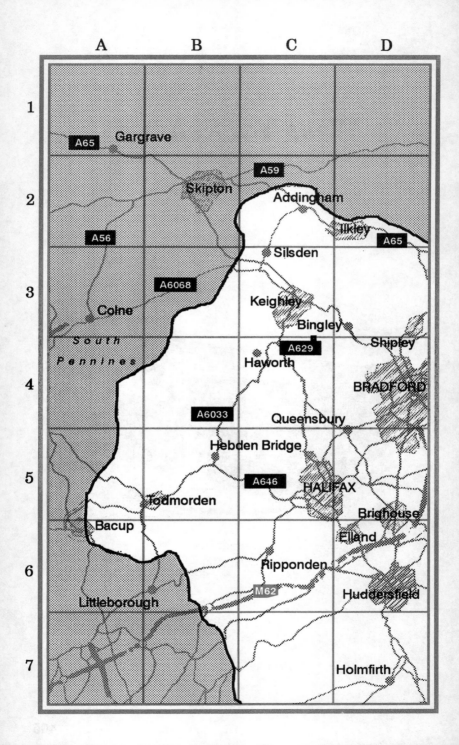

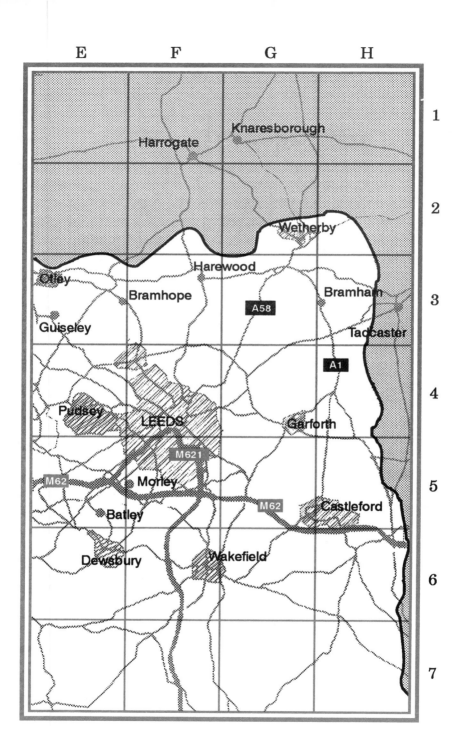

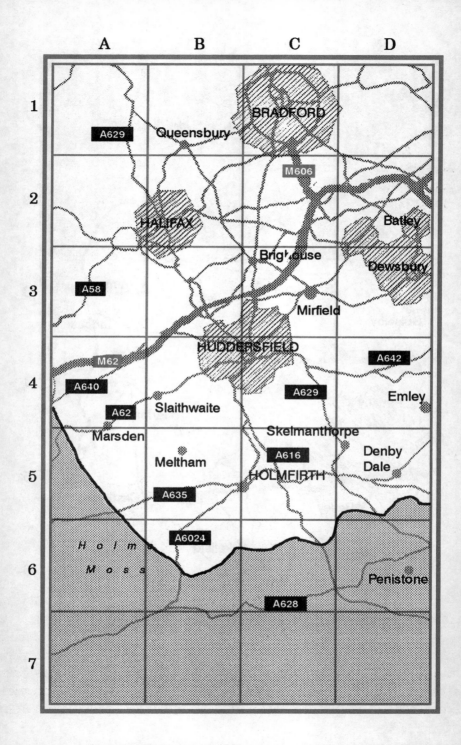

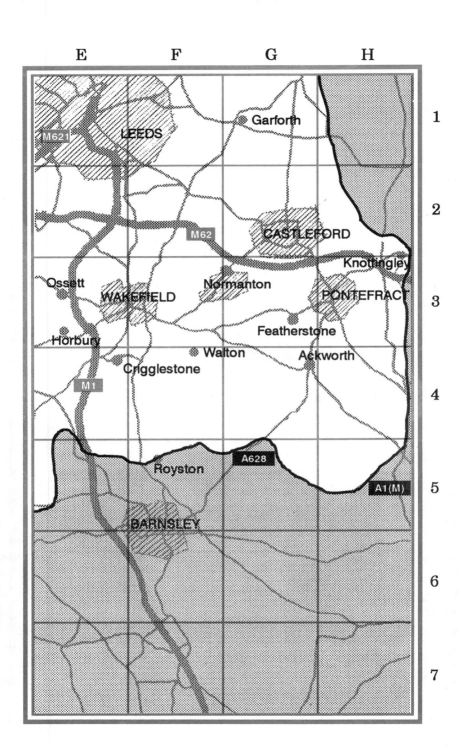

Ilkley

CHAPTER EIGHT

West Yorkshire

Ilkley to Halifax

At the junction of the rivers Worth and Aire is the bustling textile and engineering town of **KEIGHLEY**. Despite its modern redevelopment, Keighley still retains a strangely nostalgic air of the Victorian Industrial Revolution, for it was that era that created the town you see today, beginning at Low Mill in 1780, when cotton spinning on a factory scale was first introduced.

Despite being reminders of hardship, the labyrinth of ginnels and terraces amid the many elaborately decorated mills hold a great deal of exploration potential. There are delightful carvings and on one early mill chimney are three heads, one wearing a top hat; in contrast is the classical French-styled Dalton Mill in Dalton Lane with its ornate viewing gallery.

The centre of Keighley is dominated by impressive Victorian civic buildings and a beautifully set-out covered shopping precinct, where the statue of legendary local giant Rombald stands. The parish church, also in the centre, is famous as the site where Patrick Brontë often officiated at marriages. The graveyard contains 15th-century headstones, as well as a crude cross made from four carved heads which is believed to be Saxon in origin. Above the town, as a means of escaping the industrial past, one might enjoy a walk in Park Woods, taking the cobbled path to Thwaites Brow, which affords magnificent views of the town below.

Outside the town centre is Cliffe Castle which, despite its deceptive name, is in fact a grand late 19th-century mansion complete with a tower, battlements and parkland, which once belonged to local mill owners, the Butterfields. It now houses a natural history museum, with fascinating information on the local topography and geology of Airedale. The decor is Victorian at its grandest, with magnificent French chandeliers. Predictably, there is also an excellent exhibition of cotton mill memorabilia and history which is well worth a visit.

A short way down the valley is East Riddlesden Hall, a National Trust Property with parts dating back to Saxon times. The main building was constructed in the 1630s by James Murgatroyd, a wealthy Halifax clothier and merchant. It is a gabled house built of dark stone with mullioned windows, original central hall, superb period fireplaces, oak panelling and plaster ceilings. The house is furnished in Jacobean style, which is complemented by carved likenesses of Charles Stuart and Henrietta Maria. East Riddlesden Hall also has one of the largest and most impressive timber-framed barns in the North of England, which now houses a collection of farm waggons and agricultural equipment.

Lying in the village of EASTBURN, near Keighley, is The White Bear Inn. The original building, which now houses the kitchens, dates back to 1770 and is solidly built of light coloured Yorkshire stone. There is a traditional tap room where you can enjoy a variety of pub games such as darts and dominoes, and the cosy atmosphere is enhanced by the settles beside the roaring fireplace. The pub also has a lounge and dining bar and a recently added conservatory, dedicated to non-smoking. There is plenty of activity here, with folk evenings and live music and various forms of Morris dancing outside during the summer months.

Run by Graeme and Vanita Jenkins the pub offers a warm, friendly welcome, however the food is far from the normal fayre of most local pubs. Vanita, the chef, comes from the Surat Jujart area of India, just north of Bombay and this has a great influence on the menu. You can expect to eat well prepared, fresh, authentic Asian food, a delightful and enjoyable experience in the heart of Yorkshire. Children are well looked after too with an indoor play area. This is an interesting place to visit, where traditional Yorkshire hospitality meets the enticing smells and tastes of India.

The White Bear Inn, Main Road, Eastburn, Near Keighley
Tel: 01535 653000

SILSDEN is a well-contained stone-built industrial town which spreads uphill from the Leeds and Liverpool canal. Rows of stone-built terraced cottages and houses lie on the steep hill sides and there is newer housing on the outskirts of the town. Silsden owes its development to the textile industry and some textile companies remain in the original mill buildings. Surprisingly the town is unspoilt.

Opposite the park in Bolton Road you will discover a truly exceptional restaurant and wine bar which is located in a converted stone-built cottage. Merlin's is owned and personally run by Chris and Cynthia Sykes and their son Howard who over the years have accumulated a wealth of training and experience in catering to the highest standard. Today, they offer their customers the very best in food and wine, both in the relaxed atmosphere of the bar and in the more formal surroundings of the restaurant.

Howard is responsible for selecting Merlin's first-class wine list which features examples from some of the world's finest lesser-known vineyards. He also chooses the daily menu for Merlin's first-class à la carte restaurant which features a variety of English, Continental and International dishes, carefully prepared from top quality ingredients including fresh fish, game in season and meat supplied by a celebrated local butcher. Meals are individually cooked to order and may take a little time to prepare, but the results are well worth waiting for. For those requiring a lighter, more straightforward meal, these are provided in the bar every evening except Saturdays. The Sykes also organise excellent value monthly gourmet wine-tasting evenings

413

which typically feature a six course meal accompanied by up to seven specially selected wines. Open Monday to Saturday, 7pm to midnight and for lunch Thursday to Saturday, 12 noon to 2pm.

Merlin's Restaurant, 7 Bolton Road, Silsden, Keighley
Tel: 01535 655995

ADDINGHAM, lying just two and a half miles on the Skipton side of Ilkley, was a prosperous mill town at the time when Ilkley was just a quiet back-water. This was mainly due to the availability of ample water-power in the locality, and for serious students of Yorkshire's early industrial history, Addingham repays exploration. Various small mills and industrial buildings demonstrate the evolution in the West Riding of the world's first textile manufacturers. In the 18th century, cottage hand-loom weavers, sharing a common house loft, began to develop the idea of a common workshop - the significant change from a cottage to a factory system. Addingham also has several old inns dating back to the stagecoach days, and it was here that the horses would be changed ready for the long ascent over Chelker Brow into Skipton. There are also some interesting craft outlets, a pottery and antique shops to browse around.

One of the most famous West Yorkshire attractions has to be Ilkley Moor, immortalised in the well-known song, and a visit is a must, if only to say that you've been there (preferably without your hat!). Like any of the Yorkshire moors Ilkley Moor can look inviting and attractive on a sunny day but ominous and forbidding when the weather takes a turn for the worse. The River Wharfe runs along the edge of the moor and through the town of ILKLEY, which is clustered within a narrow section of the valley, in the midst of heather moorland, craggy gritstone and wooded hillside.

Originally an Iron Age settlement, Ilkley was eventually occupied by the Romans, who built a camp here to protect their crossing of the River Wharfe, and who named the town that sprang up Olicana, giving rise to the present name, with the familiar "ley" (Anglo-Saxon for pasture) added. Behind the medieval church is a grassy mound where a little fort was built and in the town's museum are altars carved in gritstone, dedicated to the Roman gods.

The spring at White Wells brought more visitors in the 18th century, and a small bath-house was built, where genteel and elderly patients were encouraged to take a dip in the healing waters of the "heather spa", as it was known. Early Victorian times saw the development of the hydros - hydropathic treatment hotels, providing hot and cold treatments based on the ideas of Dr Preissnitz of Austria who, in 1843, opened Britain's first hydro at nearby Ben Rhydding.

The coming of the railway lines from Leeds and Bradford in the 1860s and 70s, during a period of growth in the Yorkshire woollen industry, saw Ilkley take on a new role as a fashionable commuter town. Wool manufacturers and their better paid employees came, not only to enjoy the superb amenities, but to build handsome villas in West Riding gritstone. If Bradford and Leeds was where people made their "brass", then it was usually Ilkley where they spent it. Even today, Ilkley sports some remarkable and opulent Victorian architecture as proof of this.

Ilkley's patrons and well-to-do citizens gave the town a splendid Town Hall, library, Winter Gardens, and King's Hall and a sense of elegance is still present along the Grove. It is still a delight to have morning coffee in the famous Betty's coffee house, and discerning shoppers will find a wealth of choice, some in a perfectly preserved Victorian arcade, complete with beautiful potted palms and balconies.

Few places in the North can equal Ilkley Moor or, more correctly, Rombalds Moor, as it should be known. The Ilkley Moor made famous in the song is, strictly speaking, only the tract of ancient open common land which lies within the old township of Ilkley. The moorland, much of it still covered in heather, is an area of national importance for its archaeology. There is a series of mysteriously marked cup and ring stones dating, like the Swastika stones, from the Bronze age. Almost in the centre of the moor is an ancient stone circle which hints at this being a site of some religious importance. Only the keen walker is likely to find these, located high up on the moor, though there is a fine example of a cup-and-ring stone in the lower part of St Margaret's Churchyard on Queen's Road.

La Sila, 7 Grove Promenade, Ilkley Tel: 01943 601908

La Sila, which can be found on Grove Promenade in the centre of Ilkley, is the best Italian restaurant in the area. It is owned and personally-run by Vittorio and Luigi who are genuinely Italian. The menus are extensive and feature the

416

Keighley and Worth Valley Railway

Brontë Parsonage, Haworth

best of traditional Italian cuisine, especially Southern Italian dishes. The atmosphere is lively and exciting and, just like in Italy, quite laid back. To complement your meal the bar stocks a good range of Italian wines and spirits. There is plenty of room but it is a good idea to book ahead at weekends.

The Moorview Hotel, 104 Skipton Road, Ilkley
Tel: 01943 600156

The Moorview Hotel is only a five minute walk from the centre of Ilkley and provides an ideal touring base for a Yorkshire Dales holiday. The house was built in 1879 as the residence of a famous Ilkley merchant and adventurer - Joseph Smith - whose initials can still be seen etched on the glass of the front door. The imposing stone building has since been carefully and tastefully converted into a hotel providing every modern convenience while still retaining its original Victorian character. The beautiful gardens run down to the Dales Way and the banks of the River Wharfe where it is often possible to observe a wide range of wildlife, including kingfishers and badgers. The bedrooms are generously proportioned and are equipped with a colour TV and drinks tray. Most have en-suite facilities and family accommodation is available. The rural setting of Moorview means that there are views of the Wharfe valley or Ilkley Moor from many

418

rooms. A comfortable guest lounge is available which features the original plasterwork, and a log fire in winter months. A selection of newspapers and business magazines are always available here too. The proprietor, Christine Head, can offer local knowledge of beauty spots and walks, with a wide range of maps and guidebooks, to help you make the most of your stay. A good Yorkshire breakfast is served each morning and packed lunches can be provided.

Riverside Hotel, Riverside Gardens, Ilkley Tel: 01943 607338

A short distance from the Old Bridge is the Riverside Hotel, a fine establishment run by Kristine Dobson and her family for 24 years. Open all day, the hotel's public bar has an attractive open log fire and French doors open onto a beer garden which overlooks the River Wharfe. The decor is traditional with stone walls and a brick fireplace. There is also a fine restaurant offering a variety of home-cooked lunches and evening meals including traditional roasts on Sundays. Behind the bar is a good selection of hand-pulled beers. There is accommodation available which is of the same high standard as the rest of the establishment. The nine en-suite letting rooms are of varying sizes and feature television and drinks tray.

The Riverside Hotel is set in the Riverside Gardens where there is a range of additional amenities. There are children's play areas including rides and a riverside cabin sells ice cream, candy floss and snacks. Between Easter and September, rowing boats can be hired for trips between the Old and New Bridges. The location makes this ideal for golfers, walkers and cyclists. This family-run hotel is well-recommended.

Looking at a map of the area, many people's attention is drawn to the curiously named Cow and Calf Rocks, which form a striking moor-edge landmark above Ben Rhydding. The Cow is a great gritstone outcrop concealing an old quarry, popular with climbers, while the freestanding Calf is a giant boulder.

To the south of Keighley, the road follows the line of the Keighley and Worth Valley Railway to Haworth. This restored steam railway line passes through some attractive small villages and some notable stations. Keighley Station itself is Victorian and the five miles of railway that runs to Oxenhope is run by volunteers.

DAMENS was at one time the smallest railway station in the world and Edwardian OAKWORTH will look familiar to many - it featured in the classic film 'The Railway Children' and "Sherlock Holmes".

The railway also has a station in that most popular of Yorkshire tourist spots, HAWORTH. Once a bleak, moorland town in a dramatic setting that fired the romantic imaginations of the Brontë sisters, it has been transformed into a lively, attractive place, with wonderful tea-houses, street theatre and antique and craft shops, very different to how it must have been in the Brontës' day. It was then a thriving, industrial town, squalid amidst the smoke from its chimneys, filled with the noise of the clattering looms, which were rarely still. It is, however, worth exploring the ginnels and back roads off the steeply rising High Street, to get a feeling of what the place was like in the days of the Brontës.

One might also choose to take the leafy paths on the outskirts of the town that lead over stone bridges and sparkling streams, past grey stone mills, with the occasional

420

steam train rushing past. The Worth Valley Steam Railway sheds always make for a fascinating visit, where you can watch the volunteers repair the huge steam engines.

The Parsonage, built in 1789, is the focus of most Brontë pilgrimages. The Brontë Society have restored the interior to be as close as possible to how it was when the sisters were here. There are exhibitions and displays of contemporary material, personal belongings, letters and portraits, as well as a priceless collection of manuscripts, first editions and memorabilia in the newer extension.

Brontë enthusiasts can also sit in the Black Bull, where Branwell sent himself to an early grave on a mixture of strong Yorkshire ale, opium and despair (although the last two are not available here these days, we can heartily recommend the ale!)

The Post Office, from where the sisters sent their manuscripts to London publishers, is still as it was, as is the Sunday School at which they all taught. Sadly the church which they all attended no longer exists, although Charlotte, Emily and Branwell, Anne is buried in Scarborough, all lie in a vault in the newer church, which dates from 1879.

The countryside around Haworth inspires the modern visitor as much as it did the Brontës. This is excellent walking country, and if you should get the chance, it is worth taking a trip via the Penistone Hill Country Park, following the rough track by old moorland farms to the Brontë falls and stone footbridge, for so long one of the sisters' favourite walks. If you are feeling energetic, you may wish to continue on to the romantic, deserted ruins of Top Withins Farm, said to have been the inspiration for the setting of "Wuthering Heights".

Half way down the historic cobbled Main Street in Haworth you will find Mamin's. This delightful tea shop is an ideal place to stop for refreshments during a busy day's sightseeing or shopping. The building was originally four small cottages with much of it dating back approximately 250 years. Some occupants of these cottages must therefore have been neighbours of the famous Brontë family. The owner, Marilyn Brophy, has obviously worked hard to create a warm and welcoming atmosphere and has succeeded. The pleasant surroundings are further enhanced by displays on the walls of original water-colours, acrylics, oils and exclusive prints, most of which were painted by the proprietor and all of which are for sale. The café offers a wide range of speciality teas, coffees served in cafétiéres, and cold drinks, as well as a good selection of delicious hot and cold meals, sandwiches, pastries and sumptuous gateaux and desserts, all served by smart and friendly staff. Particularly recommended are the BIG Yorkshire Puddings and the home-made jam and cream scones. This is an exceedingly friendly establishment with a homely feel to it - discover it, and you are sure to return.

Mamin's, 52 Main Street, Haworth Tel: 01535 647370

About two-thirds of the way down Haworth's old cobbled Main Street, in one of the terraced rows which pre-date the Brontës but still retain their original style, is Spooks, a rather unusual shop. It specialises in the sale of books on the Paranormal, including such subjects as Dowsing, Divination and Psychic Development, and has a complementary range of Pendulums, Crystals, Cards, Crystal Balls, as well as a range of quality Aromotherapy Oils.

Unlike many shops which deal in the Occult, Spooks presents a light interior and the staff actively attempt to de-mystify the subject, believing that many people can benefit by developing their natural psychic abilities.

Services available include Tarot Reading, Clairvoyance and Palmistry, as well as healing and other therapy demonstrations. People often ask "why Spooks?" and "why in Haworth?". The staff say that the name was chosen for its simplicity and humour, to lighten what is sometimes taken as a rather contentious subject; and why in Haworth - well, the Brontës were well acquainted with ideas of survival of the spirit so why not Spooks?

422

Spooks, 22 Main Street, Haworth

The village of **OXENHOPE** lies to the south of Haworth and contains over 70 listed buildings, including a Donkey Bridge, two milestones, a mounting block, a cowshed and pigsty. The early farmhouses had narrow mullioned windows which gave the maximum light for weaving and some had a door at first-storey level so that the 'pieces' could be taken out. The first mill was built in 1792 and during the 19th century there were up to 20 mills producing worsted. 'The Railway Children' was made here in 1970, using local views and local people.

Between Halifax and Keighley is a wide expanse of moorland and the unusual sight of one of Britain's few wind farms.

Nearby is the mill-town of **HEBDEN BRIDGE**, characterised by the stepped formation of its houses which are stacked one on top of the other up the hill and reminiscent of a Cornish fishing village. A little known fact is that Hebden Bridge was one of the first purpose-built industrial towns in the world. It has seen many changes of fortune and today stands as a proud monument of an era which changed the entire world. Once filled with factories producing trousers and corduroy, it is now a place of

423

The Brontës

No lover of literature can possibly visit Yorkshire without making a trip to Haworth, former home of the famous Brontë sisters. Situated in a valley on the edge of rugged moorland to the south of the Aire Valley lies the small, bleak West Yorkshire village and it was to the Georgian parsonage that the Brontë family came in 1820 and where the sisters lived and wrote until 1849. It is now a museum containing such belongings as Charlotte's sewing box and Branwell Brontë's spectacles. Other old haunts include the Black Bull Inn at the top of the hill and the favourite footpath of the sisters to the Brontë Bridge and Waterfall.

Why not walk in the steps of the Bronte sisters on 'The Bronte Way'? It is a 40 mile middle distance linear footpath with a series of four guided walks available, linking those places which provided inspiration to the sisters. It was, for instance, Oakwell Hall near Batley which gave Charlotte her setting for Shirley Keeldar in the novel, 'Shirley'. A more exhilirating excursion could be taken to Top Withins, just outside Haworth, with has associations with 'Wuthering Heights'.

The route takes into account a great variety of scenery, from wild moorlands to pastoral countryside, triggering real images which the sisters so vividly brought to life in their work.

bookshops, antique shops, restaurants and a market, all open on Sundays.

One popular attraction is Automobilia, a traditional moorland textile mill converted to house a remarkable collection of Austin and Morris cars, motoring memorabilia, early cycles and motorbikes. The museum also has an unusual hire service, and for a fee, you can glide along the Pennine roads in an Austin Seven or Morris Eight to the envy of passers-by.

Overlooking the Rochdale Canal and Marina in the heart of this Pennine town lies **Hebden Lodge Hotel**. Owned and run by Michael and Layala Hatfield, the modest exterior of the building hides a wealth of true professional hotel management where the comfort and care of the guests is paramount. All of the 12 bedrooms are en-suite and the downstairs rooms have been thoughtfully adapted for disabled guests. From the Marina Bar you can relax and watch the working horses in harness pulling colourful barges along the Rochdale Canal. The restaurant offers a candlelit atmosphere in which to enjoy the five course dinners, choosing from a menu which changes daily. A friendly and comfortable place to stay in the heart of some wonderful countryside.

Hebden Lodge Hotel, New Road, Hebden Bridge
Tel: 01422 845272

While in this area, one should not miss out on a visit to HEPTONSTALL, a lovely, quiet and traditional moorland village, filled with winding, cobbled streets of cottages with mullioned windows, courts, inns and chapels. There is a famous old Grammar school, which houses an exhibition of Heptonstall's textile past, and the wonderful ruined church of St Thomas à Becket, which dominates the skyline. The blackened remains, with crooked towers, are a little eerie.

Curious travellers may feel compelled to visit the cheekily-titled village of SLACK BOTTOM. The inhabitants hereabouts must have had a bizarre sense of humour - the surrounding hills having been given such names as Back of Behind, Too To Hill, and others that cannot be repeated!

Following the River Calder and the Rochdale Canal to the southwest, along the A646, you will soon arrive in TODMORDEN. The town lies in a surprisingly open vale and from Todmorden Edge a wide panorama takes in a sweep from Bridestones Moor in the north to Walsden Moor in the south. When the canal was built by the Rochdale Canal Company, Todmorden began to grow and it quickly became an industrial town.

Several famous names are linked with Todmorden. Sir John Crockroft, who received the Nobel prize for splitting the atom in 1932, came from the town as did John Fielden, MP for Oldham. John Fielden is probably noted in history for obtaining the 'Ten Hour Act' making it illegal to work for more than ten hours a day thus improving factory conditions.

Among the various visitor attractions in the town there is the Amateur Astronomy Centre offering tours of the site (to groups only) including camera obscura and a planetarium show.

The town enjoys a fine Victorian legacy of which the Town Hall, sometimes called the 'Parthenon', is the centrepiece. Opened in 1875 it initially straddled the Yorkshire/Lancashire border due to the location of the river which passes underneath it! The classically styled pediment depicts figures which represent cotton and wool manufacture and agriculture. Guided tours and teas are available on occasions.

Sandwiched between the River Calder and the Rochdale Canal, just outside Todmorden, you will find the **Calderbank Guest House**. Owned and run by Marilyn Wardroper, this converted mill owner's house, built in 1860, stands in one and a half acres of garden. Now a charming guest house, with five large, spacious rooms, it enjoys outstanding views over the Calder Valley and is a delightful place in which to relax and be taken care of. The garden, with lawns, outdoor seating and plenty of shrubbery, is a haven for birdlife and ideal for children. Barbecues are held out here when the weather permits and there is also a tea garden, famous in the area for its cream teas. A relaxed and friendly establishment with a flexible approach to meal times.

Calderbank Guest House, Shaw Wood Road, Todmorden
Tel: 01706 816188

The A646 on the other side of Hebden Bridge will take one to **MYTHOLMROYD**, home to the World Dock Pudding Championships which are held here every spring.

Dock Pudding is unique to this small part of the country and is made from the weed 'Polygonum Bistorta' or sweet dock (which must never be confused with the larger docks that are commonly used for easing nettle stings). In spring the plant grows profusely and local people pick it by the bagful; the docks are then mixed with young nettles and other essential ingredients and cooked to produce a green and slimy delicacy the appearance of which is found by many to be rather off-putting. It is often served with bacon after having been fried in bacon fat and is believed to be an essential spring medicine which reputedly cures acne and cleanses the blood.

Nearby HALIFAX has one of Yorkshire's most impressive examples of municipal architecture, the large and beautiful Piece Hall. It possesses a large quadrangle, where regular markets are held, surrounded by colonnades and balconies, behind which is a host of interesting shops and commercial outlets. There is also an art gallery with a varied programme of contemporary exhibitions and workshops. Built in the 17th century, it was originally utilised for the selling of cloth or pieces, and in the 18th century, after having been allowed to fall into disrepair, was renovated with the permission of Lord Ingram.

The Town Hall is another notable building, designed by Sir Charles Barry, who also designed the Houses of Parliament. and there is an attractive Borough Market, constructed in cast-iron and glass, with an ornate central clock.

In Gibbet Street stands a grisly reminder of the past - a replica of a guillotine - the original blade being kept in the Piece Hall Museum. There are a lot of hidden places in old Halifax to explore; from Shear's Inn, an old weavers' inn below the centre, one can walk up the cobbled Boy's Lane, very little changed from Victorian times; or trace out the ancient Magna Via, a medieval path to the summit of Breacon Hill.

Halifax also has the largest parish church in England, of almost cathedral sized proportions, which dates from the 12th and 13th centuries, although most of the present building is from the 15th century. There is a lovely wooden ceiling which was constructed in 1635, and visitors should look out for "Old Tristram", a life-sized wooden effigy of a beggar, reputedly based on a local character, which was once the church poor box.

The Calderdale Industrial Museum, which houses still-working looms and mill-machinery, the "Horses at Work Museum" at Dobbin's Yard and the Bankfield Museum are all worthy of a visit. A new addition is Eureka!, which introduces children of all ages to science with a host of hands on exhibits and do-it-yourself experiments.

Shibden Hall and Park, about two miles out of town, is somewhere very special that should not be missed. The Old hall itself lies in a valley on the outskirts of the town and is situated in 90 acres of parkland. The distinctive timber-framed house dates from 1420 and is deliberately furnished to reflect the various periods of its history. The 17th century barn behind the Hall houses a fine collection of horse-drawn vehicles and the original buildings have been transformed into a 19th century village centre with a pub, estate-worker's cottage, and saddler's, blacksmith's, wheelwright's and potter's workshops.

Mountain Hall, Brighouse and Denholme Road, Queensbury
Tel: 01274 816258

A couple of miles north of the town is QUEENSBURY where you will find Mountain Hall. The hall was constructed in 1913 by a local mill owner in the village of

429

Mountain, as a 'social and educational institute' for his workforce, and was known as The Speak Institute. Although maintaining its exterior appearance the building has recently been fully modernised and now, as well as functioning as a hotel for special interest practical courses including such subjects as Psychic Awareness, Complementary Therapies, Hypnotism, and Past Life Regression, it is also hired to groups for their own seminars.

The hotel is thought to be the highest in Yorkshire, being situated at 1200 feet, and affords spectacular panoramas by day or night. In keeping with its current use, there is a resident (but innocuous) ghost! The hotel, and the courses held there, are under the personal supervision of the proprietors.

Huddersfield and Holmfirth

HUDDERSFIELD may seem an unlikely visitor centre of this region, but its streets and Yorkshire stone buildings, blackened with years of industrialisation, have an honest, no-nonsense charm that have a certain appeal.

It has a gritty, industrial atmosphere with steep, often cobbled streets, a mixture of terraced houses, older millstone grit cottages and larger Victorian dwellings, some interesting pubs and a skyline dominated by the scars and marks of its industrialisation. The wealthy lords of the manor hereabouts were the Ramsdens, and much of the grand architecture in the centre is due to their efforts. There is a very impressive railway station, designed by James Pigott of York and built between 1846-50. Other buildings of interest include the Italianate Town Hall, the neo-Gothic Parish Church of St Peter and Bryam Arcade. The Brook Street market is another pleasant place to wander around.

The outskirts of the town are interesting, and many visitors may decide to head towards the highest point in the area, Castle Hill, about two miles south of Huddersfield. It is

430

considered one of the most important archaeological sites in Yorkshire. The hill, a high moorland ridge overlooking the Colne and Holme Valleys has been occupied as a place of defence since Stone Age times, circa 20,000BC, by what are believed to be Neolithic herdsmen from mainland Europe - simple tools, flints, bone needles, combs and pottery have been unearthed to substantiate this. The magnificent ramparts of the Iron Age Fort, built here in 600BC, later destroyed by fire, can still be seen. In 1147 the Normans restored the earthworks, building a motte and bailey castle here which was apparently used as a base for hunting. The hill was also used as a beacon during the times of the Armada and also during the Napoleonic wars. At present it is crowned with the Jubilee Tower, built in 1897, to celebrate Queen Victoria's reign. It stands at just under 1000 feet above sea level and apart from offering wonderful panoramic views of the valleys, it also houses an exhibition of the hill's long history.

The Lodge Hotel, Birkby, Huddersfield Tel: 01484 431001
Fax: 01484 421590

Dating back to the mid-19th century, the magnificent Lodge Hotel, purchased by Garry and Kevin Birley in 1989, has gradually been restored to its former glory. Designed by Edgar Wood, a prominent architect of the time, the hotel is the epitome of grandeur. The hotel boasts eleven magnificent en-suite rooms of very high quality and the restaurant has an intimate atmosphere in which to enjoy the exceedingly fine cuisine. The table d'hôte lunch and dinner menus make use of fresh seasonal produce and feature innovative dishes. To complement your meal there is an extensive wine list which includes classic European and popular new world wines. Set in beautiful grounds with a private car park, The Lodge is also ideal for small conferences, weddings and private dinner parties and in summer, traditional cream teas can be enjoyed on the lawn. Located just five minutes from the M62, the hotel is an ideal base for exploring the area.

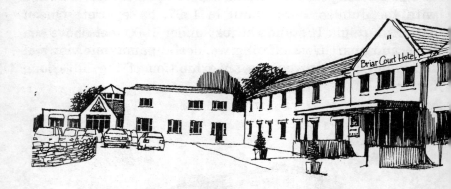

Briar Court Hotel and Da Sandro Pizzeria Ristorante,
Halifax Road, Birchencliffe, Huddersfield
Tel: 01484 519902/512845

In a convenient location just off the M62 motorway, on the road to Huddersfield lies the Briar Court Hotel. This purpose-built hotel offers a warm and friendly welcome and provides all its guests with the highest standard of service to ensure their stay is enjoyable. There are 47 bedrooms all with en-suite facilities and an array of creature comforts. The comfortable lounge bar and tastefully decorated restaurant are open to guests and non-residents. Alternatively, you may choose to dine in the extremely popular adjoining Italian

432

restaurant, Da Sandro, where there is a mouth-watering menu of pizza and pasta along with traditional Italian dishes and, of course, heavenly desserts. Briar Court Hotel is within a short drive from Haworth, Holmfirth and the attractions of South Yorkshire.

Situated in the Huddersfield suburb of LOCKWOOD, close to the local railway station, is the aptly named Railway public house. Solidly built in the mid 19th century of eye-catching Yorkshire stone this charming pub has been run by Kevin Schofield since December 1994. The comfortable lounge bar, tap room and inviting games and function room have been completely redecorated and Kevin has made great efforts to attract a clientele from all walks of life. There is a good range of drinks to tempt you, cider, stouts, lagers and hand pulled ales and lunchtime food will soon be available. This is very much a locals' pub, but all visitors can expect a warm and friendly welcome.

The Railway, 1 Park Road, Lockwood, Huddersfield
Tel: 01848 540290

Tolson Memorial Museum is Huddersfield's History Book. Situated in Ravensknowle Park, the museum concentrates on the history of the town from prehistoric times to the present. The many exciting displays cover 'Going Places', the story of transport and travel, and 'Comers-In' which tells of the first inhabitants of the area. The days of industrial revolution, so important in the growth of the town, and of political protest are also faithfully recreated. With a year-round programme of special events and activities this is certainly a museum not to be missed.

Tolson Memorial Museum, Ravensknowle Park, Wakefield Road, Huddersfield Tel: 01484 530591/541455

Nearby **ALMONDBURY** has a charming old part with several interesting 17th-century buildings. The Church of Old Hallows dates from the 13th century, with lovely 15th-century stained glass windows. However, if you get the chance, look up at the ceiling and observe the wonderful carved bosses, representing the instruments of passion, in grotesque faces, a half-moon, a face with two tongues and a head with three eyes and two noses.

GOLCAR, less than three miles from Huddersfield to the west, was once an important woollen weaving centre, and one can still see the weavers' cottages with their long mullioned windows. It is also the home of the Colne Valley Museum, based in 19th century cottages converted to their original state. One loom chamber has been turned into a gas-lit cloggers' workshop, whilst the ground floor is a Victorian parlour. The village is also the start of the 12 mile Colne Valley circular walk along paths and old tracks between moorland farms to Marsden and beyond - an interesting place to discover the hidden places of the Valley which can be done in stages, sometimes using public transport. A booklet explaining it is on sale in the museum.

Situated high up in the Pennines on the main Huddersfield to Rochdale road, at **SCAMMONDEN**, is the **Lower Royal George Inn**. Built at the end of the last century, this quaint establishment has breathtaking panoramic views of the surrounding moorland. Stephen and Margaret Lowe came here 13 years ago and have really stamped their own personality on the place. Tastefully

434

Holmfirth

decorated and furnished, a warm, friendly welcome awaits all visitors, new or regular. The bar is stocked with fine ales and the menu offers a range of good wholesome food. This inn, where good old fashioned values matter, is well worth finding.

Lower Royal George, New Hey Road, Scammonden, Huddersfield Tel: 01848 842455

Also in the village of Scammonden lies the Moorland Lodge. Dating back to the late 18th century the building, formerly a coaching inn on the Rochdale to Huddersfield road, offers fine views of the deep valley and Scammonden Dam. The picture postcard setting is rivalled by the outstanding interior of the establishment; beautiful woodwork, fine decoration and carefully chosen ornaments and pictures.

For the past 19 years Mary Lockwood and her daughter, Alison, have been offering superb home-cooking and excellent accommodation from the Lodge. The restaurant, open at the weekends and by special arrangement, offers beautifully prepared dishes; Mary has a fine reputation for her cooking. The five very individual, cosy bedrooms all enjoy the same spectacular views of the surrounding countryside and the well tended gardens. Guests are greeted in the morning with a full farmhouse breakfast, setting them up for the day. The

Lodge is in an ideal position to visit the many attractions of the area.

Moorland Lodge, New Hey Road, Scammonden, Huddersfield Tel: 01484 843398

The nearby village of SLAITHWAITE is situated in the valley of the River Colne, five miles west of Huddersfield. The moor capped hills rise on either side of the wooded valley with streams fed by numerous springs. Parallel to the river is the Huddersfield Narrow Canal which was constructed in 1795 linking Huddersfield with Manchester. This was the main form of transport until a road was built in the 1820s.

Smuggling was at one time rife in this valley and this led to the legend of the 'Moon Rakers'. Contraband goods were sometimes hidden from excise officers in the canal and on one occasion men were caught when pulling the item out again. They supposedly evaded the officers by claiming that they were trying to capture the reflection of the moon! This event is celebrated to this day at a Moon Raking Festival held each February.

Further along the valley lies MARSDEN whose name means 'boundary valley', appropriate as it happens, lying as it does at the head of the Colne valley near to the Yorkshire border. Nearby STANDEDGE is a natural point at which to cross the Pennines because at 1,300 feet it is the lowest point

437

on the watershed. The packhorse road, the earliest known route over Standedge, can still be followed on foot and the first turnpike road made in 1759 by John Metcalf ('Blind Jack' of Knaresborough) is still to be found by various landmarks in the village. The Standedge Trail, running from the north of Marsden, has a unique concentration of remains from canal, rail and turnpike eras. Standedge Tunnel is the longest canal tunnel in the country, carrying the Huddersfield Narrow Canal, but is now derelict. A railway tunnel runs parallel with the canal tunnel extending 3 miles through the sandstone bedrock between Marsden and the village of Diggle in Greater Manchester.

The Coach and Horses Hotel, Manchester Road, Marsden, Huddersfield Tel: 01484 844241

Situated high up on the A62, just a couple of miles outside Marsden and with breathtaking views in every direction, is the Coach and Horses Hotel. This is a former coaching inn, as the name implies, on the Pennine route between Lancashire and Yorkshire. There are 11 comfortable, double bedrooms, all with en-suite facilities. The smashing restaurant offers an interesting and varied menu with special provision for babies and young children. Open for lunch and dinner during the week and all day at weekends, this is a super family inn.

438

MELTHAM is situated five miles southwest of Huddersfield and nestles in the Pennine hills below West Nab. The name is quite ancient; 'Melt' signifies a moor covered with cloudberry bushes - so Melt-ham is 'the home amidst cloudberry bushes'.

Three of the village's customs have been carried on for many years; the distribution of free sweets to the children by the shopkeepers on Collap Monday, the day before Shrove Tuesday; the singing of carols with the band in the centre of the village on Christmas Eve; and the annual Whitsuntide Walk around the village by the different congregations of churches and chapels, accompanied by the local brass band.

The Will's O'Nat's, Blackmoorfoot Road, Meltham,
Huddersfield Tel: 01484 850078

Any inn with a name such as **Will's O'Nat's** arouses the curiosity and attracts the attention. The origin of the name goes back to days when nicknames were used to distinguish son from father and brother from uncle, a custom sometimes used even today. 'Will's O'Nat's' meant simply 'William, son of Nathaniel', but as a name for a fine old country inn it could hardly be bettered.

Standing high up on the hills above Meltham, with views on all sides across open country, the pub's setting

Hebden Bridge

Piece Hall, Halixfax

complements its name. Deer Hill and Blackmoorfoot Reservoir can both be seen in the distance across the valley.

Kim and Anne Schofield are rightly proud of the hospitality they provide and the excellent food on offer. Freshly prepared and cooked, all dishes are listed on the blackboard and offer something to suit everyone, with a wide range of hot and cold dishes. A particular speciality is the beef, mushroom and red wine casserole. The large lounge area is pleasant and comfortable with wonderful views of the countryside. For added interest, in the lounge are the many photographs of old Huddersfield showing trams, horse and carts and buildings that have long since gone. Will's O'Nat's makes both an intriguing and a satisfying stop-over for visitors to the area.

While in this area, many will no doubt feel compelled to visit HOLMFIRTH, best known as the location of the television series "Last Of The Summer Wine", and despite the commercialisation, their trip will not be disappointing.

Visitors can take a trip past the real Sid's Café, Nora Batty's cottage and sit in the famous pub. The rest of the town offers a network of side lanes, courts and alleyways with some interesting shops and cafés besides. The terraces of weavers' cottages are typical of a town famous for its production of wool textiles. As with so many of these moors villages, there is a lot of water surrounding and in its time, Holmfirth has suffered three major floods, of which the flood of 1852 was the worst. The nearby Bilbury Reservoir burst its banks, killing 81 people and destroying mills, cottages and farms at the cost of 7,000 jobs. A pillar near the church records the height of the waters.

The lovely Georgian church was built in 1777-8 in neo-classical style to the designs of Joseph Jagger. The gable faces the street and the tower is constructed at the eastern end against a steep hillside. Also in Holmfirth is the delightful Holmfirth Postcard Museum (above the library), based on nearby Balmforth's - the country's leading producers of the traditional saucy seaside postcard. The displays also include cards from over nearly a century, including patriotic cards from World War I, less sentimental ones from World War II and a moving audio-visual documentary presentation of the 1852 flood.

The Old Bridge Hotel was built from scratch in the mid 1980s by the owners, Hervey and Dorothy Woodhead. This charming hotel and restaurant in Holmfirth provides the very best in luxury dining and accommodation. All the 20 bedrooms have been individually designed to the highest standard and offer the latest in comfort. There is also a comfortable lounge area and a large lounge bar, as well as a friendly restaurant, all with views overlooking the River Holme. The menus are imaginative and include a wide variety of dishes from home and abroad, all freshly prepared. Hervey and Dorothy also cater for banquets and receptions. A warm welcome awaits all visitors.

Old Bridge Hotel and Restaurant, Holmfirth, Huddersfield
Tel: 01484 681212

The small surrounding villages, such as UPPERTHONG, NETHERTHONG and THONGSBRIDGE are worthy of exploration. Thong, which is common to all three names, comes from the Danish 'thing' meaning a place of military gathering. The prefix of 'nether' may seem inappropriate for a village that is 700 feet above sea level, but in relation to its neighbour, Upperthong, it is indeed lower!

The **Holme Valley Camping and Caravan Park** is built on the site of an old dyeing and finishing mill once owned by the Lancaster family. Nothing remains of the mill now except for the picturesque dam, fringed with silver birch, and the stone-built store, now converted into one of the park buildings. The park is spread over 8 acres of woodland and includes a large lake, stocked with carp, tench, roach, rudd and bream. Fishing rights are available to the park patrons with a day ticket. As well as accommodating touring campers and caravaners, the owners, Hazel and Philip Peaker have a small number of static vans for hire and, for those little emergencies, the site shop is there to satisfy your all requirements. The picture postcard setting and the luxurious amenities available, including a solarium, make this a splendid base from which to tour the surrounding 'Last of the Summer Wine' countryside.

Holme Valley Camping and Caravan Park, Thongsbridge, Near Holmfirth Tel: 01484 665819

DENBY DALE, a few miles to the east, is famous for its production of gigantic meat pies, a tradition which was started to celebrate King George III's recovery from mental illness. Several have been produced since then, to celebrate

443

such occasions as the Battle of Waterloo and the repeal of the Corn Laws. One of the most recent was in 1964, when the pie measured 18 feet in length and weighed six and a half tons. The last one was made in 1987 and the dish used is now on display just outside the village.

The Grove Freehouse, 1 Station Road, Skelmanthorpe, Huddersfield Tel: 01484 863082

Situated in the heart of the village of **SKELMANTHORPE** is **The Grove Freehouse**. This magnificent building dates back to the early 18th century, when it was listed as a farm and an inn - at one time in its history the building was used as a slaughterhouse! Today the inn, solidly built of fine Yorkshire stone, is quaint with a homely and welcoming atmosphere. Four years ago the then tenants, John and Margaret Drury, decided to buy the inn and went into partnership with John and Jess Ogden. They have not looked back since. There is a cosy intimate restaurant and the excellent home-cooked food can either be served here or in the main bar where there is a selection of fine ales from which to choose. When the partners took over the inn they added five comfortable and superbly furnished bedrooms to the rear of the original building. With full facilities the rooms have the added bonus of being part of the inn and its wonderful hospitality.

444

Situated within easy reach of the M1 motorway near the village of SCISSETT and lying in 40 acres of beautiful parkland is Bagden Hall Hotel. Owned by Robert and Mandy Braithwaite, this grand old country house was created by Robert's father from a semi-derelict state. The glorious grounds include a nine hole, par three, golf course. All the 17 bedrooms have been magnificently furnished and include all the modern day comforts; there are a number of period rooms including a honeymoon suite and a room with a four poster bed. The restaurant, open for lunch and dinner, is tastefully decorated creating an wonderful atmosphere to complement the delicious food. The cuisine, prepared by an expert chef, is a mix of traditional and modern English food with a hint of classical French. This is an excellent hotel with plenty to enjoy.

Bagden Hall, Wakefield Road, Scissett, Near Huddersfield
Tel: 01484 865330

The minor country roads to the south of the A642 Wakefield to Huddersfield Road lead to the lovely village of EMLEY, three miles east of KIRKBURTON. Like many other villages in the area, Emley has become a mixture of old and new houses. The famous TV mast, which is one of Europe's tallest structures, stands on Emley Moor and is over 1,000 feet high.

445

The village was granted a royal charter in 1253 to hold a weekly market and an annual five day fair. The remains of a market cross stand in the centre of the village and each May, on the occasion of Emley Feast, it is painted with whitewash.

The Green Dragon, 30 Church Street, Emley,
Near Huddersfield Tel: 01924 848275

Situated in the village centre, and originally a row of early 18th-century cottages, is the beautiful country inn, the **Green Dragon**. This used to be the house of the well known village family of James Gill, a joiner from Pontefract, who moved to Emley and became an innkeeper, calling his house the Green Dragon. The establishment remained in the family for many years but is now run by Amanda Rowley and her partner Steve. The beamed ceilings add to the cosy feel of the pub interior where there is always a warm welcome. As you would expect in this part of the country the menu provides an excellent choice of dishes, including the famous Yorkshire Pudding to start the Sunday roast lunch. A popular hostelry with locals and visitors.

On the outskirts of Emley you will find **White Cross Farm**, a working farm with beef cattle and sheep, which also offers first-rate farmhouse bed and breakfast accommodation. The house which originally occupied this site was constructed in the 11th century and was inhabited by Cistercian monks from Byland Abbey near Helmsley. The splendid present-day farmhouse dates back to the 16th century and was once the home of a Royalist captain who was captured by Cromwell following the fall of Wakefield on Whit Sunday, 1644.

White Cross Farm, Ash Lane, Emley, Nr. Huddersfield
Tel: 01924 848339

The present owner, Marie Gill, offers her guests comfortable accommodation in three rooms, one en-suite, with wonderful Yorkshire hospitality.

Yorkshire Sculpture Park

447

Bretton Hall, a handsome neo-classical mansion built in 1720, stands in the private grounds of Bretton College. This superbly landscaped estate of enclosed parkland and mature trees is open to the public and contains miles of walks, lakes and gardens. Part of the gardens is taken up by the Yorkshire Sculpture Park, a unique outdoor setting for permanent and changing exhibitions of important works of sculpture. The Park was founded in 1977, and as well as being known for its major exhibitions, it is also famous for its permanent collection of sculptures by artists such as Henry Moore, Elizabeth Frink and Barbara Hepworth.

At certain times it is possible to see sculptors working on site and visitors can also create their own pieces in one of the public sculpture workshops. In recent years, the Yorkshire Sculpture Park has taken a further step forward by opening an Access Sculpture Trail which has been specially designed for disabled and elderly people. There is also disabled access to the park shop and Bothy Café. The Country Park is open daily and is best reached from the small car park and visitor centre which is situated just off the A637 north of junction 38 on the M1. The entrance to the Sculpture Park is in **WEST BRETTON**, a short distance further north.

Although situated in the lovely South Yorkshire village of **HIGH HOYLAND**, the **High Hoyland Centre** is located in a former church that was once part of the Wakefield Diocese and has close connections with West Yorkshire. It is now a popular self-catering centre not far from Bretton College. The College administrates the transformed church which is available for parties of up to 24 people. Further details from Rachel Davies, Administrator, Bretton Hall, West Bretton, Wakefield. Tel: 01924 830240.

Situated on a ridge of hills in the village of **WHITLEY**, south west of Dewsbury, lies **The Woolpack Inn**. Well over 200 years old, the inn was originally one room in a series of back to back cottages and it remained this size until 1966 when the property was bought by a local businessman. As and when the cottages became vacant the inn was extended

Friends' School, Ackworth

to provide a cocktail bar, a small snug (the Pine Bar) and in 1968 the Rosewood Grill was created. In 1990 the building was totally refurbished and extended to provide larger facilities and 15 en-suite bedrooms. The inn is now owned by Ralph Williams whose enthusiasm and hard work has ensured that the reputation of the establishment has grown to greater heights. The Head Chef, Bart, has been working here on and off for 25 years and he and his team provide an interesting and enticing menu, served in the cosy and intimate restaurant. Snacks are available in the bar where you can also sample a pint of one of the six different ales on tap. The Woolpack's aim is to provide the customer with a perfect setting and a perfect meal and this they certainly achieve with the help of Manager, Pepe, and Deputy Manager, Jennie. A delightful place to stay, run by a professional and friendly team.

The Woolpack Inn, Whitley Road, Whitley, Dewsbury
Tel: 01924 499999

MIRFIELD, to the southwest of Dewsbury, has some interesting buildings and a popular canal basin from where there is a summer waterbus service to nearby Brighouse, of brass-band fame. The town also has Brontë associations; Emily and Charlotte went to Roe Head School near here and

Emily based her novel "Agnes Grey" on Blake Hall, where she was governess.

If you happen to be a keen gardener, a truly top class garden centre can be found beside the A62 near Mirfield. Whiteley's Garden Centre in Leeds Road was named the Regional Garden Centre of the Year by the Garden Centre Association for three years in succession, between 1988 and 1990. The trophy is now on permanent display as Whiteley's was named outright winner when the competition came to an end in 1990. It has also recently been awarded the National Plant Centre of the Year, 1994/5.

Whiteley's Garden Centre, Whitegate, Leeds Road, Mirfield
Tel: 01924 495944

The centre is owned and managed by Dennis and Linda Whiteley who, along with their twenty friendly and well-trained staff, strive to offer their customers the widest range of top quality plantse. The centre employs a flair for display more commonly seen at the Chelsea Flower Show and takes great pride in introducing new and unusual varieties of garden and house plants. Dennis and Linda have successfully created a relaxed and unpressured environment, both in their indoor showrooms and in their beautifully maintained outdoor plant areas. They also offer their customers a range of garden furniture, fish and aquatics, barbecues, terracotta

451

pots, floral art arrangements, books and other gifts. Whiteley's Garden Centre is open every day, Monday to Saturday until 8pm and Sunday 10.30am to 4.30pm, throughout the spring and summer (closing at 5.30pm in Autumn and Winter) and can be found on an attractive green-belt site on the northern side of the A62 Huddersfield to Leeds road. It is easily reached by taking exit 25 off the M62, driving south for one mile, then picking up the eastbound A62 for another mile.

Geordie Pride Restaurant and New Inn, Child Lane, Roberttown Tel: 01924 402069

In the rural village of **ROBERTTOWN**, just off the A62, lies the family-run **Geordie Pride Hotel and New Inn**. The inn, formerly a farm, dates back to the 17th century and is a real must for beer lovers with a choice of five real ales. The old farm out-buildings have been converted into a delightful and elegant restaurant and a typical warm Yorkshire welcome is extended to all those who dine here. Keep an eye out for the collection of clock plates; there were over 70 at the last count. Across the road is the hotel, built of the local Yorkshire stone, where the same welcome is extended to overnight visitors. The cosy rooms have all the usual facilities and are designed with comfort in mind. A perfect oasis of hospitality in the heart of Brontë country.

Dewsbury to Pontefract

Inside a large bend of the M62 lies DEWSBURY, which probably has even less of a reputation as a tourist magnet than Huddersfield. It is an extremely old town which once had considerable influence. It remains the centre of Yorkshire's heavy woollen industry, filled as it is with old mills and warehouses. It has one of the region's oldest town centres with an imposing Town Hall designed by Henry Ashton and George Fox. It also has a number of other notable public and commercial buildings and a substantial shopping centre with a famous market.

The Church of All Saints is situated, according to legend, at the point where Saint Paulinus baptised converts in the river Calder. It dates from the 12th century although the tower was designed by the eminent York architect John Carr in 1767. The interior is interesting with several intriguing features, including fragments of an Anglo-Saxon Cross and coffin lids. It is, however, best known for its custom of tolling the Devil's Knell on Christmas Eve to ward off evil spirits with the bell that is known as Black Tom. Patrick Brontë was the curate of Dewsbury between 1809-11 and Charlotte taught at Wealds House School nearby which was run by Miss Wooler, who later gave her away when she married.

One place of interest to visit while in the town is Crow Nest Park, a landscaped park with a Victorian mansion which contains the Dewsbury Museum of Childhood, including a reconstructed classroom and a wonderful display of toys and dolls.

Dewsbury, famous as the home of Betty Boothroyd, Stan Laurel and Eddie Waring, now boasts one of the best hotel and restaurants in West Yorkshire. Heath Cottage dates back to the mid-19th century and the present owners, Peter and Molly Williamson, turned it into a hotel in 1983. Since then, the outdoor stabling has been converted into bedrooms

453

and a conference centre, built using stone from a disused mill, was added just last year. Through all their hard work Peter and Molly have created a wonderful establishment full of character and atmosphere.

Expertly decorated and furnished throughout, there are a total of 28 bedrooms all en-suite, spacious and well-equipped. A high quality restaurant, which is open to non-residents, is intimate and cosy. The food is of an excellent standard offering both a table d'hôte (Monday to Friday) and à la carte (daily except Sunday) menus. The bar area and lounge are colourful and cheery, ideal for a drink before or after your meal. The gardens and terrace are carefully tended and well-stocked with attractive flowers so in warmer weather drinks can be enjoyed outside.

Heath Cottage, Wakefield Road, Dewsbury
Tel: 01924 465399 / 457136

On Briestfield Road is the Shoulder of Mutton public house and restaurant run by John and Beryl Lodge. Dating back to the early 19th century the building was once part of the Armytage Estate. The restaurant area has been expertly converted from the old village forge and retains the high ceiling and rafters creating a charming room in which to eat and enjoy an excellent selection of dishes. Meals are served at lunchtime and evening and there is a lighter menu of bar

454

snacks. A traditional set price, three-course roast lunch is available on Sundays and children are catered for at all times. The restaurant can get busy and it is advisable to book at weekends and essential for Sunday lunchtime.

The games room is decorated with interesting pictures of local activities including many on sheep dipping, a traditional event which takes place annually and in which most villagers take part. In the pub is an extensive collection of Toby jugs and paintings by a local artist that are for sale. The beers are from the Websters brewery and there are occasional guest ales.

The Shoulder of Mutton, with its friendly atmosphere and excellent service, is an ideal place in which to take a break from sight-seeing and relax amid pleasant and peaceful countryside.

The Shoulder of Mutton, Briestfield, Dewsbury
Tel: 01924 848297

To the north of Dewsbury is BATLEY, with its pleasant cobbled market-place, handsome Town Hall and Library. The Central Chapel in the Square, built in 1869, was known as "Shoddy Temple" because of the amount of business done by local textile merchants on the steps after Sunday morning service (shoddy being a cloth made from old rags reworked with new wool - a technique of recycling materials to make a

Wragby Church

Chantry Chapel, Wakefield

cheaper cloth, hence the association with the term of abuse "shoddy"). The technique was discovered by Benjamin Law, later known as the "Shoddy King", who lies buried in the church.

Alder House is a very secret hotel, hidden away in the middle of busy Batley. Once you pass through the gates you feel as though you are miles away from the busy town and in the heart of the countryside. The hotel dates back to the early 18th century when the original Georgian building, from which the hotel was created, was known as Healey House. The house was converted into the elegant hotel that you see today in 1982 with a major extension added in 1991.

Alder House Hotel, Towngate Road, Healey Lane, Batley
Tel: 01924 444777

There are now a total of 21 bedrooms, all comfortably and tastefully furnished. The seven new executive rooms are even more luxurious with the additional features of a trouser press, hair dryer and teletext television. The hotel bar is warm and welcoming and features an open log fire for those cold winter evenings. The restaurant, Mulberry's, has an established reputation for serving fine traditional and French cuisine complemented by an extensive wine list. The restaurant is open to non-residents and is open every day except Sunday evening. The surrounding gardens extend to two acres and add to the peaceful and relaxed atmosphere.

Bagshaw Museum, Wilton Park, Batley Tel: 01924 472514

Situated in Wilton Park the Bagshaw Museum was started in the early 20th century by the local JP, Walter Bagshaw. His original idea of a small local history museum in one room of his extraordinary Gothic mansion was soon outgrown due to the enthusiasm of the local people of Batley. Today the local history collection sits alongside more exotic displays from around the world. The brilliant colours of the Far East are represented in Chinese and Japanese pottery and porcelain and there is a tantalising array of objects from Asia, Africa and the Americas. The Enchanted Forest exhibit transports you to the tropical rainforests and helps explain this complex environment. A visit to the museum is indeed an experience.

In BIRSTALL on the northern outskirts of Batley, Oakwell Hall Country Park is set in 100 acres of beautiful Yorkshire countryside in what was the estate to the Hall. There is plenty to occupy the whole family here; an equestrian arena, an orienteering course, many marked walks, picnic spots, a beautiful walled garden, herb garden and arboretum. Oakwell Hall, originally Elizabethan, is furnished in the style of the 17th century and featured in the

458

novel 'Shirley' by Charlotte Brontë. The original outbuildings contain an Environmental Discovery Centre and the shop is full of imaginative crafts and gifts. After exploring all the Hall and Park have to offer you will be ready for a visit to the Oak Tree Café!

Oakwell Hall Country Park, Nutter Lane, Birstall,
Near Batley Tel: 01924 474926

In **GOMERSAL** is the **Red House**, so called because of its unusual red brick construction which set it apart from the surrounding houses built of local Yorkshire stone.

Red House Museum, Oxford Road, Gomersal
Tel: 01274 872165

Built in 1660, the house was home to the Taylor family until 1920 and features as 'Briarmains' in Charlotte Brontë's novel 'Shirley'. In fact Charlotte was a visitor here in the 1830s as she was a friend of Mary Taylor. This era is beautifully recreated inside the house and gardens, with a mixture of original and reproduction furniture and other antique pieces, now open to the public as a museum. A stroll round the tranquil gardens will take you past the 'rose basket' and the 19th-century herb garden. This is a real step back in time to a fascinating, bygone age.

Prospect Hall Hotel, Prospect Road, Cleckheaton
Tel: 01274 873022

Prospect Hall Hotel was originally a private house built in Victorian times in the heart of CLECKHEATON. In its time it has been owned by the Trades Union Movement and used as a Trades Hall and, during the 1950s, it was the place to go to for dinner dances. In the mid 1980s the property, considerably rundown, was purchased by Jack Brook and, along with manager Sonia Hall, they have returned the hotel to its former glory. There are 40 bedrooms, 20 in a recently completed extension, all beautifully decorated and with all the modern facilities you would expect. The restaurant menus are extensive and along with the bar meals there is something to tempt everyone. Although this is a large hotel it has retained a friendly and personal feel and is an ideal place from which to tour the surrounding area.

Just off the main Dewsbury to Wakefield road lies the Spangled Bull pub, a delightful oasis where you are guaranteed a warm welcome by your hosts Beryl and Malcolm Flowers. The pub building dates back to the 17th century and was formerly Home Farm House where, later, beer was brewed. The interior houses a fine collection of gleaming brasses which can be enjoyed while relaxing on the traditional wooden settle seating. A visit at lunch time will enable you to sample the delights of honest Yorkshire home-cooking, including Yorkshire Pudding, accompanied by one of the fine ales from the bar. In summer, Malcolm decorates the exterior with hanging baskets which ensure that the picturesque pub is a sight worth visiting.

The Spangled Bull, 6 Town Street, Earlsheaton, Dewsbury
Tel: 01924 462949

The attractive town of OSSETT is midway between Wakefield and Dewsbury, close to junction 40 of the M1. Here, make a point of calling in at the Wellgate Centre, a new development of eleven shops and offices which has been carefully designed and constructed to blend in with the original architecture of the old town. The Centre is built around a well which was discovered on the site during

461

Thomas Chippendale

Thomas Chippendale was the first cabinet-maker to have a style of furniture named after him - previously this privilege went only to a reigning monarch. He was the chief exponent of the English 'Rococo' style - a style in which the decoration takes the form of seemingly living organisms alongside an often unnatural and assymetric mixture of vegetables and rock-like features. The style allowed great freedom and Thomas later adapted it to fit in with the new neo-classical style which came into fashion in the 1760s. It is this style which has given his work such fame today.

Thomas was a poor son of a Yorkshire joiner who worked alongside his father and served his apprenticeship at Otley, West Yorkshire. The Chippendales made furniture for the owner of Harewood Estate, from oak grown on the estate, and these superb examples of their work can be seen at Harewood house to this day.

It was as a result of this opportunity that Thomas gained the ambition he needed to travel to London with his bag of tools to begin a prosperous and rewarding career.

Further examples of Chippendale furniture can be seen at Newby Hall, and at Nostell Priory.

Thomas Chippendale died in London in December 1779, aged 61.

construction and which has now been turned into an attractive wishing well.

Continuing east the next big town is WAKEFIELD, one of the oldest towns in Yorkshire, which was a focal point even in Anglo-Saxon times. The town stands on a hill guarding an important crossing of the River Calder, which has been a major routeway ever since that period. Its defensive position has always been important too and indeed it was the Battle of Wakefield in 1460, when the Duke of York was defeated, that gave rise to the song "The Grand Old Duke of York".

There are also some strong arguments that Robin Hood came from this area - according to the Court Rolls, one Robin Hode lived here in the 14th century with his wife Matilda before fleeing to become an outlaw.

Wakefield is also well-known for its cycle of medieval miracle plays, which explore New and Old Testament stories in vivid language. The cycle is performed on the precinct in front of the Cathedral as part of the city's annual festival.

There are three main streets in the city - Westgate, Northgate and Kirkgate which still run exactly where they did in medieval times. The tiny Chantry Chapel on Chantry Bridge (the old Wakefield Bridge) dates from the mid-14th century and is the best of only four such examples of bridge chapels in England. It was believed to have been originally built by Edward IV to commemorate the brutal murder of his brother Edmund.

This modern city, close to the great Yorkshire coalfields, remains an important industrial and administrative centre and until 1974 was the county town of the West Riding. The status that this brought the town is evident in some of the grand architecture that can still be seen. Just north of the centre, on the site of the medieval town (where there are still old inns and courtyards) are some stately Georgian and Regency terraces and squares. There are fine civic buildings too, most notably the Town Hall, the County Courts and the huge County Hall, a beautiful building with a sumptuous interior, and the recently restored Edwardian Theatre Royal.

The town centre is mostly pedestrianised and dominated by the Cathedral with its 247 foot spire - the highest in Yorkshire.

There are some award-winning shopping centres, and much more to see in this lively, friendly town. The Elizabethan Grammar School, in Brook Street, near the market, has been superbly restored as an exhibition centre and small art gallery.

Wakefield Art Gallery, Wentworth Terrace, Wakefield
Tel: 01924 305796 Minicom 01924 305769

The Wakefield Art Gallery in Wentworth Terrace is located in an attractive former Victorian vicarage just a short stroll from the town centre. Collections include many early works by locally-born sculptors Henry Moore and Barbara Hepworth and important work by other major British modern artists.

Wakefield Museum, Wood Street, Wakefield
Tel: 01924 305351 Minicom 01924 305769

Wakefield Museum is located in an 1820s building in Wood Street, next to the Town Hall. Originally a music saloon and then a Mechanics' Institute, it now houses collections on the history and archaeology of Wakefield and its people from prehistoric times to the present day. There is also a permanent display of exotic birds and animals collected by the noted 19th-century traveller and naturalist Charles Waterton who lived at nearby Walton Hall where he created the world's first nature reserve. The museum hosts about six exhibitions every year.

Other museums to visit are the Stephen G Beaumont Museum, which houses an unusual exhibition of medical memorabilia, and the Yorkshire Mining Museum at Overton. Those looking for more outdoor diversions could take a walk through Thornes Park, with its lovely open parkland and gardens in which the remains of an early motte and bailey castle can be discovered amid the shrubbery.

Fayre Do's, 13 Silver Street, Wakefield Tel: 01924 291200

Situated in the little shopping-mall at 13 Silver Street is Fayre Do's, a delicatessen and tea-room. Owned by Barbara Hicks for the past three years, the shop offers specialist teas, coffees, cheeses, jams and cakes as well as home-made salads of many varieties. This delightful establishment is open all day but closes early on Wednesdays at 3pm. Barbara is also able to offer outside catering.

Fayre Do's provides a lunchtime delivery service of high quality sandwiches, salads, 'lunches-in-a-tub' and desserts, also available in the tea-rooms where the menu changes weekly and there is a tea-room special daily. Sandwiches are made with an international choice of bread and offer a wide range of fillings such as salami, smoked turkey breast, pastrami or cheeses. Fresh salads can be accompanied by onion bhajis and vegetable samosas and the intriguing 'lunch-in-a-tub' might contain garlic pasta or spiced chicken with apricots and almonds. Pies, tarts, gateaux, cheesecakes, baklava, strudel - whatever your taste, it's definitely worth making a detour to Silver Street!

Inns of Court, King Street, Wakefield Tel: 01924 375560

In the centre of Wakefield, opposite the Town Hall and close to the Crown Court, is the magnificent Inns of Court public house. Dating from the late 18th century and formerly called the Royal Oak, this building is as impressive inside as it is outside. Though it has been brought up-to-date in many ways your hosts, Barry and Wendy Spencer, have ensured that it still retains its charm and character. The inn is open all day during the week and at normal hours at the weekend, serving fine ales and weekday lunchtime bar meals. The outstanding quality of this establishment is extended to the four bedrooms; a super place to stay with the personal touch.

On the southern outskirts of the town is SANDAL, an attractive suburb of the town, with a remarkably well-hidden castle which should be visited by all lovers of medieval

466

history. This Norman motte and bailey structure was a stronghold for the Norman Manor of Wakefield, that covered most of the Calder Valley, and had been captured from the Saxons. This was the scene of the historic Battle of Wakefield which was fought in the midst of a snowstorm in December 1460, when the Duke of York was killed by Lancastrian forces and his head displayed at Micklegate Bar in York.

There is a Victorian monument to the battle on Castle Road, where flowers appear each year to commemorate the battle. The castle was garrisoned by Charles I's forces during the Civil War, and after a siege was demolished on the orders of Parliament. Little now remains apart from the foundations of this once impressive fortress.

Waterton Park Hotel, Walton Hall, Walton, Wakefield
Tel: 01924 257911

Waterton Park Hotel in WALTON, otherwise known as Walton Hall, is a beautiful Georgian mansion, located on an island surrounded by a 26-acre lake, once the ancestral home of Charles Waterton, an eccentric 19th-century traveller and naturalist. Following extensive travel, particularly in South America, Waterton returned to the family home at Walton Hall where he set about managing the estate as a protected environment for wildlife. It is thought to have been the first nature reserve. Today, guests to the hotel can benefit from

467

Waterton's legacy. The hotel is magnificent, set in 200 acres of parkland and overlooking a lake, with exquisite decorations and furnishings, wonderful food and, for the more energetically inclined, a leisure centre complete with swimming pool, solarium and sauna as well as golf and fly-fishing. This is an ideal location from which to visit the surrounding area, but the delights of the hotel will make it hard to leave.

Nearby is Pugneys Country Park, an area of man-made lakes created out of old mine subsidence areas where land has been cleverly reclaimed and restored for various leisure activities. Other areas of similar interest nearby are Newmillerdam, a nature and water reserve, based around an old mill dam, Wintersett Reservoir and the walks along the old Barnsley Canal.

Nostell Priory, some six miles south-east of Wakefield on the A638 Doncaster road, is one of the most popular tourist venues in this area. The word "priory" is misleading, and evokes the picture of an ecclesiastical structure, as it is in fact a large Palladian building that was built on the site of an old Augustinian priory. The land was originally owned by Ilbert de Lacy, and donated by his son Robert to the order in the 1100s, who dedicated it to St Oswald. The monks here were a mining fraternity and worked the local seams. At the time of the Dissolution, the Priory was owned by Sir Thomas Gargrave, Speaker of the House of Commons during the reign of Elizabeth I. It passed through various hands, the original building being used until 1733, when Rowland Winn commissioned James Paine to build a new house near the old priory, which was then pulled down. Paine was only 19 at the time and this was his first large project.

A further wing and extensions to the riding school and stables were added by Robert Adam in the time of Sir Robert's son, the fifth baronet, and more help was enlisted by James Rose, Antonio Zucchi and Thomas Chippendale.

The interior of the house is truly beautiful, with some of the most skilfully executed of Chippendale's works, including

468

Nostell Priory

the fascinating Doll's house, made in 1735, with some intricate and tiny pieces of furniture made by the great craftsman still inside. Of Nostell's many art treasures, perhaps the celebrated portrait of 'Thomas More and his Family', by Holbein, is the most famous. The grounds are also of outstanding beauty, with rose gardens, a lake, a summer house, beautiful trees and the 16th century Wragby Church. Facilities include a large adventure playground and picnic area, a craft centre in the stables, camp-site for tents and caravans, excellent coarse-fishing and a conference and banqueting suite located in the converted riding school. The Priory is still the home of Lord and Lady St Oswald, although the main part was donated to the National Trust by the late Lord St Oswald in 1953.

The rich, rolling countryside hereabouts is the home for many a picturesque village, and lovely ACKWORTH, with its famous 18th-century Quaker School, is one of these. Here, there are some lovely 18th- and 19th-century houses, as well as some notable Georgian almshouses. There is also a Victorian church at High Ackworth with a 15th-century tower. One sad reminder of the village's old history is the Plague Stone situated at the cross roads, where the unfortunate natives were required to leave money in vinegar in exchange for food.

The Beverley Arms, located at the crossroads of the A638 and A628, was built earlier this century although its prime location would lead one to believe that there has probably always been a inn on the site. Owned by the Mansfield Brewery, this is another of their high quality establishments.

The decor is traditional in styling and the welcome is warm and friendly. The menu offers a good selection of traditional fayre with many dishes available in smaller portions for children or grown-ups with a small appetite. The fine restaurant is mainly non-smoking making this an ideal stop for families. There is also a comfy bar area where you will find top quality ales - Riding Bitter, Mild and Old Bailie.

There is an attractive garden to the rear and plenty of car parking.

The Beverley Arms, Doncaster Road, Ackworth, Pontefract
Tel: 01977 615945

A couple of miles southeast lies the equally picturesque village of BADSWORTH, famous as the burial place of Sir John Bright, Cromwell's right hand man at the battle of Selby and the siege of Pontefract, whose grave can be found at St Mary's Church. Local legend has it that the church had, at one time, beautiful stained glass windows. During the Civil War when the Parliamentary forces were approaching the windows were apparently removed for safe-keeping. Unfortunately, the man responsible for their burial died in the battle that ensued and they were never found.

Set in glorious countryside, Rogerthorpe Manor is a Jacobean house that has been restored to create a luxurious hotel offering the best quality and value for money. From the minute you arrive, via the long drive through green lawns and colourful flower beds, you will sense the special character of this hotel. You will be welcomed in the reception hall that boasts moulded ceilings above a medieval fireplace and is furnished with comfortable leather suites. The twelve bedrooms are spacious and stylish, all are en-suite, and furnished in a style in keeping with a grand country house

471

including a superb four-poster room. Many improvements have been carried out by the present ownerssuch as the fine mahogany bar. The oak-panelled dining room is also splendid and here you can enjoy fine cuisine from the extensive à la carte menu. The setting of Rogerthorpe Manor and the standard of the attractive gardens make this an ideal setting for weddings. Dinners and banquets are also well catered for and other special events include the murder mystery weekends which have become so popular. For a house of this age it is not surprising to learn that it is haunted, but guests need not worry unduly, as the ghost has not been seen for many years! For detailed instructions on how to find the hotel, ring 01977 643839.

Rogerthorpe Manor, Thorpe Lane, Badsworth, Pontefract
Tel: 01977 643839 Fax: 01977 641571

Situated opposite the railway station in SOUTH ELMSALL is the aptly named Railway Hotel. Originally, the hotel was built in the 1870s by the side of the busy main line between Doncaster and Wakefield and was, in its time, one of the big railway inns of that era. It was purchased in 1992 by Roy Gainey who has, bit by bit, been returning the establishment to its former glory. There are nine comfortable and inviting bedrooms, all with en-suite facilities. Downstairs there is a lively bar and lounge; the lounge is half panelled with a feature fireplace and beautifully decorated and furnished. The bar is open all day on market days to non-residents and as well as serving well kept ales, offers bar snacks. Evening meals are available to guests only.

The Railway Hotel, Station Road, South Elmsall, Pontefract Tel: 01977 642839

The village of WENTBRIDGE lies in a steep valley, four miles south of Pontefract. A quiet place, little traffic passes through it, most people now using the A1(M). The quietness belies its history; until the 1960s the village lay on the Great North Road and was a traditional route north dating back to Roman times. However, to local historians, the village is more famous as the supposed home of Robin Hood. An interesting outlook on the story of this famous outlaw, subtitled 'The Case for the Wentbridge Robin Hood', can be bought locally.

Bridge Guest House is situated in the heart of this now peaceful village. Dating back to the 1600s, the building was formerly a coaching inn and stable being located on the old Watling Street. In later years it has been a shop, garage, post office and guest house and it is the latter two that still apply today. It is a beautiful house run by Jennifer Adams and her family. There are eight outstanding letting rooms which are characterful and cosy and with plenty of facilities. One of the downstairs rooms is even located within the old shop! There is no doubt that all guests will be well looked after here.

Bridge Guest House, Wentbridge, Pontefract
Tel: 01977 620314

Sitting beside the Old Great North Road at Wentbridge is **The Swiss Cottage**. The location is hard to match as there are impressive panoramic views of the surrounding countryside from the windows of the restaurant. The present owners are Allan and Denise Jones, and Allan's story just goes to show that hard work can really take you to the top! He started work at the Swiss Cottage in the 1950s as a young boy with an ambition to own the restaurant for himself. Many years later, having worked here intermittently for many years, his dream came true. Despite having now made it to the top, Allan will often roll up his sleeves and assist in all departments while Denise looks after the front of house. Built and decorated to mimic a Swiss alpine lodge the Swiss Cottage is full of character. The food served is exceptional with a rustic feel to the menu. The meals are reasonably priced and feature only the freshest ingredients while the table d'hôte menu is supplemented by a blackboard of specials. If you want to try somewhere that is a little bit different, then The Swiss Cottage is well worth a special visit.

474

The Swiss Cottage, Wentbridge Tel: 01977 620300

Although the industrial heritage of the towns here may not be hidden, it could be said that much of their ancient and inspiring history is, and **PONTEFRACT** must be amongst the foremost of these.

Shakespeare alluded to the town in his plays as "Pomfret", a place of influence and power, often visited by kings and their followers. The great shattered towers of its castle still stand on a crag to the east of the town. Built by Ilbert de Lacy in the 11th century it was one of the most formidable fortresses of the Norman forces. In medieval times it passed to the House of Lancaster and became a Royal Castle and Richard II was imprisoned here and tragically murdered in the dungeons on the orders of Henry Bolingbroke, as described in the play by Shakespeare.

The Castle became a major Royalist stronghold during the Civil War, after which it was destroyed by Cromwell and today it remains as a gaunt ruin with only sections of the inner bailey and the lower part of the keep surviving intact. There is an underground chamber, part of the dungeons where prisoners carved their names so that they might not be forgotten completely. Perhaps even the unfortunate King Richard may have lived here for the years he was imprisoned

475

Kirkstall Abbey

within these very walls. The oldest parts are the foundations of St Clement's Church and part of the 12th century bailey wall with the postern gateway. The Keep, or Round Tower, dates from the 13th century and was hewn from the solid rock.

Many of the streets of this town evoke memories of its medieval past, with such names as Micklegate, Beast Fair, Shoe Market, Salter Row and Ropergate. Sadly, though modern development has masked much of old Pontefract, behind the accoutrements of 20th-century civilisation lies a fascinating array of historical relics and architecture. There are still many old Georgian buildings, winding streets and the old Butter-cross, the focal point around which the weekly street market revolves.

Pontefract Museum, Salter Row, Pontefract
Tel: 01977 797289

The most famous product the town has to offer, though, has to be the celebrated Pontefract Cakes. Liquorice-root has been grown here since monastic times, and a few roots of the plant are still grown in the local park for the sake of continuity. Naturally the cakes and liquorice allsorts are still a firm favourite with the tourists.

Pontefract Museum is housed in a flamboyant art nouveau building. The displays cover the history of the town

477

and its castle and include coal measure fossils, medieval pottery and even the colourful history of liquorice. An outstanding 17th-century painting shows the castle in its heyday. Changing exhibitions are available throughout the year.

Malt Shovel Hotel, 1 Cornmarket, Pontefract
Tel: 01977 702604

Situated in the heart of the town is the very impressive **Malt Shovel Hotel**. This wonderful black and white timber framed building is medieval and also has a crypt. Inside there are plenty of oak beams which add to the cosy, friendly atmosphere generated by your hosts, Steve and Sheila Jow. As well as offering a selection of fine beers and ales there is an excellent menu of home cooked food ranging from the daily carvery to freshly made sandwiches, and keep an eye out for the daily blackboard specials. The hotel accommodation comprises five individual bedrooms. A super place to stay.

The Elephant Hotel, Market Place, Pontefract

Also in the heart of the town is the turn-of-the-century establishment, **The Elephant Hotel**, a typical town centre inn. Among its outstanding features are the wood panelled
478

walls in the bar area, its tastefully decorated and well-appointed letting rooms, its delicious, well-kept ales and food, but above all, the warmth and hospitality extended to all visitors.

There are six letting rooms in all, three twin, and three singles, and they are available all year. Food is served at lunch times, Monday to Saturday, with a set menu and daily specials. The inn also opens early on Saturdays for breakfasts. Ideally situated, it is only a mile or so from junction 32 of the M62 and very close to the A1.

Leeds and Bradford

The city of LEEDS is the largest urban development in Yorkshire and can certainly lay claim to being the economic capital of the county. Leeds developed rapidly in the early 19th century as the inland port on the Leeds-Liverpool and Aire and Calder Navigation canals. The city formed a central link between Liverpool and Hull, from where goods were exported world-wide. The Canal Basin, which formed the link, rapidly grew, providing extensive wharves, warehouses, boat-building yards and wet and dry docks where boats could be repaired. Although the water-based trade sadly declined, as first the railways then the roadways took over as the trade routes, interest in the long-neglected warehouses and waterways, with their rich and historical tradition, has been rekindled. The Canal Basin has been designated a Conservation Area, and the once derelict buildings redeveloped into sought-after offices and shopping areas, as well as providing a venue for street-shows, markets and landscaped water-side areas.

There are many interesting and hidden places in this fascinating area, well worth exploring for their historical value. The Redevelopment Programme has taken pains to maintain as much as possible, and familiar landmarks such as the cargo-cranes, famous buildings and the twin towers (modelled on Italian campaniles) have been preserved as interesting focal points.

The canal itself is also enjoying a new lease of life with a wide variety of leisure craft increasingly evident on its waters. In response to the enormous interest in the site, a trail with an environmental theme is being developed, which is available to disabled visitors, and a Visitor Centre is now housed in the former Canal Office.

Another excellent way to discover Leeds' remarkable early industrial heritage is to follow the Museum of Leeds Trail along the towpath of the canal through the Kirkstall Valley. This takes the visitor from the Canal Basin past warehouses and mills, bridges, locks and canal architecture, to the Leeds Industrial Museum at Armley Mill, once the largest textile mill in the world. It now houses a museum of the textile, clothing and engineering industries of which Leeds is still a major centre. The story of the development of the clothing industry in Leeds is told in a reconstruction of the Jewish tailoring quarter and one of the few surviving water-powered fulling mills in Europe can be seen.

Leeds city centre offers a great deal to occupy its visitors as well as offering some of the most beautiful baroque civic architecture in the North. There is plenty of shopping available, with wonderful arcades and a large market and other attractions include a regional theatre, the Opera House and the City Museum and Art Gallery. The latter houses the Henry Moore Sculpture Gallery, founded by the late sculptor who was born in nearby CASTLEFORD. The Museum has been in existence for over 170 years and its collections are among the finest outside London. The exhibits range from coins to wildlife, dinosaurs to minerals, costumes to Greek and Roman marbles. The Natural History galleries are especially fascinating and include the largest egg in the world.

Kirkstall Abbey, to the north-west of the city, is one of the most complete ruins in this part of Yorkshire. Building started in 1152 by the Cistercians and was finished within a

480

generation, thus Kirkstall is regarded by many to reflect Cistercian architecture at its most monumental. It was executed with the typical early Cistercian austerity, as can be seen in the simplicity of the outer domestic buildings but the bell-tower, a 16th-century addition, was in contravention of the rule that there were to be no stone bell towers as they were considered an unnecessary vanity.

Travelling from Leeds out to the east, one may decide to call in at Temple Newsam House, set back off the A63, at the GARFORTH turn-off. There has been a mansion here of some sorts since a couple of Anglo-Saxon thanes, Dunstan and Glunier, set their claim to the land. The house has had a great many owners, including the Earl of Pembroke, the Darcy family, the Ingrams and the Marchioness of Hertford. It was purchased in 1922 by Leeds City Council.

In its time such names as John Carr, the Adam brothers, Chippendale and Capability Brown have contributed to its improvement, and it houses some incomparable collections of antiques within its walls. The view of the house is impressive, set amidst huge expanses of rolling grassland. The grounds cover 1200 acres, and include the Home Farm, where there is a rare breeds centre. There is ample car-parking and it is worthwhile noting that admission to the grounds is free and that there are concessions for the unemployed, elderly, students and children for admission to the House.

Situated in the nearby village of OULTON, you will come across the New Masons Arms. Once discovered, you will never forget this classy establishment which is run by a very likeable couple, Maureen and Paul Whiteley. The exterior is delightful - literally covered with flowering plants in a multitude of colours - so it will come as no surprise to learn that the New Masons Arms has received a number of awards for being the most attractive inn in the Leeds district. The interior is just as attractive with a feature fireplace of exposed brick and a collection of pitmen's lamps hanging from the ceiling.

In an adjacent building, converted from old stables, there are four magnificent bedrooms all en-suite and individually decorated. Back in the inn, food is served at lunch times (Monday to Saturday) and early evening(Tuesday to Friday). The menus offer a good selection of traditional pub fayre and the food is reasonably priced. The traditional, well-kept ales are of an equally high standard.

New Masons Arms, 26 Aberford Road, Oulton, Leeds
Tel: 0113 282 2334

Lotherton Hall, due east of Leeds and just off the A1, is another stately house, dating from the 19th century, owned by Leeds City Council. Originally the ancestral home of the Gascoigne family, it contains many fine features, including a 12th century chapel.

In the centre of ABERFORD, on the Old North Road, is the 16th-century former coaching inn, The Swan Hotel. If you drive too fast through the village it is easily missed, but it is worth slowing down for because it is excellent. Very traditional in its decor and furnishings the owners, Otto and Ann Kreft, have created a friendly and very jolly atmosphere that is much enjoyed by all visitors. The Swan Hotel has a well-earned reputation for the high standard of its food which can be selected from an impressive menu - impressive both because of the choice of dishes, which is quite overwhelming, and in its actual physical size! The dishes originate from all four corners of the globe as well as from the home county of Yorkshire. It would be impossible to name some of the dishes as there are so many, but rest assured, everyone is sure to find something that will appeal, even vegetarians and children get a better selection than in most top restaurants. All dishes are reasonably priced and freshly prepared to order. In addition, should you need more choices, there is a carvery every lunch time and a table d'hôte menu Monday to Friday evenings.

If you can't drag yourself away, Otto and Ann can offer bed and breakfast accommodation in the six en-suite bedrooms. They are comfortable and cosy, very good value, and just think - there's breakfast to look forward to in the morning!

The Swan Hotel, Great North Road, Aberford, Nr. Leeds
Tel: 0113 2813205

Travelling up the A1 towards Wetherby, one might think to call in at BRAMHAM and nearby Bramham Park, one of the loveliest villages in this part of lower Wharfedale. Bramham Park is one of Yorkshire's most exquisite country houses and is special for a number of reasons. The house itself dates from the Queen Anne era, built by Robert Benson, Lord Bingley, between 1698 and 1710, and superbly proportioned in an elegant and restrained classical style. The finished effect is more French than English, with tasteful gardens, elegant furniture and paintings by such famous artists as Kneller and Sir Joshua Reynolds. In fact, the gardens were modelled on Louis XIV's Versailles, with ornamental canals and ponds, beech groves, statues, long avenues and a prized arboretum with a collection of rare and unusual trees.

You will come to BOSTON SPA just before you reach Wetherby and it is another town well worth stopping in. It's a gracious, inviting place, whose growth began in 1744, through the discovery of its spring by a labourer called John Shires. A guidebook of 1853 tells of the pure and bracing air to be had at Boston Spa, where one might either drink or bathe in the waters, by visiting one of the pump-rooms and variety of baths. Nowadays, it no longer functions as a spa town, and is better known as a popular fishing ground.

Completely unspoilt by industry is WETHERBY, situated on the Great North Road at a point nearly midway between Edinburgh and London. Hence it is renowned for its coaching inns, of which the two most famous were the Angel and The Swan and Talbot. It is rumoured that serving positions at these inns were considered so lucrative that employees had to pay for the privilege of employment in them!

The town has a quaint appearance and in the centre is a market place that was first granted to the Knights Templar, who were allowed to hold a market here every Thursday and an annual fair lasting three days. Many of the houses in the town are Georgian, Regency or early Victorian. Apart from its shops, galleries, old pubs and cafés, there is also a popular racecourse nearby. Another feature is the renowned 18th-century bridge with a long weir which once provided power for Wetherby's cornmill and possibly dates from medieval times.

Along the A659 HAREWOOD is a village that grew up around the famous Harewood House, and which was moved to its present site in the 1760s. The House, renowned for its royal connections, was originally owned by Henry Lascelles,

484

Harewood House

a wealthy 18th-century merchant, who during his lifetime in fact lived at nearby Gawthorpe Old Hall, across the valley from Harewood. It was his son Edwin, however, who became the first Lord Harewood, and who built the Harewood house we know today.

The last occupier of the house was the Princess Royal, only daughter of King George V and Queen Mary, who married Lord Harewood and lived on at the house until her death in 1965, when the National Trust acquired the property which is now open to visitors. The grounds are truly breath-taking, with Royal rhododendron gardens, bird gardens and Tropical Rain Forest area - certainly not to be missed. The interior is also stunning in its elegance and beauty, as befits its prestigious list of contributors.

Continuing along the A659 one will eventually arrive at OTLEY, a medieval market town, which keeps its individual character with a busy cobbled market-place, little alleyways and courtyards. There are still ancient mileposts in the wilds of the moors which mark the distance to Otley market. To keep the hoards of merchants and farmers well-lubricated a large amount of inns sprang up, some 27 in number, which even for Yorkshire is something of a record! One of the survivors has been made famous as The Woolpack in ITV's 'Emmerdale'.

On the front of the 17th-century former Grammar school building in Manor Square is the plaque and statue of Thomas Chippendale, the great furniture maker who was born in Otley in the early 1700s. The Parish church dates from Saxon times, the main body, though, having been constructed in the 11th century. An unusual memorial, close by, is a stone model of Bramhope Railway Tunnel, with its crenellated entrance portals on the Leeds-Thirsk Railway (the present Leeds-Harrogate line), built in the 1830s. Over 30 men lost their lives in the construction, due to inadequate safety precautions, and the model stands to commemorate this.

The scenery in these parts is both idyllic and magnificent, and there are plenty of walks from the town along the River

Wharfe and up onto Otley Chevin. If all that walking has built up an appetite, just to the south of Otley is the small town of GUISLEY and the world's most famous 'chippie', Harry Ramsden's. Though today there are Ramsden's franchises as far apart as Hong Kong and New York any Yorkshireman will tell you there's only one true Harry's.

BRADFORD is a city with a lot of entertainment to offer its visitors. Among these is the National Museum of Photography, Film and Television, which houses IMAX, one of the largest cinema screens in the world, as well as a wealth of exhibitions on capturing images. One of Britain's major museums, it shouldn't be missed.

The city has an excellent pedestrianised centre, indoor market and a wide choice of Asian restaurants and supermarkets, selling everything you might need for cooking that authentic curry for discerning friends.

Another area worth exploring is Little Germany, the historic merchants' quarter, with its tall, handsome warehouses situated behind the Cathedral. The streets are worth exploring if only to spot some of the stone carvings that were added to already ornate buildings to reflect the wealth and prestige of the owner. Many of the buildings have in fact been listed for their architectural and historical significance.

The jewel in Bradford's crown must be Lister's Mill. Its huge ornate chimney dominates the city skyline and according to local legend is wide enough at the top to drive a horse and cart around. The mill fell silent some years ago, though its exterior has been cleaned and there are plans to use it to house a museum to the industry that bought the city its wealth - wool.

A rather quirkier sign of the city's former riches is Undercliffe Cemetery. Here the wool barons were buried, each in a more opulent gothic mausoleum than the last. It is easy to spend an hour here admiring the Victorian funereal art on show with the cityscape laid out before you.

The fact that Bradford has a Cathedral is an indication of its historical importance as a city. The first evidence of worship on the site comes from the remains of a Saxon preaching cross and today the Cathedral contains many items of interest, including beautiful stained glass windows, some of which were designed by William Morris, carvings and statuary. The old parts of the building are well worth exploring for their curiosities as well.

Travelling a small way out of the city centre, there are various places of interest, including, at FULNECK, a settlement originally founded by a German religious sect called the Moravian Brotherhood in 1742, which has kept much of its 18th-century village atmosphere. One of the cottages has been restored and is now used as a museum.

Nearby TONG is interesting for the Tong-Cockerdale Country Park, an area of reclaimed coal mines, ironworks, railways and mill-races which form a lovely semi-natural area with footpaths and walks. The village is situated on a minor road two miles to the south of PUDSEY which is itself located midway between Leeds and Bradford.

Lapwater Hall, Westgate Hill, Tong, Bradford
Tel: 01274 681449

Anyone looking for a special night out should make a point of finding the impressive restaurant at Lapwater Hall in Westgate Hill, in Tong. This fine establishment specialises in providing excellent value all-inclusive evening meals and
488

traditional Sunday lunches in splendid elegant surroundings. Meals are accompanied by music from a resident DJ who is only too pleased to accept requests, with diners being able to dance until late. Lapwater Hall welcomes party bookings and also provides catering for weddings and functions of up to 120 people.

The towns to the north of Bradford, SHIPLEY, SALTAIRE and BINGLEY, are interesting for a number of reasons. Although Shipley is mainly industrial, Shipley Glen is a very popular area for tourists with a tramway set in a narrow woodland valley with steep sides and huge millstone grit boulders, flanked by a plateau of moorland; there is a Japanese Garden and lake created in the 1890s, as well as various amenities for visitors such as tea-rooms and gift-shops.

Saltaire is the model village created by the famous Titus Salt for the workers at his mill. Salt was a very benevolent employer, and determined to provide his workers with everything essential for a decent standard of living, unlike many other mill-owners who only saw their workforce in terms of profit. The facilities in the village were designed to cater for all his people's needs - health, leisure and education - but there were no public houses. Their spiritual needs were attended to by the elegant Congregational church, described as the most beautiful Free Church in the North of England. Salt's statue stands in nearby Robert's Park, (where swearing and gambling were banned) above the figures of a llama and an alpaca, whose wool he imported for spinning in his mills. The Victoria Boat House was built in 1871 and has been beautifully restored, with an open fire, pianola and wind-up gramophone, all recreating a traditional parlour atmosphere, which serves cream teas and runs special Victorian Evenings in fancy dress.

Saltaire also has an unusual Reed Organ Museum with a collection of over 45 instruments, including harmonicas and an American organ, which are demonstrated, and some are available for visitors to try.

Salt's Mill, built in 1853, is a very impressive building, modelled on a 15th-century Italian palace. Through sponsorship by local businessmen, the mill's interior has been beautifully transformed into the world's biggest Hockney art gallery.

Congregational Church

Bingley is a medieval town renowned for its staircase locks on the Leeds-Liverpool Canal, the "Three-rise" and "Five-rise", which each take at least take half an hour to negotiate. They were built in the 1770s and much of the mechanism is still in workable order. The lock gates are of English Oak and are built to withstandthe pressure of 90,000 gallons of water. This area has some lovely walks, leading into the centre of Bingley via a path with the curious title of "Treacle Cock Alley".

South Yorkshire

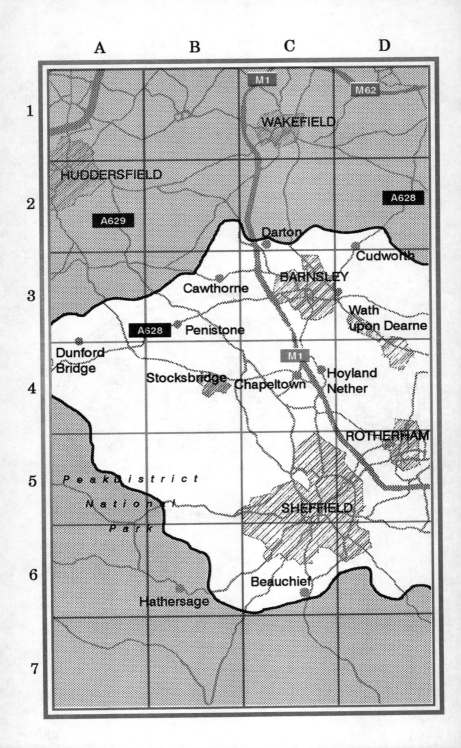

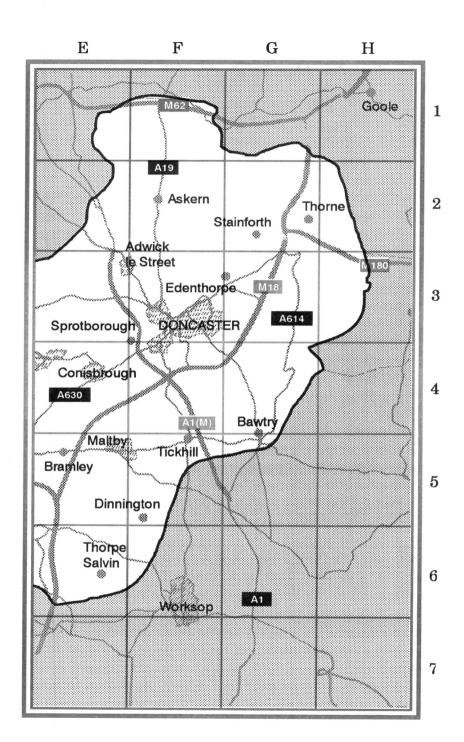

Roche Abbey

CHAPTER NINE

South Yorkshire

Barnsley

There are not many people who would consider a holiday in these parts, but as ever, South Yorkshire holds many surprises.

In the town of BARNSLEY, as with so many of the places in this character-filled county, one does not need to scratch too far below the surface to find many interesting places to visit and experience. It was the wealth of coal that shaped the town and the lives of the inhabitants and the proximity of the mines were of vital importance to the iron and steelworks of its neighbours.

In the centre of Barnsley lies the Cooper Gallery, a centre for the arts, which hosts a lively programme of contemporary exhibitions throughout the year as well as housing a fine permanent collection.

Cooper Gallery, Church Street, Barnsley Tel: 01226 242905

Just a couple of minutes away from the town centre, in a quiet road, is The Limes, an excellent restaurant. Opened in October 1994 by Jason and Adele Reader, the restaurant is housed in an 18th-century, grade two listed building which has formerly been a private house, a convent and a dentists! The bar area on the first floor is reached via a wooden staircase passing a beautiful stained glass window. The restaurant, on the ground floor, is bright and intimate and can seat 60 people. All the food is cooked to order from top quality, fresh ingredients with the emphasis being on

495

traditional British fare. Closed on Mondays, The Limes is open each evening and for lunch at weekends.

The Limes, 102 Dodworth Road, Barnsley Tel: 01226 244990

The many satellite towns and villages are also steeped in history. The village of MONK BRETTON is famous for its ruined priory, the only remaining settlement of the Cluniac Order of monks. It was started in 1154, colonised from the wealthy Pontefract Priory, although a dispute later led to a rift between the two. It achieved independence in 1281, which led to its affiliation with the Benedictine Brotherhood. The plan of the priory, which includes the foundations of both infirmary and guest house, is unusually complete. The Prior's lodgings, based on the first floor of the west claustral stage are particularly interesting due to the fine detailed chimney piece. Also of interest are the two gatehouses and the curious administrative building in the outer court, one of the few to have survived in this country.

Nearby CAWTHORNE is a pretty village with a 16th-century church that sports an octagonal font rescued from Roche Abbey.

This is the location of the Victoria Jubilee Museum, with its remarkable collections of natural and local history exhibits, founded in a local cottage in 1884 and expanded in the year of the Queen's Golden Jubilee.

As in any close-knit community there are a number of tales that have been passed down the generations. One concerns two local families that lived side by side near to Tanyard Beck. They shared an earth closet which was set some way from their houses. The head of one family would take his pipe to smoke while he was using the closet, dropping spent matches down the hole. After a feud, the opposing family took their revenge by pouring paraffin down the closet hole just before the smoker paid his daily visit. The resulting effect has not been documented and will be left to the reader's imagination!

Nearby is the **Cannon Hall Country Park and Hall** set around a Georgian house with 70 acres of beautiful and serene parkland. Now a museum, the hall's rooms are furnished in a variety of styles from Jacobean to Victorian. There is an interesting glassware collection which amongst other things, contains such oddities as glass rolling pins and walking sticks. Cannon Hall also houses the Regimental Museum of the 13th and 18th Royal Hussars, whose part in the Charge of the Light Brigade in 1854 is recalled in a series of stirring displays. There are outstanding collections of 17th- to 19th-century furniture, pottery, glassware and major paintings by such artists as Constable.

Cannon Hall Museum and Country Park, Cawthorne, Barnsley Tel: 01226 790270

Situated directly behind Cannon Hall is **Cannon Hall Open Farm** a modern, family run, working farm which attracts over 100,000 visitors a year with many organised school visits. Roger Nicholson, his wife Cynthia and sons Richard, Robert and David along with daughter-in-law Julie, have put in a lot of effort to ensure that there is plenty to do and see - all year round. The emphasis is very much on the animals and all visitors are encouraged to touch and hold them and there are always staff on hand to provide information and assistance. The farm keeps many smaller animals, such as chipmunks, chinchillas, canaries, wallabies and turkeys as well as the more usual farm animals - goats, sheep, cattle, pigs, ponies, donkeys and llamas. Additional facilities on the site are the tea-room and gift shop. There is always something going on here and this is a wonderful place to take children.

Cannon Hall Open Farm, Cawthorne, Barnsley
Tel: 01226 790427

Also located close to Cannon Hall lies **Beatson House**, known throughout Britain for its excellent cuisine. The building dates back nearly four hundred years and was formerly three houses, the interior retaining many low beams and being full of character. The restaurant is owned and personally run by Peter Lightfoot, the chef, and his partner

Wendy. Dining in a romantic and intimate room you can expect the very best; the menu is carefully chosen, using only the freshest of ingredients, offering traditional dishes in new and interesting versions such as pork with a cream and apricot sauce and salmon thermidor. The chef's specials are a gastronomic delight! The house also has three beautiful and quaint bedrooms. This is without a doubt a very special place to visit.

Beatson House, 2 Darton Road, Cawthorne, Barnsley
Tel: 01226 791245

SILKSTONE, not far away, is a historical village that dates from the time of the Roman occupation and said to have received its name from the word 'salix' which refers to the willow trees that surrounded the village at the time. At the south end is a hill which leads to the common land where the villagers once took their animals to graze. A railway station was sited here in 1854 and the village of SILKSTONE COMMON was born.

A visit to the Church of All Saints reveals a sad reminder of the exploitation of child labour in the grim days of the Industrial Revolution, for in the churchyard is a monument to the 26 children who drowned in the Huskar Pit Disaster of 1838.

What better way can there be to see the countryside of Yorkshire than from the back of a horse? **The Silkstone Equestrian Centre**, in the village of Silkstone Common and on the edge of some wonderful riding country, aims to teach would-be riders the skills of horsemanship in a relaxed and safe environment. The centre is owned and run by Charles and Diana Baxter who have had a lifetime with horses, starting the riding school some 30 years ago, and with their daughter Sue they give qualified instruction to all levels. They have an indoor and an outdoor school with plenty of horses to suit everyone's needs. Also on the same site is the **Throstle Nest Saddlery**, run by David Baxter and his wife Jayne which has one of the finest collections of riding wear, saddlery, country clothing and gifts, displayed within seven rooms. In fact, all you and your horse could possibly wish to have. Whether you are experienced or a beginner, this is a splendid establishment in which to learn about the art of riding.

Silkstone Equestrian Centre and Throstle Nest Saddlery,
Throstle Nest, Silkstone Common, Near Barnsley
Tel: 01226 790422/790497

PENISTONE, a small South Yorkshire town with a character all of its own, forms a gateway to the Peak District. It is situated 700 feet above sea level, in the midst of moorland landscape, and has an agricultural heritage that it is careful to preserve. There are some interesting public buildings, including the 17th-century Dissenters' Chapel, an 18th-century Cloth Hall, and a Parish Church with a 15th-century tower, where ancestors of the poet Wordsworth are buried.

In the centre of the village, on Shrewsbury Road and opposite the church, you will find the **Old Vicarage Guest House and Tea Rooms**. This is a fine old building set within beautiful mature gardens and the adjoining village post office is housed in the Old Vicarage's former coach house.

Owners Joyce and Paul Clibbens have nine beautifully appointed guest rooms available, some with en-suite facilities. They also run an attractive tea room which offers delicious home-made cakes and snacks, including their celebrated cinnamon tea cakes and the 'Penistone Parcel', a mouth-watering savoury surprise invented by Joyce. A recent addition is a small gift shop adjacent to the tea rooms. Here you will find a good range of gift ideas and souvenirs and a good selection of Hidden Places titles.

The Old Vicarage, Shrewsbury Road, Penistone, Sheffield
Tel: 01226 370607 Fax: 01226 766521

Tucked away down a long driveway off Royd Lane, in the nearby village of MILLHOUSE GREEN, and hidden amongst trees is **Millhouse Guest Centre**. When Pat and Ken Worboys moved here over 20 years ago the buildings were nearly derelict, with no roofs, running water or electricity. Their hard work has paid off; not only do they have a wonderful house but they have converted the old barn into the very well equipped Guest Centre. Bed and breakfast, self-catering and bunkhouse accommodation is available; breakfast is taken at the house and evening meals, packed lunches and flasks are available on request. Set in 24 acres of outstanding countryside high up in the Pennine hills, the views from the centre are magnificent and its charm and character irresistible.

Millhouse Guest Centre, Carr House Farm, Royd Lane,
Millhouse Green, Penistone Tel: 01226 762917

Set in 50 acres of grounds and perched high up overlooking the Peak District National Park in **LANGSETT**, **Aldermans Head Manor** is a beautiful and isolated country house hotel dating back to the 16th century. In the 13th century the land was owned by the monks of Kirkstead Abbey and was believed to have been used as a grange for their farming activities. Towards the end of the 1200s, the Lord of the Manor was granted the rights to hold a market and the annual medieval fair was held under a great yew tree somewhere near the river.

502

The present owners, Ann and Philip Unitt, have spared no expense in providing outstanding accommodation in this historic setting with four, very individual, bedrooms. In fact, the decor and furnishings throughout the establishment add to the overall atmosphere of days gone by. The food is also very imaginative with all the dishes prepared from the freshest of ingredients. If you are looking for a relaxing and welcoming atmosphere with delicious home-cooking and superb accommodation this is the place to stay.

Aldermans Head Manor, Hartcliffe Hill Road, Langsett, Stocksbridge, Sheffield Tel: 01226 766209

Nearby THURLSTONE developed when the first settlers realised that the nearby moors provided extensive grazing for sheep and the lime-free waters of the River Don were ideal for the washing of wool. Today it still contains some fine examples of the weavers' cottages which sprung up during the early 19th century, the best of which can be seen on Tenter Hill. Here the finished cloth would have been dried and stretched on 'tenters', large wooden frames placed outside on the street, which gave the road it name.

The village's most famous son was Nicholas Saunderson, born in 1682, who was blinded by smallpox at the age of two. He taught himself to read by passing his fingers over the tombstones in Penistone churchyard - 150 years before the

503

introduction of Braille. He went on to attend grammar school and ultimately became Professor of Mathematics at Cambridge University.

To the west, just north of the busy Woodhead pass, lies **DUNFORD BRIDGE**, a hidden place that nestles in a deep fold of the surrounding hillsides, where once the trains halted before entering the now redundant Woodhead tunnel.

The Waggon and Horses, Sheffield Road, Oxspring,
Near Sheffield Tel: 01226 763259

On the B6462 road, south-east of Penistone, is the village of **OXSPRING** where you will find the **Waggon and Horses**. This charming 18th-century building was once a farmhouse, farm and smithy. At the coming of the railways, the old barn was home to many of the navvies. The establishment became an inn in the early 19th century and it has remained so to this day. In 1992, Barbara and Stan Barley came here to run the pub and in a short time have turned it into a quality establishment. The old barn has been converted into a 60-seater restaurant and function room, with exposed stone walls and original beams it creates wonderful atmosphere. The lounge and bar area are exceedingly comfortable and horse memorabilia is displayed on the walls. This is a very characterful inn serving excellent food and drink in congenial surroundings.

504

At nearby THURGOLAND is the only ironworks of its kind in Britain still on its original site, Wortley Top Forge, which dates from the 17th century. Complete with its dam, sluices and waterwheels there is also a rare example of an 18th-century water-powered forge hammer.

Hidden away in the tiny hamlet of CRANE MOOR is the outstanding Rock Inn. The original building is believed to date back to the 18th century and when Richard and Mary Kirkham arrived here in the mid 1980s it was very much on its last legs. Together they have refurbished the building, adding to it in places, to create this wonderful establishment with eight enchanting bedrooms. The bar area is full of character and charm and has an aviation theme; the magnificent mural was painted by a local artist and is signed by "Johnnie Johnston" the highest scoring fighter pilot of World War II. Richard and Mary have also added an intimate and cosy restaurant where the most delicious freshly prepared food is served. Once found, this is a place you will want to return to time and time again.

The Rock Inn, Crane Moor, Sheffield Tel: 0114 288 3427

On the south side of Barnsley lies Worsbrough Mill Museum. The mill was recorded in the Domesday Survey of 1086 and the present building, a water powered corn mill, was probably built in about 1625. The mill has been fully

505

restored to working order and is now an industrial museum with a rare 1911 Hornsby hot bulb oil engine driving the once steam-powered machinery. The land around the mill is now a country park and on the north side is Wigfield Farm. This is a great favourite with all children, young and old. The Farm Trail starts at the farm buildings and from here explores the rest of the farm, explaining farming practices and identifying the animals and machinery along the way. The farm is home to many rare and traditional breeds.

Worsbrough Mill Museum, Worsbrough Bridge, Barnsley
Tel: 01226 774527

WORSBROUGH village stands at the head of the parkland which rises from the A61 to Barnsley overlooking the beautiful scene of a valley with a reservoir, now known as Worsbrough Country Park.

In the centre of the village is a 13th-century Church of St Mary built of crumbling sandstone. It contains a splendid oak monument which looks very like a double-decker bed, the base of which is carved with heraldry. A knight lies on the upper ledge and below is a skeleton - both are carved in wood and painted.

The canal, built in the valley during the Industrial Revolution, is now used for recreation. At one time a colliery, iron and brass foundry and a glass and chemical works, were

506

located on its banks, the canal being the main source of transportation for all these industries.

Wigfield Farm, Haverlands Way, Worsbrough Bridge, Barnsley Tel: 01226 774581

Situated near to the old canal basin in **WORSBROUGH DALE** is **The Boatman's Rest**, a real gem of a place.

Boatman's Rest, Worsbrough Dale, Barnsley Tel: 01226 286620

Originally two houses, the building dates back to the 17th century and, in oldest parts, the owners, John and Pat Stainsby, have on display a fine array of mining memorabilia.

507

The restaurant and lounge areas of this splendid establishment are beautifully decorated and furnished and simply ooze charm. This is a real family business, John, a retired professional footballer, runs the place along with daughter Lisa, the Restaurant Manager. The delicious, plentiful and reasonably priced food is prepared by Pat and their son, Mark. Once you have tasted the warm hospitality of this inn you will most certainly want to return.

On the A61 in the village of **WORSBROUGH BRIDGE**, lies the charming **Red Lion Inn**. Built in the mid 19th century, this old coaching inn is still very busy, open all day to serve food and drink and offering accommodation. It is also home to the second largest bat colony in South Yorkshire and two friendly ghosts. Inside, the decor is very Victorian, with fireplaces, high decorative ceilings, a comfortable, raised dining area and a well stocked bar. Entertainment is laid on most evenings and the menu is full of delicious dishes all home-cooked to order. The inn also has four individual bedrooms. A popular pub with locals and visitors alike.

The Red Lion Inn, Park Road, Worsbrough Bridge,
Barnsley Tel: 01226 282639

The earliest written record of the village of **TANKERSLEY** is within the Domesday Book of 1086. St Peter's Church is mostly 14th-century with a tower that was built later. Inside are a number of cannonballs found after a Civil War battle between Royalist and Parliamentary troops in Tankersley Park.

During the mid-19th century the coal mining industry started to grow here with the Wharncliffe Silkstone Colliery working the seams in Tankersley Park from 1854. The colliery closed in 1971. Today, the woods of Hood Hill, Bellground, Westwood and Upper Tankersley conceal most of the scars on the landscape and an industrial park covers the site of the colliery yard. Interestingly, on the same industrial site, is a pond that is a protected area since it was discovered that it was home to a number of Great Crested Newts.

Tankersley Manor Hotel, Church Lane, Tankersley, Barnsley Tel: 01226 744700

In the centre of the village you will find the splendid **Tankersley Manor Hotel and Restaurant**. This former 17th-century manor house has been lovingly restored to offer hospitality of the highest quality. The 40 individual en-suite bedrooms were designed with customer comfort very much in mind and one bedroom has been fully adapted for disabled guests. Situated on two levels, the restaurant caters for all tastes with a mouth-watering menu of both traditional and lighter, more contemporary dishes, all cooked to the same high standard. Finally, the bar area acts very much as the 'local' for the village and with its open log fires and old oak beams, provides a traditional warm welcome to accompany your pint.

Situated in the nearby village of **HOYLAND COMMON**, on the eastern side of the M1 motorway, is **The Cross Keys**. Run by partners Stuart Jackson and Glenn Fraser this is a delightful place to stop and have a meal or take a drink. Both inside and outside this inn is a real picture. In several places the interior resembles Grandma's parlour, with beautiful cast iron fire places; there is also a wonderful, bright conservatory extension and a separate family room. The menu is outstanding with plenty of imaginative dishes and not surprisingly the cuisine is renowned throughout the area. Approximately one third of the premises is non-smoking and the inn has gained the Roy Castle Good Air Award.

The Cross Keys, Sheffield Road, Hoyland Common, Barnsley
Tel: 01226 742277

Returning to the west side of the M1 again, and there you will find the small village of **CHAPELTOWN**. The village developed mainly following the arrival of the railway and the building of its own station. In 1897 the line was extended to Barnsley and the station is still used today by commuters.

In the heart of the village is the outstanding **Greenhead House Restaurant**. The magnificent building is over 350

510

years old and has, in its time, been a vicarage and a private house. In 1986 Neil and Anne Allen bought the place and have turned it into an impressive restaurant with a widespread, well earned reputation. There is a cosy lounge for pre-dinner drinks and after-dinner coffee or, if the weather is good, there is a delightful garden for the diners. The restaurant itself, open Wednesday to Saturday evenings, is intimate and cosy with beautifully laid tables offering imaginative and delicious food. Neil is the chef of the partnership and the ever-changing menu is a joy to read. All the dishes are chosen to reflect what is in season and prepared in a mixture of traditional and modern British cuisine styles with continental influences. This is a superb restaurant and a complete dining experience.

Greenhead House Restaurant, Burncross Road, Chapeltown, Sheffield Tel: 0114 246 9004

Sheffield

On the northern outskirts of Sheffield and minutes away from the busy M1 motorway is The Regency Hotel, a haven of peace and tranquillity. Dating from the mid-19th century this imposing old mansion house in the quiet village of

511

ECCLESFIELD has been sensitively extended and refurbished to provide a luxurious base for any traveller, whether on business or pleasure.

The Regency has been in the hands of the Rusby family for many years and it was originally a garden nursery. Robert Rusby senior open a restaurant here in 1968 and the bedrooms were added in 1982. This is a really special place, full of character and charm, and also offering a highly professional service. The restaurant is stylish and intimate with an interesting and mouth-watering menu complemented by an extensive wine list that has been carefully chosen. Little wonder this is one of the most popular dining rooms in South Yorkshire. All of the 19 double bedrooms are en-suite and provide top class accommodation with a full range of extras at your disposal.

The hotel can also meet all your business and conference needs through its range of function and syndicate rooms. You can be assured that every detail of your meeting arrangements will be taken care of in a discreet and professional manner.

The Regency Hotel, High Street, Ecclesfield, Sheffield
Tel: 0114 246 7703

For anyone who enjoys horses then Barnes Green Equestrian Centre is a must. Set in the village of **BARNES**

GREEN, not far from GRENOSIDE, the centre offers many styles of riding and has an outdoor arena, its own cross-country course, side saddle instruction and accompanied hacking through nearby Forestry Commission land. Owned by Carol Walker, herself an experienced rider, and with Sarah Ellis as Chief Instructor the safety of all their clients is an important feature of the centre and they work very hard to ensure that your visit is a very enjoyable one as well. Whatever your age and ability Carol and Sarah have the horse for you and they are very happy to arrange disabled riding with prior notice.

Barnes Green Equestrian Centre, Woodseats Farm,
Barnes Green, Grenoside, Near Sheffield Tel: 0114 240 2548

Tucked away in the village of Grenoside itself is the charming Middleton Green Farm. However, if you imagined this to be a working farm you would be wrong - this wonderful country house accommodation is only a small-holding. When Lynn and Kevin Mennell arrived here in 1987, there was a small disused cottage and a working cow shed both dating back to the 17th century. With much hard work Lynn and Kevin have turned the buildings into very attractive premises offering a high standard of accommodation in an idyllic setting. The interiors are beautifully decorated and furnished with a cosy, friendly

513

atmosphere. There are three superb en-suite bedrooms, one with a Jacuzzi and sauna. Pets are welcome here too, by prior arrangement, and the Mennell's have two dogs of their own. Surrounded by open land this is a tremendous place to stay.

Middleton Green Farm, Cinderhill Lane, Grenoside, Sheffield Tel: 0114 245 3279

Set in over 60 acres of magnificent scenic grounds, just four miles from Sheffield City centre lies the outstanding **Middlewood Hall Hotel**. This Grade Two listed building was built in the 19th century for a wealthy local businessman who, at the time, owned Wilsons Snuff of Sheffield. The impressive exterior is equalled by the interior, which features high ornate ceilings and carefully chosen furnishings. Since buying the hotel in 1993, Wesley McKeith and his dedicated, professional team have put this hotel on the map. The restaurant seats 80 comfortably and provides an excellent menu of delicious dishes. The 17 bedrooms have also been carefully restored to reflect the era of the building and some lie in the converted former Coach House. This is a delightful place to stay whether on business or to use as a base for exploring the surrounding countryside.

Middlewood Hall Hotel, Mowson Lane, Worrall, Sheffield Tel: 0114 286 3919

Visitors to the village of WORRALL, located just off the A6102, on a Sunday in November and December, may hear some strange sounds coming from the local pub. A long-practised tradition is the 'Christmas Sing' which takes place from 12noon until 2pm every Sunday from Armistice Day until Christmas, including Christmas Eve, Christmas Day and Boxing Day. Many of the carols date back to the rise of the non-conformist movement and are sung across the country though most of the tunes are local to this area. The 'sing' is increasing in popularity with folk singers travelling from as far away as the south coast to take part. Years ago women were not expected to participate, being branded as 'pudding burners' if they did.

The Blue Ball is a typical old English village pub, retaining the charm and character of its 300 year history. The establishment is run by Janet and Michael Sievewright who offer a warm welcome to both locals and visitors alike. There are three different and equally attractive rooms; a well decorated lounge bar, a tap room and a cosy snug with feature fireplace and a collection of cottage pottery. As well as serving well-kept real ales, bar snacks are available at lunchtime. In the evening the place really comes alive with ladies nights, quizzes and live jazz music. This wonderful pub provides a super meeting place in this small village.

The Blue Ball, 320 Haggstones Road, Worrall, Sheffiel   d
Tel: 0114 286 2099

The settlements of HIGH BRADFIELD, LOW BRADFIELD and BRADFIELD DALE make up BRADFIELD. Lying 7 miles from the city of Sheffield they are now located within the city boundary, and with the building of four dams here, the area has become known as the 'Sheffield Lake District'.

The Church of St Nicholas in High Bradfield dates back to the 12th century and was originally a chapel dependent on Ecclesfield with the priests having to walk across the moors

515

to take services. The watch house was built in 1745 to combat the body snatchers who were very active at this time.

There is a curious story about the church papers. It was discovered that a large number were hidden in a room of an adjoining cottage, the door to which had been covered over. The two ladies that lived in the cottage were not willing for the doorway to the opened up but following their death the hidden room was uncovered. It was found to contain a large number of documents which are now kept at the Council Offices for safe keeping.

Foxholes Farm, Hoar Stones Road, Bradfield, Sheffield
Tel: 0114 285 3047

Situated on a hillside overlooking the picturesque villages of High and Low Bradfield, amid beautiful countryside and with spectacular views, lies Foxholes Farm, a Grade II listed building sympathetically converted into holiday apartments. The farm buildings are built around an attractive courtyard with a large garden that is ideal for children. The seven apartments are all self-catering and vary in size. With excellent facilities they are all decorated and furnished to a high standard and there is a laundry on the site. The farm stands in the Peak National Park and this is a wonderful location from which to explore all the park has to offer.

516

Overlooking the village stands the magnificent Woodseats Farm, set in over 200 acres of beautiful land. The house dates back to 1634 and is still run as a working sheep and beef farm by Gillian Robinson and her son David. The impressive farmhouse, as well as having two en-suite bedrooms, also has a very comfortable residents' breakfast room and lounge and there are fantastic views from all sides of the house. Make sure you are up early in the morning as Gillian's breakfasts are enormous and absolutely delicious. Packed lunches and flasks are available on request. This is a marvellous place to stay, very friendly and in a beautiful setting.

Woodseats Farm, Bradfield, Sheffield Tel: 0114 285 1429

The once greatest steel-making town in the world SHEFFIELD does not, on the surface, seem a likely prospect for the sight-seer. Its busy, modern heart though, on closer observation, finds time to recall the history of its days as a steel-making capital. There is nowhere in the world that you will not find some item made of Sheffield steel, and such a heritage has made a deep mark indeed.

Sheffield is not often credited with the fact that it contains more parks within its boundaries than any other European city, second only to Glasgow - the rich steel barons of the town needed somewhere to promenade their ladies after all! At

Weston Park, is the City Museum, with the world's greatest collection of cutlery, dating from the Palaeolithic Age to the present day.

The Harley, 334 Glossop Road, Sheffield Tel: 0114 275 2288

The Harley Hotel occupies an attractive corner position in the centre of Sheffield. The hotel was named after Harley Street, London because of the many medical practitioners who lodged here while attending the hospitals of Sheffield. The hotel is also close to the University campus. This is very much a business traveller's hotel and there are no provisions for young children. The hotel has recently been beautifully redecorated and furnished throughout. The restaurant is excellent, with a cosy intimate atmosphere and imaginative lunchtime and evening menus offering classic English cuisine with a French influence. On Friday and Saturday evenings there is also a pianist and singer to add the finishing touch to a special dining experience.

Site Gallery, 1 Brown Street, Sheffield Tel: 0114 2725947

The Site Gallery is a photographic centre situated in Sheffield's developing cultural quarter, on Brown Street. As a gallery and resource centre open to all, it provides a forum for critical debate, and stimulates and challenges people's ideas

518

on photography and the visual arts. The aim of the centre is to inform, educate and encourage its audience to engage in all forms of photography in a supportive environment.

The Rutland Arms, 86 Brown Street, Sheffield
Tel: 0114 272 9003

Near to the Site Gallery, in a cultural corner of Sheffield, is the distinctive Rutland Arms. This eye-catching building was constructed at the turn of the century for Duncan Gilmour and Co. Ltd. and the building still bears that name. Stepping inside you enter a different world. The interior faithfully recreates the feel of the Edwardian era, with richly coloured decor, prints and paintings adorn the walls and plates and porcelain figurines pack the plate racks close to the ceilings. There is something of interest everywhere you look. The Rutland Arms is a member of CAMRA, also featuring in the Good Beer Guide 1995, so you are assured of the fine range of hand pulled real ales which include Tetleys, Marstons Pedigree, Burton Ale and William Youngers No 3. The food too is first class; the menu is extensive and there are also daily specials listed on blackboards around the pub. All the dishes are freshly cooked in a mixture of traditional and modern British styles. The evening meals are served until 7pm and a traditional Sunday lunch is served between noon and 2.30pm on Sundays. Run by Philip McKenna, this is a super inn to visit and, with six bedrooms for overnight guests, a wonderful place to stay.

Graves Art Gallery, Surrey Street, Sheffield
Tel: 0114 2735158

Graves Art Gallery, which opened in 1934, is housed on the top floor of the City Library. Concentrating on British and European paintings from the 16th century to the present day, a highlight is The Grice Collection of Chinese Ivories. There is a lively exhibition programme throughout the year.

Ruskin Gallery, Norfolk Street, Sheffield Tel: 0114 2735935

The award-winning **Ruskin Gallery**, which houses the collection of "The Guild of St George", was founded by John Ruskin for the working people of Sheffield in 1875. The collection comprises paintings, minerals, medieval illuminated manuscripts and a fine library. The adjoining Ruskin Craft Gallery offers an exciting programme of exhibitions of a wide variety of contemporary crafts and workshops.

City Museum and Mappin Art Gallery, Weston Park,
Sheffield Tel: 0114 2726281

Situated in Weston Park, the City Museum and Mappin Art Gallery house major collections of Applied and Fine Art, Archaeology and Ethnographs and Natural History. There is a changing programme of exhibitions both from the City's collections, contemporary art and touring exhibitions. The Mappin Art Workshops and the Education Service provide exciting practical workshops and events based around the permanent displays and temporary exhibitions.

Discover 'The Story of Sheffield' at Kelham Island Museum. From a sliver plated penny farthing made for the Tzar of Russia to the mighty Bessemer Converter, that could turn 25 tonnes of iron into steel in 20 mintues. Inside another giant of the industrial age, the 12,000 horse power River Don Engine can be seen in steam. Displays show the people and skills that built the city and, as befits a 'living' museum, Sheffield craftspeople can be seen practising these skills that earned the distinction 'Made in Sheffield'.

Sheffield Industrial Museum, Kelham Island,
off Alma Street, Sheffield Tel: 01142 722106

Nearby, is one of the few buildings of national importance left unused in Sheffield, The Globe Works. It was built in 1825 by cutlery and tool manufacturers Henry and William Ibbotson. Here is an unusual example of an industrial building which also incorporates a domestic residence. The interior includes a magnificent circular staircase and fine plaster mouldings, which have now been adapted to provide prestigious office accommodation. The original factory areas have been given over as craft workshops, and other additions, such as a visitor centre, restaurant and public house help to make this beautiful building a busy visitor attraction as well. The whole of the Kelbrook Island area has, in fact been designated a conservation site by Sheffield City Council.

In a timber-framed Tudor yeoman's house, built on high ground commanding a panoramic view over Sheffield, is the Bishop's House Museum. Developed to include fine examples of 17th-century oak panelling and plasterwork, there are furnished rooms, displays of Sheffield during Tudor and Stuart times, and a programme of ever-changing exhibitions.

Bishop's House, Meersbrook Park, Norton Lees Lane, Sheffield Tel: 01142 557701

Just two miles out of the centre of the city of Sheffield, in a pleasant and quiet area, is the Roslyn Court Hotel. This small, friendly hotel offers fine accommodation with excellent food and drink. All the 20 bedrooms have en-suite facilities, are very cosy and have been decorated and furnished in an attractive style. The hotel bar, called the Psalter Tavern, is reminiscent of a Victorian grand parlour and as well as serving a variety of fine ales, an exciting range of bar meals are available at lunch times and most evenings. Additionally, the hotel serves a traditional Sunday lunch in its comfortable restaurant.

Roslyn Court Hotel, 180 Psalter Lane, Sheffield Tel: 0114 266 6188

Near the centre of Sheffield is the Nags Head, a busy town public house which was built at the turn of the century as a coaching inn. Today horses and carriages have been replaced by the Sheffield Super Tram network which now runs nearby. Inside the red bricked building the inn reflects its Victorian past. There are beautiful, tiled period fireplaces, overflowing bookshelves and displays of china plates which give this inn a friendly, cosy atmosphere. Very much a meeting place for locals, all visitors are given a warm welcome, especially by the hosts Anita and Tony Holland. Accommodation comprises four en-suite bedrooms and a fine selection of bar meals are served each lunch time except Saturdays. A lively and welcoming establishment.

The Nags Head, 325 Shalesmoor, Sheffield
Tel: 0114 272 6626

In the heart of **WHITLEY WOODS** is the Shepherd Wheel, a water-powered grinding shop which dates from the 16th century, and now restored to full working order. Whitley Woods are part of a 10 mile round walk through public open spaces in the south and south western districts of the city. The signposted way starts at Endcliffe Park and leads by wooded paths to Graves Park which, at 300 acres, is the largest of Sheffield's parks. The Park, gifted to the city in 1926 by Alderman J. G. Graves, houses a Rare Breed Survival Centre, with a number of rare domestic breeds on show, the Norton Nursery and Chantryland, Sheffield's first theme park. There is a famous plant associated with and created at the Nursery, namely the Chantryland Viola, created by H. D. Widdowson and now grown all over the world, which speaks of the reputation of this celebrated horticultural centre that regularly holds places in the finals of the "Britain in Bloom" competitions.

The name of Chantry was originally that of Britain's most prolific sculptor, Sir Frances Leggot Chantry, known in his lifetime as "Sculptor of the Great". Born at Norton he achieved such status that he was, on his death, interred at Westminster Abbey. In celebration of his works part of Chantryland has been dedicated to a Sculpture Trail, created by local artists in co-operation with the famous Graves Art gallery. Here, there are permanent exhibits, such as the Green Man sculpture by Rod Powell and several temporary ones.

Rafters Restaurant, 20 Oakbrook Road, Nether Green, Sheffield Tel: 0114 230 4819

Sheffield's Nature trails do not attempt to hide their industrial links, but rather seek to highlight them, as on the Rivelin Nature Trail, where one will see hundreds of discarded mill grinding wheels lying by the river's edge. Evidence of heavier industrial relics can be found on the city's East End Trail.

Tucked away in a curiously shaped building on Oakbrook Road in Sheffield is a delightfully elegant restaurant called **Rafters**. Small and intimate this first floor establishment is owned and run by Wayne and Joanne Bosworth, along with Wayne's brother Jamie. The rafters are evident, of course, in the dining room, along with beautifully laid tables with crisp cloths, and a fine array of period furniture. Both Wayne and Jamie have excellent culinary credentials, having worked at the Savoy, London and in Paris. Joanne has a lovely personality and manages affairs at the front of house with charm and grace. This is certainly a wonderful place to dine with all the food freshly prepared to order and being mostly modern British cuisine with a Mediterranean influence. The restaurant even bakes its own delicious bread. Whenever you pay a visit be sure to book as this is a very popular place.

Since Victorian days, the citizens of Sheffield have sought an escape from the hustle and bustle of the busy steel town in the wonderful Botanical Gardens, located on the western edge of the city.

Occupying 19 acres, the Botanical gardens comprise rose gardens, rockeries, heather gardens, a wilderness area, as well as many specialist and rare trees and plants. An unusual feature is an entire area set aside for the disabled. The beautiful glass and metal 19th-century structures no longer contain exotic botanical specimens as they did in Victorian times, but now house an aquarium and aviary.

Close to the Universities and Botanical Gardens, in a leafy suburb of Sheffield, lies the **Westbourne House Hotel**. This memorable and inexpensive country house hotel is owned and run by Mary and Mike Pratt and is a delightful place to stay. A former Victorian gentleman's house, it was built in 1860 and has been beautifully restored and refurbished. All ten bedrooms have been individually furnished in different, stylish themes including Indian, French and American and they all offer en-suite facilities. The guest lounge, with polished wooden floor and period furniture overlooks the wonderful sweeping gardens. Mr and Mrs Pratt also have a self-catering flatlet available in the same conservation area of the city.

Westbourne House Hotel, 25 Westbourne Road, Broomhill, Sheffield Tel: 0114 266 0109

As befits a city of the former glory and stature of Sheffield, it has a Cathedral, of which the most famous feature is the famous Te Deum Window, designed by Christopher Webb, depicting Christ surrounded by his prophets and apostles.

Considered in a similarly reverential manner by devotees of the game of snooker, do not overlook the famous Crucible Theatre, so often the venue for the game's many well-attended finals and sponsored events. The Crucible is situated in the heart of the city.

Abbeydale Hamlet, Abbeydale Road South, Sheffield Tel: 0114 2367731

Abbeydale Industrial Hamlet is situated 4 miles southwest of the centre of Sheffield. The site dates back to the 18th century and in its heyday was one of the largest water-powered sites on the River Sheaf. Today it is a tranquil place where you will find a group of sandstone buildings set around a courtyard in a steep wooded valley. Houses and workshops of the Victorian era have been sensitively restored. There are working craftsmen and on several weekends a year special events and exhibitions are held.

Just three miles from the centre of Sheffield and close to the trans-Pennine routes, lying in a superb position next to a golf course, is the Beauchief Hotel. Run by Michel and Edwige Limon, with their dedicated and professional team, the hotel is a splendid base from which to explore the surrounding countryside and the attractions of Sheffield. The oldest part of the building date back to the late 1800s and there is a pretty stream, teaming with trout and home to many ducks, which runs between the restaurant and the inn. The attractive restaurant is well known in the area and provides a varied and imaginative menu with a choice of wines to match. All the 41 bedrooms have an en-suite bathroom and some even have four poster beds. The charming and attractive decor of the public rooms is mirrored throughout the hotel. Residents can also visit the wonderful sauna, solarium, spa bath and mini-gym facilities.

The Beauchief Hotel, 161 Abbeydale Road South, Sheffield
Tel: 0114 2620500

Conferences, business meetings and receptions are also catered for, the intimate atmosphere and the efficient staff allowing you to concentrate on your event with confidence in its success. Whether you are on business or pleasure, the warm, friendly welcome, excellent food and wines and luxurious comforts of this establishment will ensure that your stay is relaxing and enjoyable.

Situated on the Derbyshire border and six miles southeast of Sheffield, in the tiny hamlet of RIDGEWAY, is the popular Phoenix Inn. The older buildings originally belonged to an 18th-century farm and the inn continues to enjoy fine views of the surrounding countryside behind the establishment. Licensed since the early 19th century, the character, charm and atmosphere of days gone by has been faithfully maintained while redecorating and refurbishment has upgraded the interior. The Phoenix Inn has a good reputation in the area for serving delicious food and well kept beer and as a measure of its popularity it is advisable to book a table in the restaurant to avoid disappointment.

The Phoenix Inn, High Lane, Ridgeway, Sheffield
Tel: 0114 248 6440

Standing proudly in the old village of MOSBOROUGH, also on the Derbyshire border, is Mosborough Hall Hotel. This historic building, set in beautiful gardens, dates back to the 11th century and has seen many visitors, including Henry VIII's pregnant mistress, Mary Boleyn, who gave birth to their son at the hall. The hotel's owners and your hosts, Mr and Mrs Nicholas, are justly proud of their property and have

528

spared no expense to ensure that every guests' stay is as enjoyable as possible. The 24 bedrooms are individually furnished and some have four poster beds to complement the room's authentic wall panelling. The John d'Arcy restaurant has an excellent reputation, offering fine food in a delightful setting. This is a magnificent hotel with plenty to offer.

Mosborough Hall Hotel, High Street, Mosborough, Near Sheffield Tel: 0114 2484353

Rotherham

Turning to the north again, just a couple of miles to the southeast of Barnsley, lies the bustling town of WOMBWELL, at the heart of which is The Horseshoe, a busy town centre public house.

Built in the 1920s, this is a large, imposing, red brick building; the original pub, now demolished, having stood on the same site. Ian and Dawn Lawcock came here in the autumn of 1993 and have worked hard to bring the inn back to its former glory. There is a large open bar area with plenty of comfortable seating and three well-kept ales on tap. The establishment boasts five bedrooms, three of them family rooms, all with television and tea and coffee facilities and there is secure car parking to the rear. A pleasant place to stay within easy reach of Barnsley.

The Horseshoe, 32 High Street, Wombwell, Barnsley
Tel: 01226 753297

Those interested in the beginnings of the industrial revolution should take a trip to ELSECAR, south of Barnsley, now transformed into a remarkable industrial village and a designated conservation area. The village was developed in the 18th and 19th centuries by the Earls of Fitzwilliam of nearby Wentworth Woodhouse. It has a fine church, stone cottages, a flour mill built in 1842 which now houses a craft centre and a series of workshops, warehouses, a canal and a train station now housing a major heritage centre. One can also follow a Heritage Trail around the village. The showpiece at Elsecar is the Newcom Engine, a late 18th-century steam powered beam engine and the only one of its kind in the country to have been retained on its original site. Its original purpose was to drain water from the local mines, which it did until 1923. At maximum power, the engine could pump out 400 gallons of water a minute.

The Milton Arms in the village of Elsecar is a wonderful establishment. Through the efforts of owners Philip and Vikki Hickling it has become a place in which to enjoy excellent ale, delicious food and most of all, discover a warm

530

and friendly atmosphere. Dating back to the mid-17th century the inn has real style and class. Philip and Vicki have been here nine years and have very obviously stamped their personalities upon the place. To the rear of the establishment, visitors can enjoy a fine beer garden. Well-tended and looked after it is as pretty as a picture and has gone some way to helping The Milton Arms become Barnsley Pub in Bloom award for 1994 and 1995.

The Milton Arms, Armroyd Lane, Elsecar, Barnsley
Tel: 01226 742278

It was the local Fitzwilliam family who made most money from the local mine workings, and it was at Wentworth Woodhouse that they spent it, a palatial 18th-century manor, set in lavish grounds, with one of the longest façades in England. It is not open to the public, but can be enjoyed from the public paths that run through the park. There is plenty to see and do nearby with craft workshops, reached through the Hauge Lane Garden Centre, and ornamental gardens to the west of the house with a grotto tunnel and bear pit. A number of follies and monuments, dating from the 18th century, are also on the estate. Hoober Stand is a 100 foot monument that was erected at the highest point of the borough to commemorate the suppression of the Jacobite Rebellion, while Keppels Column, nearby, rises to 115 feet, in remembrance of the acquittal of Admiral Keppels who was court-marshalled for failing to beat the French in 1778. There is also the Needles Eye in Lees Wood, which consists of a tower pierced by a carriage way. The story goes that it was built after a wager by the Marquis of Rockingham to prove he could drive a horse and carriage through the eye of a needle. The Wentworth Mausoleum, also not open to the public, was constructed in 1788 in memory of the second Marquis.

Le Bistro Wentworth, Mainstreet, Wentworth, Rotherham
Tel: 01226 746162

In the heart of the picturesque and historic village of **WENTWORTH** is the outstanding **Le Bistro Wentworth**. Since opening the business here in the autumn of 1994, Angela Hawkins has built up an excellent reputation for good food and you never know who may be sitting at the next table. The building has seen many uses over the years including a cowshed and a blacksmiths. The exposed brick walls and forge area in the bistro along with lots of decorated exposed beams all add to the atmosphere and give the place a real continental feel. Whether you are here just for morning coffee, a light snack or an intimate dinner, when booking is advisable, the food and service will be second to none. With a wide range of delicious, home-cooked dishes from which to choose you are sure to return here time and time again.

While you're here, you could make a point of calling in at the Rockingham Arms, also in Wentworth. This is a splendid example of a 17th-century country inn with ivy-clad walls and a wonderful traditional atmosphere.

Standing on the edge of Wentworth Park, the inn's interior is decorated in charming rural style with open log fires burning in winter months. There is a cosy dining room and family room where children are welcome. The bar offers a fine selection of traditional hand-pulled ales, including Youngers and Theakstons. There are also 12 comfortable, newly-decorated letting bedrooms in the quaint stone cottage opposite the main building. All rooms are en-suite and some rooms have been upgraded to a luxurious standard.

Rockingham Arms, 8 Main Street, Wentworth, Rotherham
Tel: 01226 742075

The town of WATH UPON DEARNE was, not so long ago, surrounded by coalpits and engineering works, today the industry has gone and the countryside is once again visible. On the edge of the town, with wide views of the surrounding area, is The Staithes free house. Formerly several cottages the building dates back to the early 18th century when it was part of the Wentworth estate and has in its time been known as The Manvers Inn and the Kiss of Life. Your hosts, Allan and Sue Walker, have built up the reputation of the

533

establishment in the last four years, and have refurbished the inn adding a conservatory area and decorating the whole interior beautifully. Brick fireplaces, flagstone floors, sparkling brasses and old photographs of the area add to the homely atmosphere. Renowned for its good food and fine ales Allan and Sue are also proud of the pub gardens for which they received an award for the most outstanding exterior in the area

The Staithes, Doncaster Road, Wath upon Dearne,
Rotherham Tel: 01709 873546

Situated high up in Wath upon Dearne, overlooking the valley, is the impressive Sandygate Hotel. Until the mid-1950s, Wath upon Dearne was a thriving mining town but the pits have now gone and, until about 15 years ago, the Sandygate was a pit owner's dwelling. Now turned into a hotel and restaurant the decoration and furnishings are all in keeping with the Victorian style of the house and though grand there is a really warm and charming atmosphere. There are 11 bedrooms, including a family room. The bright and airy restaurant offers a wide variety of dishes, all imaginative and beautifully presented, the house speciality is a 32oz rump steak, not a choice for the faint hearted! A delightful place to stay with a excellent accommodation and hospitality.

The Sandygate Hotel, Sandygate, Wath on Dearne
Tel: 01709 877827

Between Wentworth, Wath upon Dearne and Swinton is the Waterloo Kiln. This kiln, located to the rear of the Rockingham Pottery (the interior of which cannot be visited), stands with the Pottery Pool as a relic of the internationally renowned porcelain works. Established in 1745 the firm ran into financial difficulties from which it was rescued by Earl Fitzwilliam; subsequently the firm took the Earl's family crest of a griffin as its trademark and adopted the name 'Rockingham'. The wares, especially the beautifully decorated tea and dessert services, became extremely popular and were exported all over the world. However, the firm never achieved financial stability and closed in 1842 - one of the last orders being a service for King William IV.

Hidden away in the picturesque village of SWINTON is a charming and delightful inn, The Travellers Rest. Dating back to the mid-19th century, this rambling building is an inn which retains many of the old values. Visitors can expect a warm welcome from the hosts, Eddie and Margaret Miles, as well as fine ales, good food and splendid accommodation. All the rooms, both public and letting rooms, are tastefully decorated, with plenty of old prints to maintain the atmosphere of bygone days. The menu is a mixture of traditional Yorkshire fare with the addition of more exotic dishes, all beautifully prepared and served with style. A credit to Eddie and Margaret this is an excellent place to stop; you are sure to leave relaxed and refreshed.

The Travellers Rest, Milton Street, Swinton, Near Mexborough Tel: 01709 582035

ROTHERHAM's past, like many South Yorkshire towns, is linked with iron. In fact, iron has been worked here as long ago as Roman times. They even built a fortress to protect their workings, at Templebrough on the banks of the Don, which included a granary and a bath house. Relics from the site, which was discovered around a hundred years ago, are on show at the Clifton Park Museum.

In the Middle Ages, the monks of Rufford Abbey also prospected for and smelted iron. In addition they planted orchards and even today, despite the proximity of so much heavy industry, agriculture is still important to the area with a large proportion remaining rural. However, it is the heavy industry, all connected with the iron ore resources, that brought Rotherham its prosperity. The famous Walker family struck on the idea of making cannons, and their wares were used in the American War of Independence and the Battle of

Trafalgar. They were also responsible for the building of Southwark Bridge in London.

A couple of famous inventors were also born in Rotherham - Sir Donald Colman Bailey, inventor of the Bailey Bridge used in World War Two was born here, and Edward Crimes, the inventor of the household screw-down tap was also from these parts.

As far as ecclesiastical buildings are concerned, Rotherham has more than its fair share. The Parish Church of All Saints is widely regarded as being one of the finest perpendicular buildings in Yorkshire and dates from the 15th century although there is evidence of an earlier Saxon Church on the site. Inside is the Chapel of Jesus built in 1480 by Thomas Rotherham who, after having been educated at Eton and Cambridge, became the first Bishop of Lincoln, then Lord Chancellor and was, at the time of his death, Archbishop of York. He was responsible for the founding of the College of Jesus in 1483, although little of this remains now as it was closed in 1547 during the Dissolution.

Clifton Park Museum, Clifton Lane, Rotherham
Tel: 01709 823635

Clifton House, in the centre of Rotherham, was built in 1783 for Joshua Walker, son of Samuel Walker the founder of the Rotherham Iron Works, a beautifully proportioned

537

mansion set in its own extensive gardens. Opened as Clifton Park Museum in 1893 by Rotherham Corporation it houses collections covering many aspects of local interest from earliest times to the present. From Rockingham porcelain to a huge South African lion called Nelson, displays of fossils, rocks and minerals to a recreated Victorian kitchen, and much more, there is plenty to see and enjoy. The museum is open Saturday and Sunday afternoons and closed on Fridays.

Housed in the Central Library and Arts Centre Building in the centre of Rotherham is Rotherham Art Gallery. Throughout the year the gallery organises lively and colourful exhibitions covering local artists, ethnic culture and the work of local groups and societies as well as highlighting global events issues. This is very much a community art gallery and well worth a visit.

Rotherham Art Gallery, Central Library and Arts Centre Building, Walker Place, Rotherham Tel: 01709 823621

Also to be found in the Central Library and Art Centre Building is the York and Lancaster Regimental Museum. This regiment had extremely strong ties with South Yorkshire and Rotherham was one of its key recruiting area. The displays of uniforms, campaign relics, weapons and illustrations are designed to tell the history of the regiment from 1758 until its disbandment in 1968. Following a tour of the museum you can take advantage of the café and licensed bar facilities on the first floor of the Arts Centre or visit the museum shop. The museum is open Tuesdays to Saturdays.

The York and Lancaster Regimental Museum, Central Library and Arts Centre Building, Walker Place, Rotherham Tel: 01709 382121

Just minutes from the M1 and close to Rotherham lies the Swallow Hotel. Purpose built in 1990, this new hotel is an excellent base for both business and leisure guests. The 100 bedrooms have been beautifully decorated and include all the comforts you would expect of a high class hotel. Several of the rooms have also been specifically designed with the disabled guest in mind. Holly's Restaurant is light and airy and offers the best in fine English regional and classical cooking. Finally, the hotel boasts a superb leisure club, with a large swimming pool, as well as gym equipment, spa bath and steam rooms. This hotel makes an ideal centre for touring the attractions of the Peak District and South Yorkshire.

Swallow Hotel, West Bawtry Road, Rotherham
Tel: 01709 830630

Situated in the heart of Rotherham's residential area and within easy reach of the M1 motorway is the splendid **Carlton Park Hotel**. This is an ideal location from which to explore the magnificent surrounding countryside or to use as a meeting venue. The hotel has 77 beautifully furnished bedrooms, with a whole floor set aside as non-smoking. The tasteful decoration and furnishings are continued into the public rooms and restaurant. There is an excellent restaurant serving delicious food and light and more informal meals can be ordered from the popular Carlton Bar. For a large hotel, this establishment has a very warm and friendly atmosphere, with special provisions made for babies and small children, and there is also a well-equipped leisure club for guests to use.

Carlton Park Hotel, Moorgate Road, Rotherham
Tel: 01709 849955

Situated opposite the now closed railway station in MASBROUGH is the Prince of Wales Hotel. A square building of Yorkshire stone, built in the Regency style, the grand proportions of the exterior are mirrored inside with fine, tasteful decorations and furnishings.

Prince of Wales Hotel, Princes Street, Masbrough,
Rotherham Tel: 01709 551366

There are 18 bedrooms, varying in size, with something for everyone. The owners and your hosts, Brian and Valerie French, run the establishment in a quiet professional manner and offer a warm welcome to their guests. In the evenings, the place comes alive. Brian, who started in show business in 1959, still maintains many of his old contacts and friends and his band often plays in the hotel. Residents and non-residents alike cannot help joining in and the popularity of the evenings ensures your visit goes with a swing.

Elton Hotel, Bramley, South Yorkshire Tel: 01709 545681

In the village of BRAMLEY, close to the many attractions of South Yorkshire on the eastern outskirts of Rotherham, lies the Elton Hotel. In its 225-year history the building has been the tanners' house to the local estate, a private dwelling and a guest house. In the mid-1980s, Peter and Wyna Keary and their family moved here and have transformed it into one of the leading hotels of the area. There are 29 exceptionally fine bedrooms, one purposefully designed with disabled guests in mind, all with full en-suite facilities and those little extras that make all the difference. The cosy, intimate restaurant serves fine English and French cuisine and has won the coveted Relais Routier Casserole Award. This is an ideal place in which to relax while exploring Yorkshire.

Nearby, the village of WICKERSLEY is the home of the Morthen Craft Workshop, a fascinating place to visit for all those interested in living country crafts. It can be reached by turning south of the A631 midway between Rotherham and Maltby onto the B6060 at Wickersley and then turning west into Morthen Lane. Open all year round with car park, tea room and herb garden, visitors can browse the gallery that houses prominent sculpture from Zimbabwe. A gift shop sells a variety of items including hand creams and oils made from herbs on the site. Both skilled craftspeople, the owners Sylvia and Brian also have pre-booked evenings for groups (between 10 and 50); these include a demonstration on topics varying from herbs to jewellery-making followed by refreshments. All visitors can be assured of a warm welcome.

Morthen Craft Workshop, Springvale Farm, Morthen Lane, Nr. Wickersley, Nr. Rotherham Tel: 01709 547346

Continuing out of Rotherham beyond MALTBY, on the A634, are the beautiful remains of Roche Abbey, a ruined Cistercian house situated in an idyllic riverside setting. The story of the monks' dismissal at the hands of Henry VIII's men is filled with pathos, for an on-site auction of all their treasures and effects was held, and the monks were forced to look on as Henry's favourites and other well-off personages haggled over their sacred artefacts. Their departure was

542

followed by an almost complete devastation of the Abbey, so that today, there are only two graceful fragments upstanding to attest to the building's former glory.

The foundations that remain of the great house, give one a clear picture of the ordered existence of the Cistercian lifestyle - the monks based on the east of the building and lay brethren to the west. One can also still see the clever drainage system, the engineering of which dictated the locations of all Cistercian houses, which caused them all to be sited next to fairly flat stream beds, which could be harnessed and diverted to their purposes. The surrounds of the decayed Abbey were landscaped in the 1770s by Capability Brown, as part of the grounds of Sandbeck Hall, home of the Earls of Scarborough.

Due south of Rotherham, accessed off the A618, is the Ulley Country Park. The park provides quiet walks, picnic places and a variety of wildlife. The conservation of wild flowers and grasses of the area is of great importance and the lake provides excellent coarse fishing including facilities for disabled anglers. A section of the lake is set aside as a nature reserve where no fishing is allowed. A number of interesting walks into the surrounding countryside can be commenced from the park and leaflets are available at the small but well-equipped Visitor Centre.

ASTON, just by junction 31 of the M1, has a collection of Georgian buildings that give an air of grace and elegance to the town. One of them, a former rectory, was the home of the reverend William Marshall, author, poet, musician and friend of Thomas Gray. It is reputedly for the reverend that Gray wrote his famous 'Elegy'. The house was designed by the celebrated John Carr, and features a number of ornamental plaster ceilings and copious fireplaces. Here Marshall would have played his coelestinette and pentachord, or perhaps devised a new dramatic scene for 'Caractacus' or 'Elfrida'.

Marked on the map and only a short drive from Rotherham, is the Rother Valley Country Park. Many watersports can be enjoyed; sailing dinghies, sailboards, canoes, rowing sculls and wetsuits can all be hired plus private boats can be launched. There are facilities for angling, cycle hire, horse riding, grass skiing and walking, plus a nature reserve and accommodation for touring caravans and camping. A new 18-hole golf course, driving range and par 3 course have recently opened. Bedgreave New Mill, situated in the Park, contains a restored water wheel and other working equipment. The mill buildings also house a Visitor Centre where the history of the park is explained, and a café.

In the pleasant village of **DINNINGTON**, tucked away near the Nottinghamshire border, is **The Squirrel**, an impressive public house. Though the pub does not have a long history, it was built in 1957, Bob and Pauline Woolley have created a warm and friendly establishment with character and charm. The inn boasts a variety of well-kept ales and delicious home-cooked food served in tastefully decorated surroundings. If this was not enough to have you coming back for more, Bob and Pauline ensure that there is something happening here every evening, from live entertainment to quiz nights, solo clubs to darts and pool. The atmosphere is electric and well worth making a detour to find.

The Squirrel, Laughton Road, Dinnington, Sheffield
Tel: 01909 562554

The magnificent olde worlde inn, the Black Lion, stands in the heart of the picturesque and sleepy village of FIRBECK, also on the Nottinghamshire border. The building dates back over 400 years and has been maintained in a beautiful condition. Inside, it is full of atmosphere and charm much of which is generated by the lovely couple, Lynne and Karl Wirth, who run the inn. There are prints and photographs decorating the walls which follow a range of themes. Famous for is delicious food and fine traditional ales. Take your pick from hot or cold imaginatively filled sandwiches, crisp salads, or traditional grilled food, you will not be disappointed. There are also special vegetarian and children's menus. A delightful place to stop and enjoy some fine hospitality.

The Black Lion, 9 New Road, Firbeck, Worksop
Tel: 01709 812575

Also in Firbeck you will find the South Yorkshire Aircraft Museum, a privately owned museum based on the history of aviation in South Yorkshire and training aircraft. The Museum contains a large collection of Rolls Royce and other aero engines plus a full frame of a Hawker Hunter and a De Havilland Vampire. There is a Scout helicopter and open-sided sections of various cockpits. A new attraction is the collection of material connected with the early history of army flying from Firbeck Airfield.

The small town of **TICKHILL**, further north, was once a place of great note in medieval times, with a castle of its own. Here, one can see the remains of an Augustinian Friary and a medieval millpond. The Buttercross, erected in 1777, was part of the impressive Church of St Mary the Virgin which was largely rebuilt in the 15th century. The Parish Rooms were originally part of St Leonard's hospital, dating from 1470, and have been used for many purposes over the years, including a school.

There are little more than the foundations remaining to tell of the former glory of Tickhill Castle, once one of the most influential castles in England at the time of the legendary Richard the Lionheart. Tickhill was garrisoned by both sides at times during the Civil War, and was probably raised afterwards to prevent its further military use.

Doncaster

North of Tickhill is **CONISBROUGH** where you will find the magnificent Conisbrough Castle. Overlooking the River Don, its mighty, white, stone keep, towers over an impressive medieval fortress which at one time stood at over 100 feet high. It is considered one of the finest examples of Norman architecture. Much of the circular keep now lies in ruins but one can still walk through the remains of several rooms including the first floor chamber, with its huge open fireplaces, giving one a fascinating insight into the lifestyle in Norman times.

Situated close to the church in the village is **Cromwell's Restaurant**. The building, in a quiet backwater of the village, looks Georgian but is in fact older, believed to have been constructed in the 17th century. For many years owned by the Church it has also been a Post Office before, in 1983, becoming a restaurant. Chef, Ian Godfrey, has been here almost from the start and has ensured that Cromwell's retains the richly deserved reputation it has for fine food and wine. The menu is outstanding with mouth-watering dishes all cooked to order from produce in season. The Cromwell theme is followed throughout the premises with rooms taking such names as Roundhead Restaurant and Royalist Room.

Cromwell's, 18 Church Street, Conisbrough, Doncaster
Tel: 01709 869291

On the edge of Conisbrough, is the Hilltop Hotel. The present building was erected here in 1890, previously it was sited across the road and formed part of the Francis Ogley Brewery. The inn is a real picture and a great credit to the hosts Harold and Ellen Sapey. Inside you will find a fine display of gleaming brasses and horse harnesses, bellows and a splendid array of plates, jugs and other china objects. As well as having a well-stocked bar, delicious food is on offer from either a set menu or from the daily specials boards. Outside the inn, in what was the old garage, four bedrooms have been created, all furnished with comfort very much in mind. Though the establishment is small, your visit will certainly leave a big impression.

In SPROTBROUGH there is a fine medieval church dedicated to St Mary, which amongst other things has some unusual burlesque pew carvings, said to represent the marital joys and disappointments of a family in Tudor times, and reported as having been executed by a local craftsman in lieu of his tithes.

The Hilltop Hotel, Sheffield Road, Conisbrough, Doncaster
Tel: 01709 862144

Built in 1652, The Boat Inn at LOWER SPROTBROUGH earned its place in history by being the house in which Sir Walter Scott wrote his novel 'Ivanhoe'. An old coaching house, it is in magnificent condition, full of interest to any visitor, and was for many years the family seat of the Copley family; their coat of arms can be seen clearly over one of the windows. Set around a courtyard the inn features flagstone floors, a variety of bygone memorabilia and a selection of fine prints. The speciality of the excellent restaurant is fresh fish of all kinds and there is a good list of high quality wines to accompany your meal. The bar attracts a strong local trade and offers a selection of hand-pulled beers and lagers.

The Boat Inn is only 3 miles from Doncaster and is splendidly situated for access to the racecourse, nature parks and local historic buildings, and narrowboat cruises on the canal operate from a base only yards from the inn's door.

DONCASTER was an important Roman Town, known as Danum, and was chosen by them because it was the lowest crossing point on the River Don. Budding archaeologists may be interested to know that there is a well-preserved piece of Roman road just west of ARDWICK LE STREET, and that many of the churches in the area have Saxon connections.

The Boat Inn, Lower Sprotbrough, Doncaster
Tel: 01302 857188

Doncaster has strong roots in several non-conformist religions - the Quaker Meeting House at WARMSWORTH was one of the earliest in the district. George Fox visited it and held rallies at nearby BALBY. It is also worth noting that John Wesley came from Epworth and William Bradford, one of the Pilgrim Fathers who sailed with the Mayflower, was baptised at Austerfield.

The town also has some impressive public buildings, including the Mansion House, the Parish Church and the Corn Exchange. The Mansion House was built in 1748, designed by James Paine, and was to be the only civic mansion house outside London and York. The Parish Church was rebuilt in 1858 by Sir Giles Gilbert Scott as an outstanding example of Gothic revival architecture. The lively shopping centre is enhanced by a stately Corn Exchange building and a market which takes place every Tuesday, Friday and Saturday.

Doncaster is also a railway town and was one of the most important centres for the production of steam engines. Thousands were built here, including both the Flying Scotsman and the Mallard, two of the fastest and most advanced engines of their day.

There is no-one connected with the racing fraternity that has not heard of the St Leger, one of the oldest classic races, which has been held at Doncaster since 1776. Doncaster, in that Yorkshire tradition, provides a magnet for all horse racing enthusiasts and there are a total of twenty-six meetings held a year, including National Hunt Flat Races.

The Earl of Doncaster Hotel, Bennetthorpe, Doncaster
Tel: 01302 361371

On the racecourse side of town lies the Art Deco Earl of Doncaster Hotel. Although there has been an Earl of Doncaster hotel for over 150 years, the present hotel was built in the 1930s but, due to World War II, it was not opened until the late 1940s. The present owners acquired the establishment in 1993 and have since been recreating the former grandeur of the 1930s. All the 53 bedrooms have full en-suite facilities and represent a step back in time in terms of style. The same style is also present in the public rooms and in particular the hotel has a magnificent ballroom with half wood panelled walls. There is also an interesting and

550

mouth-watering menu served in the restaurant. This is an excellent hotel ideally situated close to the centre of Doncaster and with countryside views to the rear.

The town has a wealth of galleries and museums for people seeking more aesthetic pleasures. The Doncaster Museum and Art Gallery is based in Chequer Road, in a modern building it has used since 1964, although the actual gallery was founded in 1909. It houses impressive collections of archaeology, regional natural history, geology, local history, European fine art, paintings and sculpture, costumes, militaria and special exhibitions. Within the gallery is the collection of the King's Own Yorkshire Light Infantry, introduced in 1987, including uniforms, medals and equipment. Queen Elizabeth, the Queen Mother, visited in 1988, in her capacity as their Colonel-in-Chief.

The Regent Hotel, Regent Square, Doncaster
Tel: 01302 364180/364336

Near the centre of Doncaster and overlooking the secluded Regency Park is The Regent Hotel, a charming Victorian building. Founded in 1935 by the Longworth family it remains with the family and, with a combination of modern day comforts and olde worlde character, the perfect atmosphere has been created to ensure your stay is pleasant and relaxing. The hotel serves the best in food and drink with

551

a wide variety of styles. Try O'Grady's Cellar Bar, where in a continental atmosphere you can sample delicious food and exotic cocktails, or the Parade Bar, where in a atmosphere of a bygone age you can enjoy a drink or select a meal from a Giant Steak menu. All the venues are popular and the hotel offers something for everyone and can also accommodate large meetings or receptions in their Cottage Suite. The family motto 'The tradition continues' is most certainly true.

Nelsons, Cleveland Street, Doncaster Tel: 01302 344550

Lying in the heart of Doncaster is **Nelsons**, formerly The Lord Nelson public house, which offers the best in food, drink and accommodation. Personally run by the owner, Andrew Langwith, this is a very popular place throughout the day and the 'in' place for the evening. In the bar and restaurant you can soak up the lively atmosphere while quenching your thirst with a drink from the well stocked bar, or sampling some of the delicious food. The menu is imaginative and follows a seafaring theme with battle rations, cabin snacks and Trafalgar salads. There is nothing rationed about the quality or quantity though! Next door, at Nelsons Dockyard Fish and Chip diner, you can eat your fill of traditional fish suppers. Nelsons also boasts ten splendid bedrooms, some self catering, and not a hammock in sight. A place with something for everyone, whatever your age.

552

The Museum of South Yorkshire Life at Cusworth Hall appeals to a wide range of ages and tastes. Cedar and strawberry trees, larches, cypress, fig, yew and bamboo all grow in the pleasure gardens around this imposing mansion while the Hall sports fine ornamental doors, windows and palladian pavilions, in one of the finest examples of early Georgian architecture. The interior is adorned with elaborate plasterwork, panelling and carved marble chimney pieces. There are permanent displays that chronicle the way of life over the last 200 years of the people of South Yorkshire, and there are interesting collections of children's dolls, whalebone corsets and decorated chamber pots!

The areas around Doncaster are full of nature reserves and conservation sites. Seven miles to the northwest is Howell Wood Country Park, which was originally planted as an 18th-century game reserve. Today, it is 140 acres of delightful woods, streams and ponds, with special consideration for the disabled. The Park also has an unusual ice-house used by former residents of Burntwood Hall to preserve food. It consists of a cylindrical well 18 feet deep which would have been packed with ice from the adjoining lake. Its double brick walls, and shade from the overhanging oak trees, helped to keep the ice frozen for up to three years.

On the northern outskirts of Doncaster, within five minutes drive of the famous racecourse, is the rural community of **EDENTHORPE** and the **Beverley Inn**. Formerly an old farmhouse it became an inn in 1990 and in 1994 was taken over by Graham and Judi Young. It offers a warm and friendly welcome to all guests and has 14 stylish bedrooms, the majority of which have en-suite facilities. There is a cosy and intimate restaurant open every lunchtime and in the evenings from Tuesday to Saturday. A carvery is available at lunch times as well as a variety of enticing specials displayed on the blackboard, and a set menu plus an à la carte menu is offered in the evenings. This is a super place to stay with a terrific atmosphere created by the hosts.

The Beverley Inn, 117 Thorne Road, Edenthorpe, Doncaster
Tel: 01302 882724

STAINFORTH is an attractive area to the north of Doncaster well worth exploring. It was once an important trading centre and inland port on the River Don, as the main thoroughfare for the Stainforth-Keadby canal, which still has a well-preserved dry dock and 19th-century blacksmith's shop. The area is built on low, marshy ground, drained by Dutch engineers in the 17th century to produce rich peaty farmland. The place has retained the air of a quiet backwater, a little-explored area of narrow lanes and pretty hamlets, drained by slow moving dykes and canals. The rich peat resources are commercially exploited in part, but are also the home of a great deal of natural wildlife.

Lying in 193 picturesque acres of scenic countryside, just a couple of miles north of Doncaster, is **Thornhurst Manor**. Eight years ago, Ian and Duncan Murray bought the land and set about creating this excellent and special place. In August 1994 the magnificent restaurant and bar was opened, followed shortly afterwards by an outstanding 18-hole golf course. Both the restaurant and course are open to non-members and there is a charming, friendly atmosphere which makes any visitor feel most welcome. From the eye-catching

554

restaurant and bar area there are fine views over the course and an extensive menu of tasty, satisfying dishes are served. There is an on-site golf shop where visitors can hire clubs if needed. This is a popular venue and booking is recommended for weekend evenings.

Thornhurst Manor, Holme Lane, Owston, Doncaster
Tel: 01302 337799

Continuing north along the A19 will shortly bring you to the village of **WHITLEY** located near the meeting point of the M62 motorway and the Aire and Calder Navigation. Located here, near to the North Yorkshire border are a couple of fine establishments offering refreshment.

The Horse and Jockey in the village of Whitley Bridge is only five minutes from the M62, off junction 34. Dating back to the 18th century it was formerly Hut Green Farm where beer was served, later becoming an alehouse, becoming the Horse and Jockey in the late-19th century. This is very much a locals' pub where visitors are very welcome. The decor is traditional with lots of unusual ornaments and items to admire. Open every lunch time and evening, food is available at every session, except Sunday evenings, in a separate restaurant area. The food is traditional pub fayre supplemented by daily specials, and for Sunday lunch there is a set menu. The beers are well-kept and there always a good choice of bitters. The owners are Matt and Paula Lake, a delightful couple, who also have a twin-bedded room available for overnight accommodation all year round.

The Horse and Jockey, Hut Green, Whitley Bridge, Nr. Goole
Tel: 01977 661295

There has been a George and Dragon Inn in WHITLEY BRIDGE for many hundreds of years with the present establishment being built in the 1940s replacing the former inn which stood nearer the road.

The George and Dragon Inn, Doncaster Road,
Whitley Bridge, Near Goole Tel: 01977 661319

The lounge is in a Tudor style with wooden beams to the ceilings and walls and there is an attractive display of old plates and crockery that the hosts, Peter and Pat Weise, have collected over the years. The inn has an excellent reputation for good home-cooked meals and live entertainment is arranged weekly. To the rear is a wonderful beer garden with plenty of seating, an aviary, children's play area, rockery and gardens. It is also a real sun trap. This is a popular pub and just the place you will want to return to again and again.

The Bay Horse Inn, Main Street, Great Heck,
Near Whitley Bridge, Near Goole Tel: 01977 661125

Situated in the picturesque village of GREAT HECK, near to Whitley Bridge, is the Bay Horse Inn, a lovely, hidden public house. Originally three cottages which date back to the 18th century, the buildings first became an inn in 1912. In 1989 Val Taylor moved here and has turned this inn into a exciting place to visit. Open every day of the week and all day on Fridays and Saturdays the Bay Horse is well known for three things; its excellent range of beer, its delicious and generous home cooked food and, above all, its warm welcome to both locals and newcomers. It is well worth making a short detour off the main road to visit this little gem!

We do hope you have enjoyed reading the book as much as we compiling it and we would like to thank all the proprietors and managers of the places we have visited for their kind hospitality. We would be grateful if you mentioned the fact that you found them via the Hidden Places, and if you do find somewhere not already mentioned please let us know and we will be happy to consider it when the book is reprinted.

Cusworth Hall

Meanwhile we leave you to discover the hidden delights of the beautiful counties of Yorkshire and Humberside.

Tourist Information Centres

BARNSLEY
56 Eldon Street, Barnsley, South Yorkshire
Tel: 01226 206757

BEDALE
Bedale Hall, North End, Bedale, North Yorkshire
Tel: 01677 424604

BENTHAM
8 Station Road, Bentham, via Lancaster, North Yorkshire
Tel: 01524 262549

BEVERLEY
The Guildhall, Register Square, Beverley, Humberside
Tel: 01482 867430/883898

BOROUGHBRIDGE
Fishergate, Boroughbridge, North Yorkshire
Tel: 01423 323373

BRADFORD
National Museum of Photography, Film and TV, Pictureville,
Bradford, West Yorkshire
Tel: 01274 753678

BRIDLINGTON
25 Prince Street, Bridlington, Humberside
Tel: 01262 673474/606383

BRIGG
The Buttercross, Market Place, Brigg, Humberside
Tel: 01652 657053

CLEETHORPES
42-43 Alexandria Road, Cleethorpes, Humberside
Tel: 01472 200220

DANBY
The Moors Centre, Lodge Lane, Danby, Whitby, North Yorkshir
Tel: 01287 669654/660540

DONCASTER
Central Library, Waterdale, Doncaster, South Yorkshire
Tel: 01302 734309

EASINGWOLD
Chapel Lane, Easingwold, North Yorkshire
Tel: 01347 821530

FILEY
John Street, Filey, North Yorkshire
Tel: 01723 512204

GRASSINGTON
National Park Centre, Hebden Road, Grassington, Skipton,
North Yorkshire
Tel: 01756 752774

GREAT AYTON
High Green, Great Ayton, Nr. Middlesbrough, Cleveland
Tel: 01642 722835

GRIMSBY
National Fishing Heritage Centre, Grimsby, Humberside
Tel: 01472 342422

HALIFAX
Piece Hall, Halifax, West Yorkshire
Tel: 01422 368725

HARROGATE
Royal Baths Assembly Rooms, Crescent Road, Harrogate
Tel: 01423 525666

HARTSHEAD
Clifton Service Area, M62, West Yorkshire
Tel: 01274 869167

HAWES
Dales Countryside Museum, Hawes, North Yorkshire
Tel: 01969 667450

HAWORTH
2-4 West Lane, Haworth, Weat Yorkshire
Tel: 01535 642329

HEBDEN BRIDGE
1 Bridge Gate, Hebden Bridge, West Yorkshire
Tel: 01422 843831

HELMSLEY
Town Hall, Helmsley, North Yorkshire
Tel: 01439 770173

HOLMFIRTH
49/51 Huddersfield Road, Holmfirth, West Yorkshire
Tel: 01484 687603

HORNSEA
75 Newbegin, Hornsea, Humberside
Tel: 01964 536404

HORTON-IN-RIBBLESDALE
Pen-y-Ghent Café, Horton-in-Ribblesdale, North Yorkshire
Tel: 01729 860333

HUDDERSFIELD
3-5 Albion Street, Huddersfield, West Yorkshire
Tel: 01484 430808

HULL
Central Library, Albion Street, Hull, Humberside
Tel: 01482 223344

HULL
75/76 Carr Lane, Hull, Humberside
Tel: 01482 223559

HULL
Corporation Road, King George Dock, Hedon Road, Hull
Tel: 01482 702118

HUMBER BRIDGE
North Bank Viewing Area, Ferriby Road, Hessle, Humberside
Tel: 01482 640852

HUMBERSIDE INTERNATIONAL AIRPORT
Kirmington, South Humberside
Tel: 01652 688586

ILKLEY
Station Road, Ilkley, West Yorkshire
Tel: 01943 602319

INGLETON
Community Centre Car Park, Ingleton, North Yorkshire
Tel: 01524 241049

KNARESBOROUGH
35 Market Place, Knaresborough, North Yorkshire
Tel: 01423 866886

LEEDS
19 Wellington Street, Leeds, West Yorkshire
Tel: 0113 247 8301/2

LEYBURN
Thornborough Hall, Leyburn, North Yorkshire
TEL: 01969 23069/22773

MALTON
58 Market Place, Malton, North Yorkshire
Tel: 01653 600048

NORTHALLERTON
Applegarth Car Park, Northallerton, North Yorkshire
Tel: 01609 776864

OTLEY
Council Offices, 8 Boroughgate, Otley, West Yorkshire
Tel: 01132 477707

PATELEY BRIDGE
14 High Street, Pateley Bridge, North Yorkshire
Tel: 01423 711147

PICKERING
Eastgate Car Park, Pickering, North Yorkshire
Tel: 01751 473791

RICHMOND
Friary Gardens, Victoria Road, Richmond, North Yorkshire
Tel: 01748 850252/825994

RIPON
Minster Road, Ripon, North Yorkshire
Tel: 01765 604625

ROTHERHAM
Central Library, Walker Place, Rotherham, South Yorkshire
Tel: 01709 823611

SCARBOROUGH
St. Nicholas Cliff, Scarborough, North Yorkshire
Tel: 01723 373333

SCOTCH CORNER
Pavilion Service Area, A1, Near Richmond, North Yorkshire
Tel: 01325 377677

SELBY
Park Street, Selby, North Yorkshire
Tel: 01757 703263

SETTLE
Town Hall, Cheapside, Settle, North Yorkshire
Tel: 01729 825192

SHEFFIELD
Peace Gardens, Sheffield, South Yorkshire
Tel: 0114 273 4671/2

SHEFFIELD
Railway Station Concourse, Sheaf Street, Sheffield, South Yorkshire
Tel: 0114 279 5901

SKIPTON
9 Sheep Street, Skipton, North Yorkshire
Tel: 01756 792809

SUTTON BANK
Sutton Bank Visitor Centre, Nr Thirsk, North Yorkshire
Tel: 01845 597426

THIRSK
14 Kirkgate, Thirsk, North Yorkshire
Tel: 01845 522755

TODMORDEN
15 Burnley Road, Todmorden, Lancashire
Tel: 01706 818181

WAKEFIELD
Town Hall, Wood Street, Wakefield, West Yorkshire
Tel: 01924 295000/295001

WETHERBY
Council Offices, 24 Westgate, Wetherby, West Yorkshire
Tel: 01937 582706

WHITBY
Langborne Road, Whitby, North Yorkshire
Tel: 01947 602674

YORK
Travel Office, 6 Rougier Street, York, North Yorkshire
Tel: 01904 620557

YORK
De Grey Rooms, Exhibition Square, York, North Yorkshire
Tel: 01904 621756/7

YORK
Railway Station, Station Road, York, North Yorkshire
Tel: 01904 643700

Index

566

567

569

THE HIDDEN PLACES

If you would like to have any of the titles currently available in this series, please complete this coupon and send to: **M&M Publishing, Tryfan House, Warwick Drive, Hale, Altrincham, Cheshire WA15 9EA**

	Each	Qty
Scotland	£5.90	____
Northumberland & Durham	£5.90	____
The Lake District & Cumbria	£5.90	____
Somerset, Avon, Gloucestershire & Wiltshire	£5.90	____
Yorkshire and Humberside	£5.90	____
Lancashire & Cheshire	£5.90	____
North Wales	£5.90	____
South Wales	£5.90	____
The Welsh Borders	£5.90	____
Thames & Chilterns	£5.90	____
East Anglia	£5.90	____
The South East	£5.90	____
Dorset, Hampshire & the Isle of Wight	£5.90	____
Heart of England	£5.90	____
Devon & Cornwall	£5.90	____
Set of any five titles	£20.00	____

TOTAL: £

(Price includes Postage and Packing)

NAME...

ADDRESS ....

....

.... POSTCODE ....

Please make cheques payable to: M&M Publishing